Lee the American

GAMALIEL BRADFORD

BLUE GRAY BOOKS
The War Between the States ™

Publisher: Ralph Roberts
Vice-President/Operations: Pat Roberts

Senior Editor: Barbara Blood
Editors: Gayle Graham and Susan Parker

Cover Design: Lee Noel
Interior Design & Electronic Page Assembly: **WorldComm®**
Photographs as indicated

10 9 8 7 6 5 4 3 2 1

Library of Congress Catalog Card Number: 98-71804

ISBN: 1-888295-06-6

Blue/Gray Books™—a division of Creativity, Inc.—is a full–service publisher located at 65
Macedonia Road, Alexander NC 28701. Phone (828) 252–9515, Fax (828) 255–8719. For
orders only: 1-800-472-0438. Visa and MasterCard accepted.

Blue/Gray Books™ is distributed to the trade by Midpoint Trade Books, Inc., 27 West
20th Street, New York NY 10011, (212) 727-0190, (212) 727-0195 fax.

This book is also available on the internet in the **Publishers CyberMall.** Set your browser
to http://www.abooks.com and enjoy the many fine values available there.

CONTENTS

Illustrations

PREFACE

The formal and final biography of Lee should be written by a competent military specialist, like Henderson. This book, although it aims to give an intelligible biographical narrative, aims much more to give a clear, consistent, sympathetic portrait of a great soul. In short, its purpose is not so much biography as psychography. Those to whom the latter term is new will find a full discussion of it, both in general and in relation to Lee, in the Appendix.

For material I have relied mainly upon the "Official Records of the Union and Confederate Armies" and the lives of Lee by Long, Jones, Fitzhugh Lee, and Captain R.E. Lee. But a complete bibliography of sources would be practically a bibliography of the war literature both Northern and Southern. I have endeavored to give in the Notes my authority for every verbal quotation and for all important or disputable statements of fact.

My thanks are due chiefly to the *Atlantic Monthly*, also to the *South Atlantic Quarterly*, and the *Sewanee Review*, for their hospitality. This has enabled me to submit all my chapters to public criticism before giving them the final revision which has certainly not eliminated all errors, but has, I hope, diminished the number.

I wish to thank also the numerous correspondents who have sent me corrections and suggestions. Some have been severe. Most have been kindly. All have been helpful. I trust they will appreciate the result of their helpfulness as much as I do.

Robert E. Lee

PUBLISHER'S FOREWORD

*L*ee *the American* is far more than just the title of this book, it is an apt description of a great man with a towering character of honesty and integrity that shines through the ages–General Robert E. Lee.

"Do your duty in all things," Lee said. "You cannot do more. You should never wish to do less."

Lee's obvious and widely perceived *character* explains his transformation from Rebel general to American icon. Indeed, no other person came out of America's Civil War so greatly and universally respected as R.E. Lee. Certainly not Lincoln nor Grant nor any other of the victors.

If one looks at all American soldiers who ever served, including those like the beloved General Omar Bradley in War War II ("the soldier's soldier"), it is Robert E. Lee who is most revered by friend and foe alike.

Why? *Character.*

Few are unaware of Lee's agony over leaving long service with the United States Army to take up arms for the fledgling Confederacy. He was not happy with either side but believed his decision was the only one possible.

"There is no sacrifice," Lee said, "that I am not willing to make for the preservation of Union save that of honor."

History has given him the overwhelming consensus of understanding and respecting his choice.

We should not be surprised that Lee came into greatness; he was of good family. His father–General Henry "Light Horse Harry" Lee– distinguished himself in another rebellion, that of the American colonists against England. The result of that rebellion? These United States.

Henry Lee gave the funeral address for George Washington containing the now immortal line, "first in war, first in peace, and first in the hearts of his countrymen."

Robert E. Lee's son—George Washington Curtis Lee—was also a general, as was his nephew—Fitzhugh Lee. After the war, Fitzhugh Lee also served as governor of Virginia.

In soul, in character, in integrity, Robert E. Lee resembles Washington perhaps even more than his father. Given a few more resources, he might have also been the father of *his* country.

Yet, the South went down to defeat and Lee—as ever—showed his greatness even while drinking the bitter dregs of defeat.

"I believe," he said, "it is the duty of everyone to unite in the restoration of this country and the re-establishment of peace and harmony."

Duty and honor were the bedrock of Lee's strong character—those precepts color his soul into blazing glory for all time.

This, then, is what this book shows. Not the dry strategy and tactics of that most uncivil of wars so oft rehashed in thousands of now-dusty tomes. We look here into the soul of Robert E. Lee and receive understanding of his greatness.

Duty. Honor. Character.

As Lee himself said, you cannot do more.

—Ralph Roberts

To the young men both of the North and of the South who can make or unmake the future of the America of Washington, of Lincoln, and of Lee.

Au reste, dans toutes ces citations je ne prétends pas endosser les passages que j'emprunte, je m'attache, comme toujours, à faire valoir et à faire connaître l'auteur que j'analyse, par ses meilleurs côtés, laissant au lecteur la balance de tout et l'arbitrage. *Sainte-Beuve.*

1

LEE BEFORE THE WAR

T he Lees of Virginia are descended from Richard Lee, who came to this country toward the middle of the seventeenth century. Richard's English affiliations have been the subject of much dispute. Early Virginia genealogists derived him from the ancient and honorable family of Shropshire Lees and thought they had identified him exactly. Grave difficulties were discovered in this connection and at one time the emigrant seemed likely to be transferred to the delightful kinship of Sir Harry Lee of Ditchley and Woodstock. But the authorities were still dissatisfied, and have now apparently returned to the Shropshire origin, though Richard's precise position in that family is not easily determined.[1]

On his mother's side Robert Lee, doubtless in common with some hundreds of thousands of others, is said to have been descended from King Robert Bruce.[2]

Like many people who have ancestors, Lee displayed a considerable indifference to them. "General Lee had never the time or inclination to study genealogy, and always said he knew nothing beyond his first ancestor, Colonel Richard Lee, who migrated to America in the reign of Charles I."[3] On having a seal cut he does indeed, with apology, show some interest about the arms, "which I have thought, perhaps foolishly enough, might as well be right as wrong."[4] But when an enterprising genealogist undertakes a Lee book, the general's comment is: "I am very much obliged to Mr. – for the trouble he has taken in relation to the Lee genealogy. I have no desire to have it published, and do not think it would afford sufficient interest beyond the immediate family to pay for the expense. I think the money had better be appropriated to relieve the poor."[5]

Which does not mean that he was not daily and hourly conscious with pride that he belonged to the Virginia Lees, a name writ as large as any in the history of the country and transmitted to him with an honor which it was his constant care never to tarnish. From the first Richard down, the Lees had always been doing something useful and often something great, and they were distinguished by the friendship as well as by the admiration of Washington.

Robert Lee's father, Light Horse Harry, fought the Revolutionary War beside Washington and Greene. He was a fiery soldier and a more impetuous spirit than his son. He took a hot and eager part in politics and had warm friends and bitter enemies. In his last lingering illness his colored nurse did something he did not like. He flung his boot at her. She flung it back and won his heart. It is a trivial incident, but it is worth a chapter in differentiating the father from the son, who flung no boots and had none flung at him.

Harry Lee was a scholar and loved literature. He read Sophocles and Racine and the Greek philosophers and commented on them in letters far more spirited and delightful than any of Robert's. The father also wrote memoirs which the son edited. Partial admirers rate them with Cæsar's. Jefferson, who hated Harry Lee politically, says of them: "I am glad to see the romance of Lee removed from the shelf of history to that of fable. Some small portions of the transactions he relates were within my own knowledge; and of these I can say he has given more falsehood than fact."[6]

Harry Lee was forty-nine years old in 1807, when Robert was born. The son was only eleven when his father died and during much of that time they had not been together. Therefore the paternal influence is not likely to have been very great. Nevertheless, Lee cherished his father's memory with deep reverence. When he was in South Carolina in 1861, he wrote, "I had the gratification at length of visiting my father's grave."[7] And Colonel Long describes the incident simply but impressively: "He went alone to the tomb, and after a few moments of silence, plucked a flower and slowly retraced his steps."[8]

Lee's relations with his mother were much more intimate and prolonged. She appears to have been a woman of high character and to have taught her son practical as well as moral excellences. She was for many years an invalid and Robert took much of the care both of her and of the household, which may have been useful training in self-sacrifice, but must have cut him off somewhat from the natural outflow, the fresh spontaneousness of boyish spirits. I think he showed the effect of this all his life.

Of his childish years we know little. He came so late to greatness that the usual crop of reminiscences does not seem to have been gathered. Perhaps he did not furnish good material for reminiscences. Who were his companions? Did he love them and they him? What were his hopes and ambitions? Was it to be said of him, as was said of his father, that "he seems to have come out of his mother's womb a soldier"?[9] We get a rare glimpse of love for sports: "In later days General Lee has been heard to relate with enthusiasm how as a boy he had followed the hunt (not infrequently on foot) for hours over hill and valley without fatigue."[10] Horses all his life were a delight to him. He himself wrote: "I know the pleasure of training a handsome horse. I enjoy it as much as any one."[11] A good observer wrote of him: "He loved horses, and had good ones, and rode carefully and safely, but I never liked his seat."[12]

On exceptional occasions some touch of boyish memory breaks through habitual reserve. "'Twas seldom that he allowed his mind to wander to the days of his childhood and talk of his father and his early associates, but when he did he was far more charming than he thought," says Longstreet,[13] with unusually delicate discrimination. Thus Lee writes, after the war, to a lady who had sent him photographs of Stratford, the fine old Virginia manor house where he was born: "Your picture vividly recalls scenes of my earliest recollections and happiest days. Though unseen for years, every feature of the house is familiar to me." And Miss Mason tells us that shortly before his death he visited Alexandria and "one of the old neighbors found him gazing wistfully over the palings of the garden in which he used to play. 'I am looking,' said he, 'to see if the old snowball trees are still here. I should have been sorry to miss them.'"[14]

We know hardly more of Lee's education than of his childish adventures and amusements. When he was thirteen years old, Jefferson wrote of Virginia generally: "What is her education now? Where is it? The little we have we import, like beggars, from other states; or import their beggars to bestow on us their miserable crumbs."[15] But Jefferson was especially deploring the lack of educational institutions. His democratic instincts could not tolerate the traditions of a country where down to the time of the Revolution "newspapers and literature at large were a proscribed commodity,"[16] and whose governor, Sir William Berkeley, said: "I thank God there are no free schools nor printing and I hope we shall not have them these hundred years."[17] Young men in Lee's station doubtless received more or less solid instruction of the classical order. In 1811 the Lees removed to Alexandria with the special purpose of educating the children. Robert's first teacher was a Mr. Leary, who lived until after the war, and to whom his pupil wrote in 1866, with kindly remembrance: "I beg to express the gratitude I have felt all my life for the affectionate fidelity which characterized your teaching and conduct towards me."[18] Later, in preparation for West Point, Lee, still at Alexandria, attended the school of Mr. Benjamin Hallowell, where his time was chiefly devoted to mathematics. Hallowell writes that "he was a most exemplary student in every respect,"[19] with other laudatory reminiscences which had probably lost nothing by the lapse of time and the growing celebrity of the subject of them.

In 1825, when he was eighteen years old, Lee entered West Point. There seems to be general, if rather indefinite, testimony to his excellent conduct and standing in the Academy. He was a good scholar and graduated high in his class; but I do not find many anecdotes from contemporaries that will help us to humanize his life there. His unquestioned temperance and self-control in moral matters appear doubly creditable, when we read the statements made by Colonel Thayer, superintendent of West Point at that time, to President Adams, as to the drunkenness and dissipation generally prevalent among the young men.[20]

Lee graduated duly in 1829, immediately received an appointment in the Engineer Corps, and was stationed for some years at Old Point Comfort. During this time he married, at Arlington, in June, 1831, Miss Custis, Mrs. Washington's great-granddaughter, and through her he later came into control of an extensive property, with farms, and mansions, and a considerable number of slaves. Although we get little account of it, his early married life must have brought him largely into contact with all the opulence and gayety and grace of that old Virginia aristocracy whose faults and virtues Mr. Page has painted so winningly that the faults seem almost as attractive as the virtues. Brave, handsome, courtly men, pure, dainty, loving, high-minded women, danced and laughed away the time, as they did in the golden world. "For all its faults, it was, I believe, the purest, sweetest life ever lived,"[21] says Mr. Page. Then the Northern reader turns to the cold, judicial narrative of Olmsted and reads of these same chivalrous gentlemen that, though "honorable, hospitable, and at the bottom of their hearts kind and charitable, they yet nursed a high, overweening sense of their importance and dignity."[22] He reads other facts in Olmsted, of a much darker and grimmer order, and cannot avoid the momentary reflection that the most graceful and charming society in the world danced and laughed in France also before the Revolution. It may be, there are some ugly things that light hearts are dancing over to-day.

By temperament Lee had none of the vices of that vanishing world and perhaps not all its good qualities. I doubt if it ever impressed him very deeply, and his wandering military life soon withdrew him altogether from its influence. One reminiscence of this period–though only a reminiscence, and no doubt colored by the event, as such usually are–has marked interest in its anticipation of what was to come. It is given by a relative. "I have often said since he entered on his brilliant career that, although we all admired him for his remarkable beauty and attractive manners, I did not

Robert E. Lee

see anything in him that prepared me for his so far outstripping all his compeers. The first time this idea presented itself to me was during one of my visits to Arlington after my marriage. We were all seated around the table at night, Robert reading. I looked up and my eye fell upon his face in perfect repose, and the thought at once passed through my mind: 'You certainly look more like a great man than any one I have ever seen.'"[23] If all those who look like great men to their female relatives attained Lee's greatness, what a great world it would be. Yet this glimpse has a crisp definiteness which makes one unwilling to pass it over.

During the years preceding the Mexican War, Lee followed his profession of military engineer in different parts of the country. Now he was in Washington, incidentally messing with Joe Johnston and others afterwards more or less notable. Now he was in Ohio adjusting the boundary between that state and Michigan; or in New York Harbor, supervising the defenses.

Perhaps the most important of his engineering labors were those at St. Louis, connected with governing and controlling the course of the Mississippi River. The interesting thing here is that at first he met with a good deal of opposition and abuse. He bore this with entire equanimity, quietly going on with his work, until his final success won

Lee The American

the approval and admiration of those who had been most ready to find fault.[24] It was the same indomitable perseverance, without regard to criticism, which he showed again and again during the war and which is most concretely illustrated in the humorous anecdote told of him in Mexico. He had been ordered to take some sailors and construct a battery to be manned by them afterwards. The sailors did not like to dig dirt, and swore. Even their captain remonstrated. His men were fighters, not moles. Lee simply showed his orders and persisted. When the firing began, the eager mariners found their earthworks exceedingly comfortable. Their commander went so far as to apologize to Lee. "Captain, I suppose, after all, your works helped the boys a good deal. But the fact is, I never did like this land fighting—it ain't clean."[25]

The value of Lee's services during the Mexican War has perhaps been exaggerated; but the direct evidence shows that they were signal and important. He began as captain, serving with General Wool at the battle of Buena Vista. He then joined General Scott and took part in the siege of Vera Cruz. He was brevetted major at Cerro Gordo, lieutenant-colonel at Contreras, and colonel at Chapultepec. At the latter place he was slightly wounded. From the beginning to the end of the war he displayed energy, daring, and resource.

Various anecdotes are told of his personal achievements and adventures, of his scouting expedition with a Mexican guide before Buena Vista, when Lee's persistent reconnaissance of the enemy's position turned a vast collection of white tents into a Quixotic flock of sheep, of his nocturnal and storm-beaten exploration of a craggy lava tract, called the Pedregal, where no other man durst venture and whence no one believed that he could return alive.

As to this last incident General Scott declared, in formal legal testimony: "I had dispatched several staff officers who had, within the space of two hours, returned and reported to me that each had found it impracticable to penetrate far into the Pedrigal during the dark. . . . Captain Lee, having passed over the difficult ground by daylight, found it just possible to return to San Augustin in the dark, the greatest feat of physical and moral courage performed by any individual, in my knowledge, pending the campaign."[26] And General P. F. Smith testifies to the same effect: "I wish particularly to record my admiration of the conduct of Captain Lee, of the Engineers. His reconnaissances, though pushed far beyond the bounds of prudence, were conducted with so much skill that their fruits were of the utmost value—the soundness of his judgment and personal daring being equally conspicuous."[27]

Scott also bears general and repeated witness to the value of Lee's labors and the excellence of his character. We have the commander's written praise of "the gallant and indefatigable Captain Lee,"[28] who was "as distinguished for felicitous execution as for science and daring."[29] We have the more emphatic, if less reliable, reported sayings, that Scott's own success in Mexico was "largely due to the skill, valor, and undaunted energy of R. E. Lee,"[30] that "Lee is the greatest military genius in America,"[31] and that "if I were on my deathbed tomorrow, and the President of the United States should tell me that a great battle was to be fought for the liberty or slavery of the country, and asked my judgment as to the ability of a commander, I would say, with my dying breath, let it be Robert E. Lee."[32]

Nor was this wholly a matter of Scott's personal partiality; for the comment of other generals is equally laudatory. Lee's "distinguished merit and gallantry deserve the highest praise," says Pillow.[33] Lee, "in whose skill and judgment I had the utmost confidence," says Shields.[34] "Equally daring and not less meritorious were the services of Captain Lee," says Pillow again.[35]

I have dwelt thus minutely on these words of contemporaries, because they come from men who thought of Lee merely as a promising captain among other captains and did not look back to his dim past through the purple haze of Chancellorsville and the Wilderness.

With the Mexican War we enter more freely upon Lee's letters to his wife and children, which from that time on form the best commentary on his life and character. He shows a keen appreciation of the beauty and richness of Mexican landscape: "Jalapa is the most beautiful country I have seen in Mexico, and will compare with any I have seen elsewhere. [Lee had traveled widely in his own land, but he never visited Europe.] I wish it was in the United States, and that I was located, with you and the children around me, in one of its rich, bright valleys. I can conceive nothing more beautiful in the way of landscape or mountain scenery. We ascended upwards of four thousand feet that morning, and whenever we looked back the rich valley was glittering in the morning sun and the light morning clouds flitting around us. On reaching the top, the valley appeared at intervals between the clouds which were below us, and high over all towered Orizaba, with its silver cap of snow."[36]

He visits a sacred shrine and blends tropical color with the formal splendors of Catholic devotion: "The 'Trees of the Noche Triste,' so called from their blooming about the period of that event, are now in full bloom. The flower is a round ellipsoid, and of the most magnificent scarlet color I ever saw. I have two of them in my cup before me now. I wish I could send them to you. The holy image was standing on a large silver maguey plant, with a rich crown on her head and an immense silver petticoat on. There were no votaries at her shrine, which was truly magnificent, but near the entrance of the church were the offerings of those whom she had relieved. They consist of representations in wax of the parts of the human body that she had cured of the diseases with which they had been affected. And I may say there were all parts. I saw many heads severed from the trunks. Whether they represented those she had restored I could not learn. It would be a difficult feat."[37]

The references to politics in these letters are interesting because they show more vehemence and ardor of expression than, I think, Lee would have permitted himself in later years. Thus, he writes of the treatment of Trist by the Administration: "I presume it is perfectly fair, having made use of his labors, and taken from him all that he had earned, that he should be kicked off as General Scott has been, whose skill and science, having crushed the enemy and conquered a peace, can now be dismissed, and turned out as an old horse to die."[38] And, again in connection with Scott: "The great cause of our success was in our leader. It was his stout heart that cast us on the shore of Vera Cruz; his bold self-reliance that forced us through the pass at Cerro Gordo; his indomitable courage that, amidst all the doubts and difficulties that surrounded us at Puebla, pressed us forward to this capital, and finally brought us within its gates, while others, who croaked all the way from Brazos, and advised delay at Puebla, finding themselves at last, contrary to their expectations, comfortably quartered within the city, find fault with the way they came there."[39]

Also, as to the general question of the war, the captain of forty speaks out with greater frankness than we find in the letters of the Confederate commander of fifty-five. "It is rather late in the day to discuss the origin of the war; that ought to have been understood before we engaged in it. It may have been produced by the act of either party or the force of circumstances. Let the pedants of diplomacy determine. It is certain that we are the victors in a regular war, continued, if not brought on, by their obstinacy and ignorance, and they are whipped in a manner of which women might be ashamed. We have the right, by the laws of war, of dictating the terms of peace and requiring indemnity for our losses and expenses. Rather than forego that right, except through a spirit of magnanimity to a crushed foe, I would fight them ten years, but I would be generous in exercising it."[40]

After the Mexican War, Lee resumed the routine life of his profession, sojourning in one part of the country or another, as duty called. He was invited by the Cuban Junta to become their military leader;[41] but he declined because he felt such a position to be hardly compatible with his training as an officer of the United States Army. He was busied for some time with the construction of a fort in Baltimore. In 1852, he was made superintendent of the West Point Academy. His diffidence about accepting this position is extremely characteristic: "I learn with much regret the determination of the Secretary of War to assign me to that duty, and I fear I cannot realize his expectations in the management of an Institution requiring more skill and more experience than I command."[42]

I find little direct evidence as to Lee's life at West Point, but his biographer declares that it was in every way successful. "The discipline of the Academy was made more efficient, . . . and a spacious riding-hall was constructed."[43] Colonel Chesney makes similar statements from personal observation: "The writer visited West Point during the time of General Lee's charge and saw the institution very thoroughly, passing some days there. He is able, therefore, to testify to its completeness, and the efficiency of the courses of study and discipline—never more remarkable, he believes, than at that period."[44] Captain Lee bears witness to his father's kindness of manner and ready tact in making the raw students feel at ease and tells one anecdote which is perfectly in character. Lee was riding one day with his son, when they caught sight of three cadets who were evidently far out of bounds and who at once retired still further. After a few moments' silence, Lee said: "Did you know those young men? But no, if you did, don't say so. I wish boys would do what is right; it would be so much easier for all parties."[45]

In 1855 Lee was appointed to a lieutenant-colonelcy in one of the newly created cavalry regiments and ceased his connection with West Point. From this time until the breaking-out of the war his service was mainly in the Western and Southwestern States, while his family remained at Arlington.

Many of the letters written during these years have been printed. As letters they are not especially brilliant or remarkable. But they are interesting for the study of Lee, as showing his gentleness, his constant care and thought for others, and his shrewd and just observation of everything that was going on about him. Playful descriptions of scenes and people alternate with deeper feeling, such as his expression of grief for a child over whose body he had been asked to read the funeral service. "I hope I shall not be called on again, for though I believe that it is far better for the child to be called by its Heavenly Creator into His presence in its purity and innocence, unpolluted by sin and uncontaminated by the vices of the world, still it so wrings a parent's heart with anguish that it is painful to see. Yet I know it was done in mercy to both–mercy to the child, mercy to the parents."[46]

To his own children he writes with gayety and grace. "Robert. . . . has been prospecting about the neighborhood for cherry trees, and their bloom on the sides of the mountains delights his vision every moment. He revels at dinner in fried chicken and mush. An elegant school, in his opinion."[47] And again he passes to sober advice, useful, if not original: "As you have commenced, I hope you will continue never to exceed your means. It will save you much anxiety and mortification, and enable you to maintain your independence of character and feeling. It is easier to make our wishes conform to our means than our means conform to our wishes. In fact, we want but little. Our happiness depends upon our independence, the success of our operations, prosperity of our plans, health, contentment, and the esteem of our friends."[48]

Then suddenly, into a life thus organized for comparative peace and quiet, burst the thunderbolt of war. It had not, of course, been unexpected, to Lee any more than to any one else. To him, more than perhaps to almost any one else, because of his position and temperament, it came full of burden and anguish, unillumined by hope. He trusts that President Buchanan "will be able to extinguish fanaticism North and South, cultivate love for the country and Union, and restore harmony between the different sections."[49] As the danger comes nearer, he finds confidence more difficult: "My little personal troubles sink into insignificance when I contemplate the condition of the country, and I feel as if I could easily lay down my life for its safety. But I also feel that would bring but little good."[50]

In October, 1859, Lee was on furlough at Arlington, and it must be regarded as exceedingly dramatic, all things considered, that he should have been the officer ordered to arrest John Brown. It was not in Lee's nature to play up to a dramatic situation, however, and his conduct of the affair was as quiet, as businesslike, as free from sensational methods, as such a thing could be. He made his preparations, called on Brown and his followers to surrender, gave the order to attack, attacked, and in a few moments all was over. His own account in his memorandum-book is perfectly dry and quiet: "Tuesday about sunrise, with twelve marines under the command of

Lieutenant Green, broke in the door of the enginehouse, secured the robbers, and released all of the [Southern] prisoners unhurt."[51] His testimony before the Congressional Committee as to the whole affair is in the same tone: "The result proves that the plan was the attempt of a fanatic or madman which could only end in failure; and its temporary success was owing to the panic and confusion he succeeded in creating by magnifying his numbers."[52] Yet a mind so shrewd as Lee's must have had some suspicion that there were more fanatics and madmen in the North who might create panic and confusion beside which Brown's would be utterly insignificant.

As we pause here for a moment, before entering on the sudden and astonishing glory of Lee's career, it will be well to form some conception of his physical qualities and personal appearance. The great doers of the world have not always been handsome or even imposing. Cæsar, when he triumphed, may have had dignity from habit of command, but there can have been little beauty in his lean caducity. Napoleon, in later years, was fat and vulgar, for all the dominating power of his glance. It pleases us to think that Grant and Lincoln could look as they did and be what they were. Yet there is undeniably something appropriate, something satisfying in the kingly stature and lineaments of Pericles and Washington. It cannot harm a royal soul to dwell within a royal body. And not Pericles nor Washington would seem in this to have been more royal than was Lee.

From the study of photographs I get a more charming impression of his later years than of his earlier. The face and figure of the captain are eminently noble, highbred, dignified; but with the dignity there is just a suggestion of haughtiness, of remoteness. Or do I only see in the picture what I imagine of the man? But in the bearded photographs of later years all trace of such remoteness has vanished. The dignity is more marked than ever, but all sweet. The ample, lordly carriage, the broad brow, the deep, significant, intelligent eyes convey nothing but the largest tenderness, the profoundest human sympathy, the most perfect love. And again perhaps I only see what I imagine.

The record of actual observers is of more interest than any comment founded on portraits, since Captain Lee tells us that "my father could never bear to have his picture taken and there are no likenesses of him that really give his sweet expression."[53] To begin with, Lee's was a thoroughly manly beauty and founded all his life on a magnificent physique. "From infancy to threescore," says an opponent who loved and admired him, "he knew no physical malady [this is not strictly correct], and the admirable symmetry of his person and the manly beauty of his countenance were the aids to his virtue which secured to him tolerance, affection, and respect from all with whom he mingled."[54] Even towards the close of the war, when he was nearly sixty, it was his habit, when the pressure was great, "to retire about ten or eleven at night, to rise at 3 A.M., breakfast by candlelight and return to the front, spending the entire day on the lines."[55]

In his earlier life he is described by General Hunt as being "as fine-looking a man as one would wish to see, of perfect figure and strikingly handsome,"[56] and by General Meigs as "a man then in the vigor of youthful strength, with a noble and commanding presence, and an admirable, graceful, and athletic figure."[57] "He had," says General Preston, "a finished form, delicate hands; was graceful in person."[58] When he became superintendent at West Point he is pictured more minutely as "five feet eleven inches high, weighing 175 pounds, hair originally jet black and inclined to curl at the ends; eyes hazel brown, face cleanly shaved, except a mustache; a countenance which beamed with gentleness and benevolence."[59]

At the time of the war, when more years had passed over him, Wise portrays him as follows: "His form had fullness without any appearance of superfluous flesh, and was as erect as that of a cadet, without the slightest appearance of constraint. His features are too well known to need description, but no representation of General Lee which I have ever seen properly conveys the light and softness of his eye, the tenderness and intelligence of his mouth, or the indescribable refinement of his face. One picture gives him a meatiness about the nose; another, hard or coarse lines about the mouth; another, heaviness about the chin. None of them gives the effect of his hair and beard. I have seen all the great men of our times, except Mr. Lincoln, and I have no hesitation in saying that Robert E. Lee was incomparably the greatest looking of them all."[60] And Alexander H. Stephens, when he saw Lee for the first time and pressed upon him the question as to Virginia's joining the Confederacy, beheld a personage well worthy to make a great decision in a great cause. "As he stood there, fresh and ruddy as a David from the sheepfold, in the prime of manly beauty and the embodiment of a line of heroic and patriotic fathers and worthy mothers, it was thus I first saw Robert E. Lee. . . . I had before me the most manly and entire gentleman I ever saw."[61]

How many men have we all met who seemed built to play heroic parts, yet did not and could not play them. It is well, perhaps, that such a part should occasionally be played by a man whom nature has moulded for it.

2

THE GREAT DECISION

The growth of a Lee legend is greatly to be deplored most of all by Lee's warmest admirers. "One may search in vain for any defect in him," says one of the latest historians of the war. "Indeed, the perfection of Lee becomes somewhat oppressive. One would welcome the discovery of a shortcoming in him, as redeeming him to humanity."[1] This is unfair, but not unnatural, when one considers the attitude of Lee's Southern admirers. "He was never behind time at his studies, never failed in a single recitation, was perfectly observant of the rules and regulations of the institution," says an old teacher.[2] "Throughout his whole student life he performed no act which his pious mother could not have fully approved," says Long.[3] I do not believe this is true. I hope it is not true. If it is true, it ought to be concealed, not boasted of. This is the sort of thing that made Washington odious to the young and remote from the mature for generations. "In all essential characteristics Lee resembled Washington," says Mr. Rhodes,[4] with much justice. But we know that, in spite of ill-judged idolatry, Washington was not a prig. Neither was Lee, but a man, of warm flesh and blood, like the rest of us. No one could have had his large and tender sympathy for human weakness who had not known human weakness himself. Above all, from the common soldier to the president of the Confederacy comes general testimony that Lee had charm. Now, no prig ever had charm. Therefore I refuse to believe that he said—at any rate, in those words— to Magruder in Mexico: "I am but doing my duty, and with me, in small matters as well as in large ones, duty must come before pleasure."[5]

After this brief reservation and protest, it must be recognized and insisted that few men have guided their actions more strictly and loftily by conscience than Lee. That he should ever have boasted about his sense of duty is unbelievable. That he turned to it and consulted it in every crisis, and especially in the profoundest crisis of his life, is certain, and whatever we may think of his judgment, it is impossible to question the absolute rectitude of his purposes.

During the years of violent controversy which intervened between the Mexican War and the secession of the South, Lee attended quietly to his military duties. Occasionally in the published letters of this period we get a glimpse of the interest he must have taken in what was going on at Washington. But it was then and always his constant conviction that a soldier should not meddle with politics. Even when he had charge of the capture of John Brown there was no passion in the matter. The work was done with military precision and quiet coolness and the captive was handed over to the proper civil authorities. "I am glad we did not have to kill him," Lee remarked afterwards to Mrs. Pickett's father, "for I believe he is an honest, conscientious old man."[6]

As the struggle of parties and principles grew fiercer, however, Lee foresaw that sooner or later he should be forced to choose. Neither party satisfied him. Each seemed to be unreasonable, selfish, inconsiderate of the rights and feelings of the other; and he believed that a larger justice ought to be able to harmonize the opposing claims without actual conflict. In December, 1860, he writes: "Feeling the aggression of the North, resenting their denial of the equal rights of our citizens to the common territory of the Commonwealth, etc., I am not pleased with the course of the 'Cotton States,' as they term themselves. In addition to their selfish, dictatorial bearing, the threats they throw out against the 'Border States,' as they call them, if they will not join them, argues little for the benefit or peace of Virginia, should she determine to coalesce with them. While I wish to do what is right, I am unwilling to do what is wrong at the bidding of the South or of the North."[7] And again, in January, 1861, "As far as I can judge from the papers, we are between a state of anarchy and civil war. May God avert from us both. . . . I see that four states have declared themselves out of the Union. Four more apparently will follow their example. Then if the border states are dragged into the gulf of revolution, one half of the country will be arrayed against the other, and I must try and be patient and wait the end, for I can do nothing to hasten or retard it."[8]

The end came quickly. Lincoln was elected. Virginia was on the point of seceding. War seemed inevitable. If Lee remained in the

United States Army, he would be forced to fight against all he loved best in the world. He was fifty years old. For more than thirty years he had served under the Stars and Stripes. Honor, advancement, profit were assured, if he clung to his old allegiance. If he abandoned it, what would come to him no one could tell. It is hard to imagine a man placed in a situation involving a profounder moral struggle or greater difficulty of decision. And, though Lee doubtless did not so think of it, the decision was as important to the country as to himself. Without assuming, with some Northern writers, that he might have prevented Virginia's secession and possibly war, it is not unreasonable to suppose that the course of the war might have been greatly different, if his military ability had been saved to the armies of the North.

In April, 1861, Lee was awaiting orders at Arlington. On the 18th of that month he had an interview with Francis P. Blair, who, with the knowledge of Lincoln and Cameron, unofficially, but it is said authoritatively, offered him the command of the United States Army, in the field. We have Lee's own account of this interview, written after the war and agreeing with Blair's. "I never intimated to any one that I desired the command of the United States Army, nor did I ever have a conversation with but one gentleman, the Hon. Francis P. Blair, on the subject, which was at his invitation and, as I understood, at the instance of President Lincoln. After listening to his remarks, I declined the offer he made me to take command of the army that was to be brought into the field, stating as candidly and courteously as I could that though opposed to secession and deprecating war, I could take no part in an invasion of the Southern States."[9]

Immediately on leaving Blair, Lee went to General Scott. Unfortunately we have no detailed account of this most important conversation from either of the principals. "I went directly from the interview with Mr. Blair to the office of General Scott, told him of the proposition that had been made to me, and my decision," writes Lee.[10] Long tells us, from a very indirect source, that General Scott "used every argument to persuade him to remain in the Union."[11] "But to all pleading Colonel Lee returned but one answer, that his sense of duty was stronger with him than any prospect of advancement, and replied to the appeal not to resign in the following words, "I am compelled to: I cannot consult my own feelings in the matter."[12]

The narrative of the only eye and ear witness who seems to have been actually present, General Townsend, exhibits Lee in a much less favorable aspect. It is so circumstantial that it must be quoted in full:—

General Scott knew that he [Lee] was at Arlington Heights, at the house of his father-in-law, Mr. Custis, and one day asked me if I had seen or heard of him lately. I replied in the negative, except that he was on leave and at Arlington Heights. Said the general, "It is time he should show his hand and if he remains loyal should take an important command." I then suggested that I should write to Lee and ask him to call at the general's headquarters. "I wish you would," replied the general. The note was written and the next day, April 19, 1861, Colonel Lee came to the office. The general's was the front room of the second story. His round table stood in the centre of the room and I had a desk in one corner. The aides were in an adjoining room with a door opening into the general's. When Lee came in, I was alone in the room with the general and the door to the aides' room was closed. I quietly arose, keeping my eye on the general, for it seemed probable he might wish to be alone with Lee. He, however, secretly motioned me to keep my seat and I sat down without Lee having a chance to notice that I had risen. The general, having invited Lee to be seated, the following conversation, as nearly as I can remember, took place. Gen. Scott: "You are at present on leave of absence, Colonel Lee"—Col. Lee: "Yes, General, I am staying with my family at Arlington."—Gen. Scott: "These are times when every officer in the United States service should fully determine what course he will pursue and frankly declare it. No one should continue in government employ without being actively employed." (No response from Lee.)—Gen. Scott (after a pause): "Some of the Southern officers are resigning, possibly with the intention of taking part with their States. They make a fatal mistake. The contest may be long and severe, but eventually the issue must be in favor of the Union." (Another pause and no reply from Lee.)—Gen. Scott (seeing evidently that Lee showed no disposition to declare himself loyal or even in doubt): "I suppose you will go with the rest. If you purpose to resign, it is proper you should do so at once; your present attitude is an equivocal one."—Col. Lee: "The property belonging to my children, all they possess, lies in Virginia. They will be ruined, if they do not go with their State. I cannot raise my hand against my children."[13]

I have cited the whole of this account, because it is a curious instance of what appears to be reliable historical evidence, yet must,

I am convinced, be substantially false. In the first place, Townsend says April 19. Lee says explicitly, writing at the time, April 18. Next, Lee says he told General Scott of the proposition that had been made him and of his decision. Nothing of the sort appears in Townsend's story. Further, Lee, writing to Mrs. Lee a few weeks later, bids his son Custis "consult his own judgment, reason, and conscience as to the course he must take,"[14] which does not seem to fit well with the argument that his children would "be ruined, if they do not go with their State." Finally, a very slight knowledge of Lee's character makes it impossible to suppose that, after weeks of careful, prayerful deliberation and moral conflict in view of the highest patriotic duties, the man who again and again refused the offers of a grateful nation to provide for his family and assure them from want, the man who wrote to his son in the midst of the struggle that "all must be sacrificed for the country,"[15] could have gone to a personal friend whom he respected as he did Scott, with nothing on his lips but the poor, the paltry, the pitiful argument for deserting his flag and his allegiance that the property of his children lay in Virginia. It is true that Scott was a Virginian and Lee had to be careful not to wound his superior in justifying himself. But no man ever lived who was capable of handling such a situation with more tact. If only we had Scott's and Lee's own versions of what passed between them on that memorable day![16]

As it is, we merely know that two days later Lee sent his resignation to Scott, with an affectionate and manly letter, expressing his regret at separating himself from the service "to which I have devoted the best years of my life and all the ability I possessed," and adding, "save in the defense of my native State I never desire again to draw my sword."[17] Immediately after this he was offered and accepted the position of commander-in-chief of the forces of Virginia.

In considering Lee's conduct at this crisis it is a mistake to tangle one's self up in the web of metaphysical casuistry which was woven about the whole constitutional question by the fine wits of a generation of legal quibblers. Cold common sense stands amazed that men should have been ready to cut each others' throats for the ingenious subtleties of Webster and Everett anymore than for those of Calhoun and Davis. It seems as if mankind would not learn by all the experience of ages that passion is never at a loss for argument, or appreciate the force of Matthew Arnold's despairing comment, "by such reasoning anything may be made out of anything."

The technical charge that Lee has to answer, the one most commonly brought against him, is that, having accepted his education and support at the hands of the United States Government and sworn allegiance to it, he broke his military oath and betrayed his trust. This charge is said to have been discussed by Lee himself. "General Lee told Bishop Wilmer of Louisiana that if it had not been for the instruction he got from Rawle's text-book at West Point, he would not have joined the South and left the old army at the breaking-out of the late war between the States."[18] Surely Lee cannot be blamed for following the lessons which he believed the Government itself had taught him. It is unfortunate, however, that this speech has come through many mouths. As for Rawle's "View of the Constitution of the United States of America," although it was undoubtedly in use during a portion of the time Lee was in the Academy, it seems impossible that it can have been given to him as a text-book.[19] Rawle was an ardent supporter of the Union. Yet he says, "This right [of secession] must be considered as an ingredient in the composition of the general government, which, though not expressed, was mutually understood, and the doctrine heretofore presented to the reader, in regard to the indefeasible nature of personal allegiance, is so far qualified in respect to allegiance to the United States."[20] Such an assertion from such a source is significant of the state of mind of many Americans in the second quarter of the century as to the metaphysical tangle of duties, loyalties, allegiances, to which I referred above, and which was inevitable in view of the peculiar organization of the United States Government. In any case, it cannot be disputed that Lee and those who took the same course he did were influenced by an imperious conception of duty as much as Scott, Thomas, and the many others whose action was most honorably different.

When the decision of Lee and his fellows is surveyed on simpler, broader grounds, one or two general considerations present themselves. In a popular government, whenever any large, distinct section of the people thinks that it is permanently oppressed by the remainder, it will revolt. No theory, no legal argument, no paper constitution will ever prevent this. And in a government made up of long-established, originally independent units, as imperfectly welded together as were the United States in 1860, such a revolt is peculiarly liable to occur. It is true that the North then felt, and probably for the most part feels now, that the South was not oppressed. The South felt that it was oppressed and did exactly what the North would have done under the same circumstances. I know of no more constant lover of the Union than Washington. Yet Washington wrote, "There is nothing which holds one country or one State to another but interest."[21]

This general justification or explanation of the Southern revolt does not, however, apply to the case of Lee. For up to the very hour of Virginia's decision, he clung to the Union and was opposed to secession, at any rate, in practice. In January, 1861, he wrote: "I can anticipate no greater calamity for the country than a dissolution of the Union. It would be an accumulation of all the evils we complain of and I am willing to sacrifice everything but honor for its preservation. ... Secession is nothing but revolution. The framers of our Constitution never exhausted so much labor, wisdom, and forbearance in its formation, and surrounded it with so many guards and securities, if it was intended to be broken by every member of the Confederation at will. It was intended for 'perpetual union,' so expressed in the preamble"–Lee, of course, here confounds the Constitution of the United States with the "Articles of Confederation"–"and for the establishment of a government, not a compact, which can only be dissolved by revolution or the consent of all the people in convention assembled. It is idle to talk of secession. Anarchy would have been established and not a government by Washington, Hamilton, Jefferson, Madison, and the other patriots of the Revolution."[22]

Surely neither Webster nor Everett ever spoke for Federal Union with an ardor more passionate than this. And after all was over, Lee testified before the Committee on Reconstruction: "I may have said and I may have believed that the position of the two sections which they held to each other was brought about by the politicians of the country; that the great masses of the people, if they understood the real question, would have avoided it. ... I did believe at the time that it was an unnecessary condition of affairs and might have been avoided, if forbearance and wisdom had been practiced on both sides."[23]

It will at once be asked, why, then, did Lee leave the Union? Because Virginia left it and he felt that Virginia was his country. And I cannot see how any citizen of the old colonial states, with all the memories and traditions of his forefathers in his heart and all the local attachments and fellowships that constitute home, can fail even now to sympathize with such an attitude. "No consideration on earth could induce me to act a part, however gratifying to me, which could be construed into faithlessness to this Commonwealth,"[24] wrote Lee's father to Madison; and at another time he expressed himself still more strongly: "Virginia is my country; her I will obey, however lamentable the fate to which it may subject me."[25] Longstreet, in describing his own decision, tells us that "a number of officers of the post called to persuade me to remain in the Union service. Captain Gibbs, of the Mounted Rifles, was the principal talker, and after a long

31

and pleasant discussion, I asked him what course he would pursue, if his State should pass ordinances of secession and call him to its defense. He confessed that he would obey the call."[26] Hon. Charles Francis Adams, who has surely done more than any one else to help Lee on to the national glory which is his due, said in his Lee Centennial address, "I hope I should have been filial and unselfish enough myself to have done as Lee did."[27] Finally, if one may quote one's own feeling as perhaps representative of many, I do not hesitate to say that in the certainly most improbable, but perhaps not wholly impossible, contingency of a future sectional separation in the country, however much I might disapprove of such separation and its causes, I should myself be first, last, and always a son and subject of New England and of Massachusetts.

There is a deeper principle involved in this attitude than the mere blind instinct of what the French call "village-spire patriotism," local attachment to home, and family, and birthplace. When the Union was first established, its founders had an intense and wholesome dread of centralized power, but the state governments were at that time so strong and the federal so weak that it was necessary to emphasize the latter in every possible way in order to sustain it at all. In the nature of the case, however, from the very beginning the federal government absorbed more and more power to itself and the states tended gradually to lose even the authority which had originally been left them. In one sense the Civil War was a protest on the part of the South against this evolution and an attempt to restore the constitutional balance as the men of 1787 had planned it. This protest had to be met, had to be crushed, or worse, incalculable evils would have resulted. But the failure of it much increased the rapidity of the evolution already in progress. To-day the citizens of the newer states and many in the older doubtless look upon the state governments as an antiquated survival, especially as this very attitude deteriorates those governments and everywhere breeds incompetence and corruption. Such people would sympathize entirely with the remark of a writer in the "Outlook": "Lee's engrossing sentiment for his native State, mildly commendable though it might have been, was a pinchbeck thing."[28]

This development of national unity, of national feeling, is probably inevitable, is in many ways excellent and admirable; but it has its very grave dangers and is in itself certainly much less promising for the future of popular government than the careful balance of local and central authority for which the Constitution originally provided. Such, at any rate, was the opinion of Lee, reiterated in manifold forms all through the war. He, at least, felt, with the most earnest conviction, that he was fighting for the ideas of Washington and Jefferson, and that in his place they would have done as he did. "I had no other guide, nor had I any other object than the defense of those principles of American liberty upon which the constitutions of the several States were originally founded; and unless they are strictly observed, I fear there will be an end to Republican government in this country."[29] Again, he says in general orders: "They [the Confederate soldiers] cannot barter manhood for peace nor the right of self-government for life or property. . . . Let us then oppose constancy to adversity, fortitude to suffering, and courage to danger, with the firm assurance that He who gave freedom to our fathers will bless the efforts of their children to preserve it."[30] And at the close of the war he is said to have expressed the same feeling quite as explicitly and solemnly: "We had, I was satisfied, sacred principles to maintain and rights to defend, for which we were in duty bound to do our best, even if we perished in the endeavor."[31]

As we read these passionate confessions of faith, we come almost to look upon Lee as one of the great martyrs of liberty, one of the heroic champions of free democracy and popular government. And then we reflect a moment and say to ourselves, was not this man fighting for negro slavery? It cannot be disputed that he was. Southern writers may quibble as they please about slavery not being the cause of the war. Nobody denies that there were other causes, many of them, causes lying deep in difference of climate, difference of breeding, difference of local temperament. But no one can seriously maintain that any of those other causes or all of them together could have led to any sectional quarrel that might not have been easily settled, if it had not been for the dark phantom, the terrible midnight incubus of slavery. As we look back now, we all see that, in the words attributed to Lincoln, "the people of the North were as responsible for slavery as the people of the South,"[32] and that honest, noble, pure spirits could advocate it as well as oppose it. We are all ready to sympathize with the words which Lincoln actually wrote: "You think slavery is right and ought to be extended; we think it is wrong and ought to be restricted. For this, neither has any just occasion to be angry with the other."[33] Nay, more, the abolitionists of the sixties went at their problem gayly, confident that if the negro were once free, all would be well. Forty years have taught us better, until some are almost ready to cry out that the South was right and the North wrong. It is not so. The future must take care of itself. The nineteenth century made many mistakes. But it showed once for all that the modern world can never again have anything to do with slavery. "I advise Senators to let the humane current of an advancing and Christian civilization spread over this continent," said Henry Wilson. Senators and other persons who fought on the side of slavery had their backs to the light and their faces turned toward outer darkness.

It will immediately be urged that Lee was no advocate of slavery. This cannot be denied. It is true that his attitude towards the negro was distinctly the Southern attitude, and, it must also be added, that of most Northerners who live long in the South. "I have always observed that wherever you find the negro, everything is going down around him, and wherever you find the white man, you see everything around him improving."[34] "You will never prosper with the blacks," he writes to his son after the war, "and it is abhorrent to a reflecting mind to be supporting and cherishing those who are plotting and working for your injury and all of whose sympathies and associations are antagonistic to yours. I wish them no evil in the world—on the contrary, will do them every good in my power, and know that they are misled by those to whom they have given their confidence; but our material, social, and political interests are with the whites."[35] Furthermore, he had no sympathy with the Northern abolitionists and believed that they were working in utter ignorance of actual conditions as well as with a disposition to meddle where they had no legal or moral right to interfere. He even went so far as to write, toward the very close of the war, that he considered "the relation of master and slave, controlled by humane laws and influenced by Christianity and an enlightened public sentiment, as the best that can exist between the white and black races while intermingled as at present in this country."[36]

This passage does not appear in the Southern biographies of Lee, and it can be justly interpreted only as a partial utterance in view of a most complicated and difficult problem. For that Lee himself disliked and detested slavery there can be no possible doubt. The few slaves that ever belonged to him personally he set free long before the war, and he took time in the very thick of his military duties to arrange at the appointed date for the emancipation of those who had been left to his wife by her father. Before the war, also, he expressed himself on the general subject in the most explicit way: "In this enlightened age there are few, I believe, but will acknowledge that slavery, as an institution, is a moral and political evil in any country."[37] The very letter from which I quoted above as to the benefits of the relation between master and slave was written to urge gradual abolition as a reward for faithful military service, and some remarks attributed to Lee after the war form a valuable comment on his pro-slavery utterance, especially in view of all that has come and gone in the last forty years. "The best men of the South have long desired to do away with the institution and were quite willing to see it abolished. But with them in relation to this subject the question has ever been: What will you do with the freed people? That is the serious question to-day. Unless some humane course, based upon wisdom and Christian principles, is adopted, you do them a great injustice in setting them free."[38]

Yet, after all, in fighting for the Confederacy Lee was fighting for slavery, and he must have known perfectly well that if the South triumphed and maintained its independence, slavery would grow and flourish for another generation, if not for another century. And it is precisely this network of moral conditions that makes his heroic struggle so pathetic, so appealing, so irresistibly human. For the great tragedies of human life and history come from the intermingling of good and evil. And Lee is one of the most striking, one of the noblest tragic figures the world ever produced. Matthew Arnold says that the Puritans, fighting for English liberty, put the human spirit in prison for two hundred years.[39] This man, fighting, as he believed, for freedom, for independence, for democracy, was fighting also to rivet the shackles more firmly on millions of his fellow men. A most striking passage in Burke's "Conciliation" brings out this contrast with a prophetic force which no after-comment can equal:—

> There is, however, a circumstance attending these colonies, which, in my opinion, fully counterbalances this difference and makes the spirit of liberty still more high and haughty than in those to the northward. It is, that in Virginia and the Carolinas they have a vast multitude of slaves. Where this is the case in any part of the world, those who are free are by far the most proud and jealous of their freedom.... Not seeing there, that freedom, as in countries where it is a common blessing, and as broad and general as the air, may be united with much abject toil, with great misery, with all the exterior of servitude, liberty looks, amongst them, like something that is more noble and liberal. I do not mean, Sir, to commend the superior morality of this sentiment, which has at least as much pride as virtue in it; but I cannot alter the nature of man. The fact is so; and these people of the Southern colonies are much more strongly and with a higher and more stubborn spirit attached to liberty than those to the northward.[40]

In Lee, no pride, but virtue all; not liberty for himself alone, but for others, for every one. And this it is that makes the tragedy of his career so large, so fatal, so commanding in its grandeur.

One element which, since Hamlet, we consider peculiarly tragic, is, however, wanting in Lee. There is no trace of irresolution in him, no faltering, no looking back. We have indirectly from Mrs. Lee her account of the way in which the first decision was made. "The night his letter of resignation was to be written, he asked to be left alone for a time, and while he paced the chamber above, and was heard frequently to fall upon his knees and engage in prayer for divine guidance, she waited and watched and prayed below. At last he came down, calm, collected, almost cheerful, and said, 'Well, Mary, the question is settled. Here is my letter of resignation and a letter I have written to General Scott.'"[41] The question was settled—finally, and in all his correspondence or recorded conversation there is nothing to indicate regret or even further doubt. "Trusting in God, an approving conscience, and the aid of my fellow citizens," he accepted the command of the armies of Virginia; and as the war progressed, his zeal for the cause and loyalty to his high ideals seemed to be ever on the increase.

Not that he showed any bitterness towards the enemy. Or at least it is only at moments that the unavoidable horror of war wrings from him a word of reproach or condemnation, as when he says of the obstruction of Charleston Harbor, "This achievement, so unworthy of any nation, is the abortive expression of the malice and revenge of a people which it wishes to perpetuate by rendering more hateful a day memorable in their calendar,"[42] or speaks of the "savage and brutal policy which he [Milroy] has proclaimed, which leaves us no alternative but success or degradation worse than death, if we would save the honor of our families from pollution, our social system from destruction."[43] His general tone in referring to "those people," as he almost always called the Northern soldiers, is wholly in the spirit of his own admirable saying, "the better rule is to judge our adversaries from their standpoint, not from ours."[44]

But over and over again, to his family, to his friends, to his army, he expresses his pride in the cause he has adopted, his absolute belief in its nobility and justice, his unyielding determination to fight for it, so long as any fighting is possible. "Let each man resolve that the right of self-government, liberty, and peace shall find in him a defender," he says to his soldiers in the early days,[45] and commendds to them "the sacred cause, dearer than life itself, of defending the honor and integrity of the State."[46] At the climax of the struggle, with the bright hope of success before him, he consoles them for their dangers: "The country consents to the loss of such men as these and the gallant soldiers who fell with them, only to secure the inestimable blessings they died to obtain."[47] And at the last bitter parting he assures them that "You will take with you the satisfaction that proceeds from the consciousness of duty faithfully performed."[48] So, in reviewing his own private conduct, when all is over, he cannot blame his choice or regret his decision. "All that the South has ever desired was that the Union, as established by our forefathers, should be preserved and that the government as originally organized, should be administered in purity and truth."[49] Or again, more solemnly, "I did only what my duty demanded. I could have taken no other course without dishonor. And if it were all to be done over again, I should act in precisely the same manner."[50]

Finally, it is to be noted that Lee's conduct from beginning to end was absolutely free from all thought of personal credit or advantage. He declined the highest standing in his profession for what was, to say the least, a dim uncertainty. He was fifty-four years old, and such dreams of glory as he may ever have cherished had doubtless long faded in the hope of peace. One consideration, and one only, the desire to do right, prompted him in all he undertook and all he accomplished. Doubtless, the same thing might be said of many a private soldier, North and South both; but Lee's exalted position gives his action a typical significance which cannot attach to that of every one. And when the fearful failure came, when all things were sinking to wreck and ruin about him, though his heart was torn for the sufferings of his people, for his own lot there was nothing but superb tranquility, a calm, unyielding, heroic self-control, which rested upon the consciousness that he had done what man could do and all the rest was God's. He might have used the splendid words of Demosthenes: "I say that if the event had been manifest to the whole world beforehand, not even then ought Athens to have forsaken this course, if Athens had any regard for her glory, or for her past, or for the ages to come." But he had words of his own, as apt, perhaps as splendid, as those of Demosthenes, the well-known and often quoted, "Duty is the sublimest word in the language";[51] the less well-known but not less noble, "There is a true glory and a true honor, the glory of duty done, the honor of the integrity of priniciple";[52] best of all the grandly tragic phrase, addressed to his son, which forms the most perfect comment on his own career, "I know that wherever you may be placed, you will do your duty. That is all the pleasure, all the comfort, all the glory we can enjoy in this world."[53]

Jefferson Davis

3

LEE AND DAVIS

I t will hardly be disputed that Lee and Davis are by far the most prominent figures in the history of the Confederacy. Stephens and Benjamin, Johnston and Beauregard, are not to be named with them. Jackson might have been a conspicuous third; but his premature death left him only a peculiar and separate glory.

Material, of a sort, for the study of Davis's character is more than abundant. His own work, "The Rise and Fall of the Confederate Government," is one of the numerous books that carefully avoid telling us what we wish to know. Half of it is ingenious argument on the abstract dead questions at issue. The other half is a history of military matters which others have told often and told better. Of administrative complications and difficulties, of the internal working of the Confederate Government, of personalities at Richmond and the Richmond atmosphere, of the inner life and struggles of the man himself, hardly a word. Happily we have Mrs. Davis's "Life" of her husband, which shows him complete, if not exactly as Mrs. Davis saw him. We have other biographies of less value, innumerable references in letters and memoirs of friends and enemies, and the constant comments of the public press. And we have the immense mass of correspondence in that national portrait gallery, the "Official Records," where the great—and little—men of a generation have drawn their own likenesses with an art as perfect as it is unconscious.

Davis, then, was a scholar and a thinker, and to some extent he took the bookish view of life, that it can be made what we wish it to be. Compromise with men and things was to be avoided, if possible. He was an orator, a considerable orator, after the fashion of the mid-nineteenth century, which bores us now, at any rate in the reading.

Lee The American

The orator in politics, though a naturally recurring figure in a democratic society, is too apt to be an unsatisfactory one,—witness Cicero. Davis never laid aside his robes of rhetoric in public. I doubt if he did in private. I think he wore them in his soul. His passion was rhetoric, his patriotism was rhetoric, his wit was rhetoric, perfectly genuine, there is no doubt of that, but always falling into a form that would impress others—and himself. He told Dr. Craven that he could not "conceive how a man so oppressed with care as Mr. Lincoln was could have any relish for such pleasantries."[1] There you have the difference between the two.

Doubtless Davis had many excellent practical qualities. For one thing, he had pluck, splendid pluck, moral and physical. It was indeed, I imagine, rather pluck of the high-strung, nervous order than the cool, collected calmness of Lee or Grant. There again is the difference in types. Nevertheless, Davis's pluck is beyond question. He had consistency, too, knew his ideas and stuck to them, had persistency. "He was an absolutely frank, direct, and positive man," said General Breckinridge.[2] And he was sincere in his purposes, as well as consistent. "As God is my judge, I never spoke from any other motive [than conviction]," he told Seward.[3] Beyond question he told the truth. He was unselfish, too, thoughtful of others and ready to make sacrifices for them. "He displayed more self-abnegation than any other human being I have ever known," says one of his aides[4] and the statement is abundantly confirmed.

But in everything he was a nervous sensitive, which is a terrible handicap to a leader of men. He suffered always with nervous dyspepsia and neuralgia and "came home from his office fasting, a mere mass of throbbing nerves and perfectly exhausted."[5] He shrank from the sight of every form of suffering, even in imagination. When the "Babes in the Wood" was first read to him, a grown man, in time of sickness, he would not endure the horror of it.[6] His sympathy with the oppressed was also intense, "so that," says Mrs. Davis, "it was a difficult matter to keep order with children and servants."[7] He was keenly susceptible to the atmosphere about him, especially to the moods of people, "abnormally sensitive to disapproval. Even a child's disapproval discomposed him."[8] And Mrs. Davis admits that this sensitiveness and acute feeling of being misjudged made him reserved and unapproachable. It made him touchy as to his dignity, also, and there are stories of his cherishing a grudge for some insignificant or imagined slight and punishing the author of it.[9]

The same sensitive temperament appears in Davis's spiritual life. That he should seek and find the hand of Providence in temporal affairs is surely not to his discredit. But I feel that his religion occasionally intrudes at the wrong time and in the wrong way. When his enemies represented him as "standing in a corner telling his beads and relying on a miracle to save the country,"[10] I know they exaggerated, but I understand what they meant.

Altogether, one of those subtle, fine, high-wrought nervous organizations, which America breeds, a trifle too fine, consuming in superb self-control too much of what ought to be active, practical, beneficent energy.

It will easily be imagined that such a temper would not always get along comfortably with rough, practical, imperious military men, accustomed to regard civil authority with contempt. That Davis had had military experience himself, both in the field and as Secretary of War, did not help matters much, since it greatly increased his own self-confidence. Subordinate officers, such as Stuart, Longstreet, and Jackson during the latter part of his career, did not have many direct dealings with the President. But the independent commanders fall generally into two classes, those like Bragg, Pemberton, and Hood, who were more or less unfit for their positions and retained them through Davis's personal favor, and those who were able and popular but whom Davis could not endure, like Joseph E. Johnston and Beauregard. Albert Sidney Johnston seems to have been both a favorite and a great soldier, but untimely death blighted Davis's choice in that instance.

The quarrel with J.E. Johnston shook the whole fabric of the Confederacy, since the omnipotent editors took part in it. Johnston was a good general and an honest man; but he was surly with a superior and his correspondence and his book are querulous. Davis is not querulous and his references to Johnston are always dignified. Mrs. Davis assures us that "in the whole period of his official relations to General Johnston I never heard him utter a word in derogation."[11] She tells us also, however, that "every shade of feeling that crossed the minds of those about him was noticed and he could not bear any one to be inimical to him."[12] Persons of this temper always exaggerate enmity where it exists and imagine it where it does not. Another of Mrs. Davis's priceless observations is as to "the talent for governing men without humiliating them, which Mr. Davis had in an eminent degree."[13] Samples of this were doubtless the indorsement "insubordinate" on one of Johnston's grumbling letters and the reply to another, "The language of your letter is, as you say, unusual; its argument and statement utterly one-sided, and its insinuations as unfounded as they are unbecoming."[14] Compare also the indorsement on a letter in which Beauregard, a gentleman, an excellent soldier, and a true patriot, who had long held independent command, wrote that he was perfectly ready to serve under Lee: "I did not doubt the willingness of General Beauregard to serve under any general who ranked him. The right of General Lee to command would be derived from his superior rank."[15]

And so we come to the case of Lee, who during the last years of the war was universally recognized as the greatest general and most popular man in the Confederacy and who held Davis's confidence and intimate affection from the beginning to the end. "General R.E. Lee was the only man who was permitted to enter the Cabinet [meetings] unannounced," says the official who secured the privacy of those august assemblies.[16]

How did Lee manage to retain his hold on the President? Pollard, who admired Lee, but detested Davis more, says plainly that the general employed "compliment and flattery."[17] This is an abuse of words. One can no more associate flattery with Lee than with Washington. Lee respected and admired Davis in many ways. With that fine insight into character which was one of his strongest points, the general appreciated the President's peculiarities and adapted himself to them for the sake of the cause to which he had devoted his life. Davis required deference, respect, subordination. Lee felt that these were military duties and he was ready to accord them. He defends Davis to others,—"The President from his position being able to survey all the scenes of action, can better decide than any one else."[18] He defers again and again to Davis's opinion: "Should you think proper to concentrate the troops near Richmond, I should be glad if you would advise me."[19] On many occasions he expresses a desire for Davis's presence in the field: "I need not say how glad I should be if your convenience would permit you to visit the army, that I might have the benefit of your advice and direction."[20] Those know but little of Lee who see in such passages anything but the frank, simple modesty of the man's nature, or who read a double meaning into expressions like the following: "While I should feel the greatest satisfaction in having an interview with you and consultation upon all subjects of interest, I cannot but feel great uneasiness for your safety, should you undertake to reach me."[21] The solicitude was perfectly genuine, as we see from many charming manifestations of it elsewhere. "I cannot express the concern I felt at leaving you in such feeble health, with so many anxious thoughts for the welfare of the whole Confederacy weighing upon your mind."[22] And there is no doubt that such sympathetic affection held the president more than even the most exaggerated military deference.

At the same time, it is certain that Davis liked to be consulted. He had a considerable opinion of his own military gifts and would probably have preferred the command of the armies in the field to the presidency, although Ropes, the best of judges, tells us that he did not "show himself the possessor of military ability to any notable extent,"[23] and Grant slyly remarks that "on several occasions during the war he came to the relief of the Union armies by his superior military genius."[24] His jealousy of independent command sometimes appears even with regard to Lee. "I have never comprehended your views and purposes until the receipt of your letter yesterday and now have to regret that I did not earlier know all that you have now communicated to others."[25] Perhaps the most delightful instance of Davis's confidence in his own talents as a general is the little indiscretion of Mrs. Davis. "Again and again he said [before Gettysburg], 'If I could take one wing and Lee the other, I think we could between us wrest a victory from those people.'"[25] One says these things to one's wife; but I doubt if Davis would have wished that repeated—yet perhaps he would.

With all this in mind, it is easy to understand Lee's procedure and to see the necessity as well as the wisdom of it. He was never free. In the early days he writes almost as Davis's clerk. To the end his most important communications are occasionally inspired by his superior, to the very wording. This subordination is trying at times to Lee's greatest admirers. Captain Battine says, "It was the commander-in-chief who had constantly to stir up the energy of the president."[27] Colonel Henderson, whose admirable judgment is always to be respected, thinks Davis's policy was the cause of the failure to fight on the North Anna instead of at Fredericksburg, and he adds more generally, "A true estimate of Lee's genius is impossible, for it can never be known to what extent his designs were thwarted by the Confederate Government. Lee served Davis; Jackson served Lee, wisest and most helpful of masters."[28] It seems to me, however, that Lee's genius showed in overcoming Davis as well as in overcoming the enemy.

One of the most curious instances of Lee's sensitive deference to the president as his military superior has, so far as I have discovered, remained unnoticed by all the historians and biographers. On August 8, 1863, a month after Gettysburg, Lee wrote the beautiful letter in which he urged that some one more capable should be put in his place (italics mine):—

I know how prone we are to censure and how ready to blame others for the non-fulfillment of our expectations. This is unbecoming in a generous people, and I grieve to see its expression. *The general remedy for the want of success in a military commander is his removal.* I have been prompted by these reflections more than once since my return from Pennsylvania to propose to Your Excellency the propriety of selecting another commander for this army. I have seen and heard of expression of discontent in the public journals at the result of the expedition. I do not know how far this feeling extends in the army. My brother officers have been too kind to report it, and so far the troops have been too generous to exhibit it. It is fair, however, to suppose that it does exist, and success is so necessary to us that nothing should be risked to secure it. I, therefore, in all sincerity, request Your Excellency to take measures to supply my place. I do this with the more earnestness because no one is more aware than myself of my inability for the duties of my position. I cannot even accomplish what I myself desire. How can I fulfill the expectations of others?[29]

It has been, I believe, universally assumed by Lee's biographers that this proposal of resignation was the result of his devoted patriotism and of temporary discouragement caused by press and other criticism of the Gettysburg failure. Such criticism there doubtless was; but it was so restrained by the deep-rooted confidence in Lee's character and ability that it appears mild in comparison with the attacks on Davis himself and on other generals. Without any reflection on Lee's patriotism, which needs no defense, I think a more important key to his action is to be found in the first sentence of his letter: "Your letters of July 28 and August 2 have been received and I have waited for a leisure hour to reply." The letter of July 28 apparently was not printed till 1897 in the supplementary volumes of the "Official Records." In it Davis writes (italics mine):–

Misfortune often develops secret foes and still oftener makes men complain. It is comfortable to hold some one responsible for one's discomfort. In various quarters there are mutterings of discontent, and threats of alienation are said to exist, with preparation for organized opposition. *There are others who, faithful but dissatisfied, find an appropriate remedy in the removal of officers who have not succeeded.* They have not counted the cost of following their advice. Their remedy, to be good, should furnish substitutes who would be better than the officers displaced. If a victim would secure the success of our cause, I would freely offer myself.[30]

It seems of course absurd to suppose that Davis intended any hint here, especially in view of the instant, cordial, and affectionate negative which he returned to Lee's suggestion. Yet I think it quite in the character of the man to feel that it would be a graceful and respectful thing for a beaten commander to take such a step and receive presidential clemency. At any rate, if Davis's remarks were not intended as a hint, they show a gross lack of tact as addressed to a man in Lee's situation; and certainly no one can doubt that Lee's letter was in the main the response of his sore and fretted humility to what seemed the implied suggestion of his superior.

It must not, however, for a moment be supposed that Lee's attitude towards Davis or any one else was in any way servile. Dignity, not pompous or self-conscious, but natural, was his unfailing character-istic. "He was one with whom nobody ever wished or ventured to take a liberty."[31] Even little slights he could resent in his quiet way. Davis himself records with much amusement that he once made some slur at a mistake of the engineers, and Lee, who had been trained in that service, replied that he "did not know that engineer officers were more likely than others to make such mistakes."[32]

Furthermore, Lee never hesitated to urge upon the president the wants of the army. Over and over again he writes, pointing out the terrible need of reinforcements. "I beg that you will take every practicable means to reinforce our ranks, which are much reduced, and which will require to be strengthened to their full extent to be able to compete with the invigorated force of the enemy."[33] His tone is roundly decided and energetic when he represents the importance of government action to repress straggling and disorder. "I have the honor to inclose to you a copy of a letter written on the 7th instant, which may not have reached you, containing suggestions as to the means of preventing them and punishing the perpetrators. I again respectfully invite your attention to what I have said in that letter. Some effectual means of repressing these outrages should be adopted, as they are disgraceful to the army and injurious to our cause."[34] As the difficulty of obtaining supplies became greater towards the end, although it was notorious that they were to be had in various parts of the country, Lee did not hesitate to side with the public at large and demand the removal of Davis's favorite, the commissary general, Northrop; and I have no doubt that this is referred to in Davis's remark to Dr. Craven. "Even Gen. –, otherwise so moderate and conservative, was finally induced to join this injurious clamor."[35]

In general political questions Lee was very reluctant to interfere. He did so at times, however. His suggestions as to finance and as to the military employment of negroes are less connected with Davis and belong more properly to the discussion of his relations with the Confederate Government. But there were matters on which he appealed to the president urgently and directly. At the time of the first invasion of Maryland, he wrote an earnest letter pointing out the desirability of proposals for peace. "The present position of affairs, in my opinion, places it in the power of the Government of the Confederate States to propose with propriety to that of the United States the recognition of our independence."[36] Again, just before the second invasion, he writes to the same effect with even more energy. "Davis had said repeatedly that reunion with the Noth was unthinkable," remarks his latest biographer. "Lee wrote in effect that such assertions, which out of respect to the Executive he charged against the press, were short-sighed in the extreme." Lee's language is in no way disrespectful, but it is very decided. "Nor do I think we should in this connection make nice distinction between those who declare for peace unconditionally and those who advocate it as a means of restoring the Union, however much we may prefer the former. . . . When peace is proposed, it will be time enough to discuss its terms, and it is not the part of prudence to spurn the proposition in advance."[37]

Also, in political matters as affecting military movements there was more or less conflict of opinion between the president and his leading general. Lee regretted deeply the absence of Longstreet before Chancellorsville. Lee was very anxious to be supported by Beauregard before Gettysburg. There is no doubt that Lee, all through the war, would have preferred a policy of more energetic concentration. And if the testimony of Long, Gordon, and others is to be accepted as against that of Davis himself, Lee would have abandoned Richmond toward the close of the struggle, had it not been for the decided opposition of the president.

In all these differences, however, we must note Lee's infinite courtesy and tact in the expression of his views. If he had lectured his superior after the fashion in which he himself was frequently addressed by Longstreet, the Army of Northern Virginia would have been looking for a commander at a very early stage. Instead of this, however decided his opinion, however urgent his recommendations, the language, without being undignified, is such as to soothe Davis's sensitive pride and save his love of authority. "I earnestly commend these considerations to the attention of Your Excellency and trust that you will be at liberty, in your better judgment, and with the superior means of information you possess . . . . to give effect to them, either in the way I have suggested or in such other manner as may seem to you more judicious."[38]

Yet with all his tact and all his delicacy Lee must have felt as if he were handling a shy and sensitive horse, who might kick over the traces at any moment, with little provocation or none, so touchy was the president apt to be at even the slightest suggestion. For instance, Lee advises that General Whiting should be sent south. Davis indorses: "Let General Lee order General Whiting to report here, and it may then be decided whether he will be sent south or not."[39] Lee objects earnestly to the organization of the military courts, offering to draft a new bill in regard to them. Davis simply comments: "I do not find in the law referred to anything which requires the commanding general to refer all charges to the military courts."[40] Davis hears gossip about Lee's expressed opinions and calls him to order in the sharpest manner. "Rumors assumed to be based on your views have affected the public mind and it is reported obstructs [sic] needful legislation. A little further progress will produce panic. If you can spare the time, I wish you to come here."[41] But the most decided snub of all came in connection with the punishment of deserters. Lee felt strongly about this and had urged upon Davis and upon the War Office the ruinous effects of executive clemency. Finally, Longstreet calls attention to the depletion of his command by desertion, which he asserts is encouraged by constant reprieval. Lee passes on the complaint with the comment: "Desertion is increasing in the army, notwithstanding all my efforts to stop it. I think a rigid execution of the law is [kindest?] in the end. The great want in our army is firm discipline."[42] Seddon refers the matter to Davis and he calmly notes: "When deserters are arrested, they should be tried, and if the sentence is remitted, that is not a proper subject for the criticism of a military commander."[43] When one reads these things, one is reminded of Mrs. Davis's delightful remark about "the talent for governing men without humiliating them," and one is almost tempted to reverse it.

That, in spite of these small matters of necessary discipline, Davis had the most unbounded and sincere affection for Lee is not open to a moment's doubt. In the early days, when Lee was unpopular, the president supported him loyally. When the South Carolinians objected to his being sent to them, Davis said, "If Lee is not a general, then I have none that I can send you."[44] And no jealousy of later glory or success prevented the repeated expression of a similar opinion. "General Lee was one of the greatest soldiers of the age, if not the very greatest of this or any other country."[45] And the praise was as discriminating as it was enthusiastic: "General Lee was not a man of hesitation and they mistake his character who suppose that caution was his vice."[46] Admiration of the general was, moreover, backed up by a solid confidence which is expressed repeatedly by Davis himself and by others. "The President has unbounded confidence in Lee's capacity, modest as he is," says J.B. Jones, at the very beginning of the war.[47] "General Lee was now fast gaining the confidence of all classes; he had possessed that of the President always," writes Mrs. Davis.[48] "I am alike happy in the confidence felt in your ability and your superiority to outside clamor, when the uninformed assume to direct the movement of armies in the field,"[49] is one among many passages which show unreserved reliance on the commander-in-chief.

Nor was Davis less keenly aware of Lee's great qualities as a man than of his military superiority. This is made abundantly apparent in both speeches and writings after Lee's death. The president extols his subordinate's uprightness, his generosity, his utter forgetfulness of self and loyal devotion. In the noble eulogy pronounced at the Lee Memorial gathering in 1870 there are many instances of such praise, none more striking than the account of Lee's attitude towards the attacks made upon him before his popularity was established: "Through all this, with a magnanimity rarely equaled, he stood in silence, without defending himself or allowing others to defend him."[50] And besides the general commendation there is a note of deep personal feeling which is extremely touching. "He was my friend and in that word is included all that I can say of any man."[51] I have not met with a single expression on Davis's part of deliberate criticism or fault-finding, and if he did not say such things he did not think them, for he was a man whose thoughts found their way to the surface in some shape sooner or later.

With Lee it is different. About many things we shall never know what he really thought. Undoubtedly he esteemed and admired Davis; but the expression of these feelings does not go beyond kindly cordiality. Soon after the war he writes to Early: "I have been much pained to see the attempts made to cast odium upon Mr. Davis, but do not think they will be successful with the reflecting or informed part of the country."[52] After Davis's release from captivity, Lee wrote him a letter which is very charming in its old-fashioned courtesy. "Your release has lifted a load from my heart which I have no words to tell. . . . That the rest of your days may be triumphantly happy is the sincere and earnest wish of your most obedient and faithful friend and servant."[53] Lee is, of course, even less outspoken in criticism than in praise of his superior. It is only very rarely that we catch a trace of dissatisfaction, as in reference to the anxiety of the authorities in regard to Richmond: "The general had been heard to say that Richmond was the millstone that was dragging down the army."[54] In the delightful–if not always perfectly reliable–memoirs of General Gordon we get perhaps the most explicit statement of what Lee's feeling about the president really was. It was at the time when Davis was said to be unwilling to abandon the capital. Lee spoke to Gordon in the highest terms of the great qualities of Davis's character, praised "the strength of his convictions, his devotion, his remarkable faith in the possibility of still winning our independence, his unconquerable will-power. But," he added, "you know that the president is very tenacious in opinion and purposes."[55]

The study of the relations of Lee and Davis grows more interesting, as the history of the Confederacy approaches its tragic close. In 1861, Davis was popular all through the country. A small faction would have preferred another president, but once he was elected the support was enthusiastic and general. With difficulties and reverses, however, there came–naturally–a change of feeling. In the first place, the Confederacy had seceded for state rights. Now war powers and state rights did not go together. Davis was constantly anxious to have law behind him, so anxious that the "Richmond Whig" sneered at his desire to get a law to back up every act of usurpation. But military necessity knows no law and the states in time grew restive and almost openly rebellious.

More than that, there came–also naturally–a bitter hostility to Davis himself. "The people are weary of the flagrant mismanagement of the government," is a mild specimen of the sort of thing that abounds in the "Richmond Examiner."[56] "Jefferson Davis now treats all men as if they were idiotic insects," says the "Charleston Mercury."[57] And Edmund Rhett, who had been disposed to hostility from the beginning, told Mrs. Chesnut that the president was "conceited, wrong-headed, wranglesome, obstinate–a traitor."[58] These little amenities were of course to be expected. Lincoln had to meet them. But the Southern opposition seems to have been more widespread than the Northern, and I imagine an election in the autumn of 1864 would have defeated Davis decisively. A moderate view of the state of things appears in a letter from Forsythe of Mobile to Bragg, January, 1865: "Men have been taught to look upon the president as a sort of inexorably self-willed man who will see the country to the devil before giving up an opinion or a purpose. . . . We cannot win unless we keep up the popular heart. Mr. Davis should come down and grapple with that heart. He has great qualities for gaining the confidence of the people. There are many who would leap to his side to fight with and for him and for the country, if he would step into the arena and make the place for them."[59]

The question now arises, How far was Davis really responsible for this state of things? Could another, larger, abler man have done more than he did, if not have succeeded where he failed? For there is good evidence that the South had men and material resources to have kept up the struggle far longer. "Our resources, fitly and vigorously employed, are ample," said Lee himself in February, 1865.[60] It was the people who had lost their courage, lost their interest, lost their hope—and no wonder. But could any people have behaved differently? Would that people with another leader? "It is not the great causes, but the great men who have made history," says one of the acutest observers of the human heart.

Such discussion would be futile except for its connection with the character of Davis. In the opinion of his detractors, the lost cause would have been won in better hands and Pollard's clever book has spread that opinion very widely. Pollard, however, though doubtless sincere enough, was Davis's bitter personal enemy, or at any rate wrote as such. The dispassionate observer will hardly agree at once with his positive conclusions. More interesting is the comment of the diary-keeping war clerk, Jones, an infinitely small personage, but with an eye many-faceted as an insect's. Jones was a hearty admirer of the president at first, but fault-finding grows and, what is more important, the fault-finding is based on facts. Davis, says Jones, "is probably not equal to the role he is called upon to play. He has not the broad intelligence required for the gigantic measures needed in such a crisis nor the health and physique for the labors devolving upon him."[61]

It is difficult, I think, not to agree with this moderate statement, unless the emphasis should be placed rather on character than on intelligence. Probably the Confederacy could never have been saved; but there might have been a leader who could have done more to save it than Davis. In the first place, the greatest men gather able men about them. Professor Hart writes, with justice: "President Davis's cabinet was made up in great part of feeble and incapable men."[62] Mrs. Chesnut tells us that "there is a perfect magazine of discord and disunion in the Cabinet!"[63] Jones, who had the best opportunities for observation says: "Never did such little men rule a great people."[64] And again, "Of one thing I am certain, that the people are capable of achieving independence, if they only had capable men in all departments of the government."[65] Mrs. Chesnut (an admirer of Davis in the main) lays her finger on the secret of the matter when she says: "He [Toombs] rides too high a horse for so despotic a person as Jefferson Davis."[66] And we get further insight, when we learn that in 1862 Davis considered making Lee Secretary of War, but thought better of it.[67] Perhaps Lee was of more value in the field than he would have been in the cabinet; but it is difficult to believe that even he could permanently have remained Davis's secretary.

There are plenty of other indications, besides his choice of advisers, to show that Davis, able, brilliant, noble figure as he was, was over-parted in the enormous role he had to play. He could not always handle men in a way to win them, as a great ruler must. In his earlier life we read that "public sentiment had proclaimed that Jefferson Davis is the most arrogant man in the United States Senate,"[68] and Mrs. Davis herself tells us, when she first meets him, that he "has a way of taking for granted that everybody agrees with him, when he expresses an opinion, which offends me."[69] "Gifted with some of the highest attributes of a statesman, he lacked the pliancy which enables a man to adapt his measures to the crisis," says his kinsman, Reuben Davis.[70] But the two most decisive comments on Davis's career that I know of are made again by Mrs. Davis, certainly with no intention of judging her husband and all the more valuable on that account. "It was because of his supersensitive temperament and the acute suffering it caused him, I had deprecated his assuming the civil administration."[71] Cromwell, Frederick, Napoleon had not a supersensitive temperament which caused them acute suffering. And later she writes: "In the greatest effort of his life Mr. Davis failed, from the predominance of some of these noble qualities,"[72] failed, that is, not by reason of external impossibility, but from causes within himself. Pollard could not have said more. Most of us would hardly say so much. Mrs. Davis certainly did not intend to, yet she knew the facts better than any one else in the world.

Whether another ruler than Davis could have saved the country or not, an immense number of people in the Confederacy thought that one man could—and that man was Lee. Everywhere those who most mistrusted the president looked to Lee with confidence and enthusiasm. At least as early as June, 1864, it was suggested that he should be made dictator. This idea became more and more popular. On January 19, 1865, the "Examiner" expressed itself editorially as follows: "There is but one way known to us of curing this evil: it is by

Congress making a law investing General Lee with absolute military power to make all appointments and direct campaigns. It may, indeed, be said that in this new position General Lee would have to relieve generals and appoint others and order movements which perhaps might not satisfy the strategick acumen of the general publick; and how, it might be asked, could he satisfy everybody any more than Mr. Davis? The difference is simply that every Confederate would repose implicit confidence in General Lee, both in his military skill and in his patriotic determination to employ the ablest men, whether he liked them or not."

This sort of thing could not be very agreeable to Davis, and Mrs. Davis is said by the spiteful Pollard to have exclaimed: "I think I am the person to advise Mr. Davis and if I were he, I would die or be hung before I would submit to the humiliation."[73] On January 17, however, before the editorial appeared in the "Examiner," the legislature of Virginia addressed a respectful appeal to the president to make Lee commander-in-chief of all the Confederate armies. Davis, knowing his man well, replied on the 18th that nothing would suit him better, and on the same day wrote to Lee offering him the position, thus anticipating the vote of Congress on the 23rd that a commander-in-chief should be appointed by the president, by and with the consent of the Senate.

It was of course the intention of Congress to take the military control entirely out of Davis's hands. It was expected and hoped that Lee would have agreed to this. What would have happened if Lee had done so, or what would have happened if such a change could have been made at an earlier date, belongs more properly to a discussion of Lee's general relations to the Confederate Government and the national policy as a whole. To have attempted anything of the sort would have meant revolution; for Davis would have fought it to the death. As it was, Lee did not hesitate a moment. To all suggestions of independent authority he returned a prompt and absolute No. The position of commander-in-chief he accepted, but he accepted it only from the hands of Davis and with the intention of acting in every way as his subordinate. "I am indebted alone to the kindness of His Excellency the President for my nomination to this high and arduous office and wish I had the ability to fill it to advantage. As I have received no instructions as to my duties, I do not know what he desires me to undertake."[74]

Thus we see that Lee, from personal loyalty or from a broad view of policy, or both, was determined to remain in perfect harmony with his chief to the end. After the war the general said: "If my opinion is worth anything, you can always say that few people could have done better than Mr. Davis. I knew of none that could have done as well."[75] And it is pleasant to feel that in all the conflict and agony of that wretched time these noble figures–both lofty and patriotic, if not equally so–could work together in the full spirit of Lee's testimony before the Grand Jury, as reported by himself to Davis: "He said that he had always consulted me when he had the opportunity, both in the field and elsewhere; that after discussion, if not before, we had always agreed, and that therefore he had done, with my consent and approval, what he might have done if he had not consulted me."[76]

4

LEE AND THE CONFEDERATE GOVERNMENT

Virginia seceded on the seventeenth of April, 1861, one day previous to Lee's critical interviews with Blair and Scott. On April 23, Lee was invited to appear before the state convention and was offered the position of commander-in-chief of the Virginia forces. He accepted in a simple and dignified speech, saying, with a sincerity which is beyond question, "I would have much preferred that your choice had fallen upon an abler man."[1]

The newly appointed general at once made ready to organize the state troops and prepare for a vigorous defense against invasion. But things moved rapidly, and on April 25, Virginia joined the Confederacy. What Lee thought of this step and what his opinions at this time were in regard to the organization and future policy of the Confederate Government is in no way revealed to us. But Alexander H. Stephens, the Confederate vice-president and commissioner to secure Virginia's adhesion, has given a most striking picture of Lee's perfect willingness to sacrifice his own position and prospects to the best interests of his state.

Stephens had an interview with Lee. "General Lee heard me quietly, understood the situation at once, and saw that he alone stood between the Confederacy and his State. The members of the convention had seen at once that Lee was left out of the proposed compact that was to make Virginia one of the Confederate States, and I knew that one word, or even a look of dissatisfaction, from him would terminate the negotiations with which I was intrusted.... General Lee did not hesitate for one moment, . . . he declared that no personal ambition or emolument should be considered or stand in the way. . . . Nominally, General Lee lost nothing; but practically, for the time

Lee The American

being, he lost everything. The Government moved to Richmond, and Mr. Davis directed General Lee to retain his command of the Virginia troops, which was really to make him recruiting and drill inspector."[2] In this way Lee worked in more or less subordinate or inconspicuous positions during the whole first year of the war, and it was not till the spring of 1862, by the wounding of Johnston, that he was given a fair chance to display his military ability.

We have seen that one of the most striking elements in Lee's attitude towards Davis was the instinct of subordination, of subjection of military to civil authority. The same thing appears everywhere in the general's broader relation to the Confederate Government as a whole. Politics were not his business. Even policy was not his business. Let others plan and order; he would execute. Wellington said to Greville that while "unquestionably Napoleon was the greatest military genius that ever existed," "he had advantages which no other man ever possessed in the unlimited means at his command and his absolute power and irresponsibility."[3] When one turns from Napoleon's dispatches to Lee's, one is instantly struck with the difference in this regard. Napoleon says, Go here; do this; let these troops be on this spot at that date. They are there. It is done. Lee suggests cautiously, insinuates courteously. But his greatest art is to keep still. It is very rare that he goes so far as the reported humorous saying, "that he had got a crick in his neck from looking over his shoulder towards Richmond." Such military command as is delegated to him he will exercise absolutely, but he draws with watchful care the line between his responsibility and that of others and is at all times reluctant to overstep it.

An interesting instance of this tendency to disclaim all interference with the civil authority is Lee's attitude toward prisoners of war. While they are on the field, they are in his charge. "He told me that on several occasions his commissary general had come to him after a battle and reported that he had not rations enough both for prisoners and the army, . . . and he had always given orders that the wants of the prisoners should be first attended to."[4] Yet even here mark the reservation, when the question becomes more general (italics mine): "*While I have no authority in the case,* my desire is that the prisoners shall have equal rations with my men."[5] Once in the military prisons, the captives were the care of the War Department, not Lee's. When he testified before the Reconstruction Committee, he was asked, "Were you not aware that those prisoners were dying from cold and starvation?" He answered: "I was not . . . As regards myself, I never had any control over the prisoners except those that

56

were captured on the field of battle. Those it was my business to send to Richmond to the provost marshal. In regard to their disposition afterwards I had no control. I never gave an order about it."[6] The most curious point in this matter of prisoners of war is Lee's correspondence with Grant, in October, 1864, as to recaptured slaves.[7] It is curious as a piece of argument in which, given the premises, both sides were logically right. It is still more curious when we find that Lee, while appearing to speak his own mind, is in reality only a mouthpiece, a department clerk, writing at the dictation of Seddon, that is, probably, of Davis.

But no matter how submissive a man may be, no matter how rigorously trained in military discipline, he cannot command a great army through a great disastrous war in a republic and not meddle with things that do not concern him. What does concern him and what does not? It is thus that we see Lee forced to advise and even to dictate sharply to his superiors, more and more as the struggle goes on. In matters semi-military or affecting other military departments, not Lee's own, this was inevitable. As at the North, the newspapers were troublesome in telling what they should not, and Lee begs the Secretary of War to control them. "I am particularly anxious that the newspapers should not give the enemy notice of our intention."[8] "I beg you will take the necessary steps to prevent in future the giving publicity in this way to our strength and position."[9]

A commander in the field may do his best to preserve discipline, but he is terribly hampered when the War Department permits all sorts of details, furloughs, and transfers, and is lenient to desertion. Again and again Lee is forced to protest vigorously against abuses of this nature.

A general may wish to confine himself to his own sphere of responsibility; but movements in the northeast are dependent on movements in the southwest and strengthening one command means weakening another. Therefore Lee is brought, as it were against his will, to make suggestions and requests as to Bragg in Tennessee and Johnston in Georgia. "I think that every effort should be made to concentrate as large a force as possible under the best commander to insure the discomfiture of Grant's army [in the west]."[10] He writes to Bragg for more men; "unless they are sent to me rapidly, it may be too late." He urges upon Seddon the utmost activity in general measures of defense: "Whatever inconvenience and even hardship may result from a vigorous and thorough preparation for the most complete defense we can make will be speedily forgotten in the event of success or amply repaid by the benefit such a course will confer upon us in the case of misfortune."[11]

The best general can do nothing with the best army, unless it is fed and clothed; and food and clothing—the accumulation, the transportation, the distribution—depend upon the energy and capacity of the Government. Lee loved his army as if they were his children. He knew they were neither clothed nor fed. He was by no means satisfied that the people at Richmond were either energetic or capable. "As far as I can judge, the proper authorities in Richmond take the necessities of this army very easily," he writes in February, 1863.[12] How could a commander give his best thought to fighting, when he saw but one day's food before him? "We have rations for the troops to-day and to-morrow. I hope a new supply arrived last night, but I have not yet had a report. Every exertion should be made to supply the depots at Richmond and at other points. All pleasure travel should cease and everything be devoted to necessary wants."[13] Sometimes he feels that other armies are preferred to his and protests vigorously. "I have understood, I do not know with what truth, that the armies of the West and that in the Department of South Carolina and Georgia are more bountifully supplied with provisions . . . I think that this army deserves as much consideration as either of those named, and, if it can be supplied, respectfully ask that it be similarly provided."[14] He is convinced that supplies are to be had and does not pick—or rather does pick—his words in saying so. "I know that there are great difficulties in procuring supplies, but I cannot help thinking that with proper energy, intelligence, and experience on the part of the Commissary Department, a great deal more could be accomplished. There is enough in the country, I believe, if it was properly sought for."[15] And finally, in January, 1865, he takes the matter into his own hands and issues a personal appeal to the farmers of Virginia, which, for the time, affords considerable relief.

From the supplying of armies to other things, equally vital, but quite as much civil as military, the steps are imperceptible, but taken with an almost logical necessity. Lee finds his soldiers refused passage on the railways and insists on their claims being recognized.[16] Passports are given indiscriminately to persons who convey information to the enemy.[17] Lee exerts his authority to control the practice. The illegal traffic in cotton and tobacco is tolerated by the Government for its own purposes. Lee gives assistance and advice as to the regulation of such traffic.[18] The greatest difficulty, of all the many difficulties of the Confederacy, was perhaps that of properly managing its finances. Lee has a word about this also, writing to urge the authorities to make treasury notes a legal tender,[19] and elsewhere, in connection with the much desired reduction of the currency, suggesting payment for certain consignments of wood in Confederate bonds.[20]

Political even more than military was the nice question of retaliation, which was made the subject of hot dispute by persons in authority and out of it. Critics of the administration [21] attacked its lenient policy, even to the point of suggesting that Davis opposed violent measures because he wished to keep well with the North in view of possible defeat. In extreme cases Lee does not hesitate to order prompt retaliatory action. "I have directed Colonel Mosby, through his adjutants, to hang an equal number of Custer's men in retaliation for those executed by him."[22] But as to the general principle he is thoroughly in sympathy with Davis, both on grounds of humanity and on grounds of policy. "I differ in my ideas from most of our people on the subject of retaliation. Sometimes I know it to be necessary, but it should not be resorted to at all times, and in our case policy dictates that it should be avoided whenever possible."[23] Lee here frankly and naturally admits that his invasion proclamations, so lauded by Southern writers, were founded as much on common sense as on lofty principle. One can admire the noble tone and still more the rigid enforcement of those proclamations, without forgetting that Napoleon also said to his soldiers in Vienna, "Let us treat the poor peasants with kindness and be generous to this loyal people who have so many claims to our esteem; let us not be puffed up by our success, but see in it another proof of the divine justice which punishes ingratitude and treachery."[24]

Although Lee does not hesitate to go outside of his own peculiar province in many of these special instances, it is very rare indeed to find him making any general criticism of the civil authorities. The following remarks as to the Confederate Congress have, therefore, a peculiar interest and significance: "What has our Congress done to meet the emergency, I may say extremity, in which we are placed? As far as I know, concocted bills to exempt a certain class of men from service, and to transfer another class in service, out of active service, where they hope never to do service. Among the thousand applications of Kentuckians, Marylanders, Alabamians, and Georgians, etc., to join native regiments out of this army, who ever heard of their applying to enter regiments in it, when in face of the enemy? I hope Congress will define what makes a man a citizen of a State."[25]

The most striking of all Lee's incursions into the realm of civil government was his effort, toward the very end of the war, to have the negroes enlisted as soldiers. The measure, was, of course, in one sense purely military; but it affected so intimately the social organization and the ethical theories on which the whole Confederacy was founded that the military significance of it was almost dwarfed by the political. As Pollard justly points out, it seemed to imply an equality between the two races which was utterly repugnant to all Southern feeling on the subject, and nothing shows more clearly Lee's immense influence than the fact that he was able to persuade his countrymen to accept his view. All his arguments are summed up in a clear and forcible letter to Hunter,[26]—otherwise extremely important as showing Lee's general position as to slavery,—and in response to this Congress voted briefly "that the General-in-Chief be and hereby is invested with the full power to call into the service of the Confederate Government, to perform any duty to which he may assign them, so many of the able-bodied slaves within the Confederate Government as, in his judgment, the exigencies of the public service require."[27] The comment of the "Examiner" on this is intensely interesting as probably summing up the opinion of hundreds of thousands of Lee's fellow citizens. After expressing frankly grave doubts as to the expediency of the measure, the editorial concludes, in words of almost startling solemnity, "This clothes him with great power, and loads him with heavy responsibility. If he is willing to wield that power and shoulder that responsibility, in the name of God, let him have them."[28]

In the name of God, let Lee save us, if he will: no one else can. There is no doubt that this was the spirit of a majority of Southerners in February, 1865. There is no doubt that this was the spirit which led to his being offered practically the military dictatorship by Congress. "The ablest officers of the Confederate States," says the "Examiner," "would, we feel assured, gladly see the supreme direction of their conduct placed in the hands of General Lee, and would receive his orders with pleasure. All citizens, and more emphatically, all soldiers, now know . . . that the one thing needful to fill the army with enthusiasm, and to inspire the people for new effort, is to feel that our military force is to be wielded by one capable hand and directed by one calm, clear intelligence."[29] Lee, however, absolutely refused to violate his subordination to the president in any way, and according to Pollard "went so far as to declare to several members of the Richmond Congress that whatever might be Davis's errors, he was yet constitutionally the president, and that nothing could tempt himself to encroach upon prerogatives which the constitution had bestowed upon its designated head."[30]

What could an ambitious, unscrupulous man have accomplished in that emergency, or even a patriot who would have been willing to override scruple for the good of his country? Would Napoleon or Cromwell have said to Davis, "You may do what I want or go," have gone direct to Congress and enforced his will, have swept fraud and incompetence out of the executive departments, have handled the whole military force like one great machine and so concentrated it as to accomplish results which seemed at that late hour impossible? "Of one thing I am certain," wrote in January, 1865, the diarist Jones, who had the very best opportunities of forming an opinion, "that the people are capable of achieving independence, if they only had capable men in all departments of the government."[31] In any case Lee preferred to remain the loyal servant of the civil authority, which was left to work out its political problems as best it could.

What interests us in our study of Lee's character is the motive which led him not only to this final refusal, but to his general attitude of non-interference with the Confederate Government. It has often been suggested–and Grant was of this opinion[32]–that he was consistent in his state loyalty and cared for Virginia only, not for the Confederacy as a whole, preferring to do his fighting to the end upon his native soil. The writer of the excellent "Nation" review of Long's "Life" (Cox?),[33] basing his conclusions on the Townsend anecdote which I have quoted in a previous chapter,[34] holds that Lee had little regard for the Confederate cause from beginning to end. Some suspicion of the kind was undoubtedly at the bottom of Pollard's harsh charges. "The fact was that, although many of General Lee's views were sound, yet, outside of the Army of Northern Virginia, and with reference to the general affairs of the Confederacy, his influence was negative and accomplished absolutely nothing."[35] Again, "His most notable defect was that he never had or conveyed any inspiration in the war."[36] And Pollard quotes from a Richmond paper after the Wilderness, "When will he [Lee] speak? Has he nothing to say? What does he think of our affairs? Should he speak, how the country would hang upon every word that fell from him!"[37]

I believe that this theory of Lee's lack of interest in the Confederacy is utterly false. Of course he remained a Virginian and would have followed his state out of the later union as he had followed her out of the earlier; but while Virginia was Confederate, he faithfully merged his duty to her in the broader loyalty. "They do injustice to Lee who believe he fought only for Virginia," said Davis. "He was ready to go anywhere for the good of his country."[38] The cheerful energy which the general showed when sent to South Carolina in the early part of the war confirms this, as does passage after passage of his correspondence. "Let it be distinctly understood by every one that Charleston and Savannah are to be defended to the last extremity. If the harbors are taken, the cities are to be fought street by street, house by house, so long as we have a foot of ground to stand upon."[39] A writer in the Southern Historical Papers asserts that "those whose privilege it was to hear the great chieftain talk most freely of the cause for which he fought, bear the most emphatic witness that it was 'the independence of the South,' 'the triumph of constitutional freedom,' for which he struggled so nobly."[40]

But by far the most striking and interesting testimony to Lee's thorough espousal of Confederate nationality and sober, earnest grasp of the whole problem before him is his conversation with Imboden near the beginning of the struggle. General Imboden declares that his report is "almost literal," but for our purpose its substantial correctness is all-sufficient (italics mine). "Our people are brave and enthusiastic and are united in defense of a just cause. I believe we can succeed in establishing our independence, if the people can be made to comprehend at the outset that they must endure a longer war and far greater privations than our forefathers did in the Revolution of 1776. We will not succeed until the financial power of the North [the political insight of this is extremely noteworthy] is completely broken. . . . The conflict will be mainly in Virginia. She will be the Flanders of America before this war is over and her people must be prepared for this. If they resolve at once to dedicate their lives and all they possess to the cause of constitutional government and *Southern* independence and to suffer without yielding as no other people have been called upon to suffer in modern times, we shall, with the blessing of God, succeed in the end; but when it will be no man can foretell. *I wish I could talk to every man, woman, and child in the South now and impress them with these views.*"[41]

No. If Lee was modest, it was from genuine modesty. If he shunned burdens and responsibilities, it was because he truly felt himself unable to undertake them. It is a most curious point in the man's character, this nice avoidance of duties that did not belong to him. "Be content to do what you can for the well-being of what properly belongs to you," he writes to Mrs. Lee. "Commit the rest to those who are responsible."[42] It is in this spirit that he is eager to make clear to the Reconstruction Committee that the Government's foreign policy was no concern of his. "I know nothing of the policy of the government; I had no hand or part in it; I merely express my own opinion."[43] Even in military matters he is careful to draw the sharpest line between his own task and that of his subordinates: "I think and I work with all my power to bring my troops to the right place at the right time; then I have done my duty."[44] He is so careful that at times one feels a certain sympathy with the otherwise negligible Northrop, when he complains: "There is, in my judgment, no isolation of the responsibility in any of the machinery of war."[45]

One wonders that a man could be so sensitive about the limits of responsibility and yet command absolutely for three years an army of fifty to a hundred thousand men, lead them again and again to victory, make such terrible decisions as that of Jackson's movement at Chancellorsville and the attack at Gettysburg. And then one reflects that it was probably just this clear sense of what others ought to do and should be left to do that made Lee's power. Smaller men fret over executive details or rush readily into what they do not understand. He knew his own training, his own character, knew his own work and did it, letting others do theirs, if they could. It is with this explanation in view that we should read his remarkable colloquy with B.H. Hill, toward the close of the war, as reported by Long:—

"General, I wish you would give us your opinion as to the propriety of changing the seat of Government and going farther South."

"That is a political question, Mr. Hill, and you politicians must determine it. I shall endeavor to take care of the army and you politicians must make the laws and control the Government."

"Ah, General," said Mr. Hill, "but you will have to change that rule and form and express political opinions; for if we establish our independence, the people will make you Mr. Davis's successor."

"Never, sir," he replied, with a firm dignity that belonged only to Lee; "that I will never permit. Whatever talents I may possess (and they are but limited) are military talents, my education and training are military. I think the military and civil talents are distinct, if not different, and full duty in either sphere is about as much as one man can qualify himself to perform. I shall not do the people the injustice to accept high civil office, with whose questions it has not been my business to become familiar."

"Well, but, General, history does not sustain your view. Cæsar and Frederick of Prussia and Bonaparte were great statesmen as well as great generals."

"And great tyrants," he promptly replied. "I speak of the proper rule in Republics, where I think we should have neither military statesmen nor political generals."

"But Washington was both and yet not a tyrant."

With a beautiful smile he responded, "Washington was an exception to all rules and there was none like him."[46]

Probably Lee underestimated his aptitude for civil government, at any rate in comparison with that of others. The patience, the foresight, above all the tact in handling men, which made him a great general, would have made him a great president also. But taking all things into account, I doubt whether he could have done more for the Confederacy than he did, or whether even Washington would have attempted to do more.

Granted, however, that Lee's modesty was the chief cause of his not interfering further in political action, I think another consideration must have influenced him to some extent. What possible future had the Confederate Government? It is really remarkable that in all the mass of Southern—or, for that matter, Northern—historical writing so little notice is taken of this vital question. Supposing the North had given in and let the South go free, what would have happened? Few soldiers or statesmen seem to have troubled themselves much about the matter, so far as I can find out. It may be said that neither did the patriots of the Revolution trouble themselves about the future. But the case was different. It was a logical necessity, a natural development for America to separate from England. Some adjustment between the colonies was sure to be found; but even with none they would be better free. For the Confederacy there would appear to have been but two alternatives. A great slave empire might have been formed, centralized for necessary strength, supporting a standing army of half a million,—not one man more than would have been required at any moment to face the military power of the United States, in disputes that would have arisen daily over territory, emigration, tariff, and especially over slavery complications. Or the absurd incompatibility of this with all the ideas for which the South originally went to war would have made itself felt. State rights would have asserted themselves everywhere. The Confederate group would have broken into smaller groups, those again would have dissolved into the original states, and these, after a probably brief period of dissension and strife, would have been reabsorbed, with humiliation and disgust, into the Union from which they had been rent away. Is it easy to paint any more satisfactory picture of the possible future of the Confederate States of America?[47]

Such speculation is useless now. It would seem to have been eminently practical and necessary for the men who were leading millions of their fellows into such an abyss of uncertainty. What did

Lee think about it? The answer is not simple; for his words on the subject are few and noncommittal. Pollard's accusation, that "never, at any time of the war, and not even in the companionship of the most intimate friends, on whom he might have bestowed his confidence without imprudence, did he ever express the least opinion as to the chances of the war,"[48] is absurdly exaggerated; but it is true that Lee had little to say about the future of the Confederacy. Before the war, before the issue was squarely presented, we know that he took much the same view as that I have indicated above. "Secession is nothing but Revolution."[49] "I can anticipate no greater calamity for the country than a dissolution of the Union. It would be an accumulation of all the evils we complain of, and I am willing to sacrifice anything but honor for its preservation."[50] Then it seemed to him that either honor or the Union must be sacrificed and he did not hesitate. But anarchy, but the accumulation of all evils must have been clearly before him. Apparently he shut his eyes to them. Do the immediate duty of the day. Get independence. "The Confederate States have but one great object in view, the successful issue of their war of independence. Everything worth their possessing depends on that. Everything should yield to its accomplishment."[51] Independence once achieved, the rest would take care of itself. Or those who, unlike Lee, had the responsibility of civil affairs, would take care of it. Or God would take care of it. Here is the key to what in much of Lee's action seems strangely puzzling to those whose standpoint is somewhat different from his. Do the plain duty. Let the rest go. God will take care of it. In this connection a conversation of Lee's with Bishop Wilmer, is immensely significant.

In what temper of mind he entered this contest, I can speak with some confidence, from personal interviews with him soon after the commencement of hostilities.

"Is it your expectation," I asked, "that the issue of this war will be to perpetuate the institution of slavery?"

"The future is in the hands of Providence," he replied. "If the slaves of the South were mine, I would surrender them all without a struggle to avert this war."

I asked him next upon what his calculations were based in so unequal a contest, and how he expected to win success; was he looking to divided counsels in the North, or to foreign interposition? His answer showed how little he was affected by the hopes and fears which agitated ordinary minds. "My reliance is in the help of God."

"Are you sanguine of the result?" I ventured to inquire.

"At present I am not concerned with results. God's will ought to be our aim, and I am contented that his designs should be accomplished and not mine."[52]

Naturally the good bishop was charmed; but an ordinary mind is tempted to hope that it is not incompatible with the deepest love and admiration for Lee to recall the candor and profoundly human truth of Barbe-Bleue's remark: "C'est en ne sachant jamais où j'allais moi-même que je suis arrivé à conduire les autres."

The object of all war is peace, and with the thousand doubts and difficulties that were pressing upon him, Lee must have been anxious from the beginning to arrive at almost any reasonably satisfactory conclusion of hostilities. Here again was a political question, yet one that it was almost impossible for a commanding general to avoid. In the earlier part of the war Lee urged a peace attitude upon Davis, with some apology "in view of its connection with the situation of military affairs."[53] The general thought the Northern peace party should be encouraged without fear of that encouragement resulting in a reestablishment of the Union. "We entertain no such apprehensions, nor doubt that the determination of our people for a distinct and independent national existence will prove as steadfast under the influence of peaceful measures as it has shown itself in the midst of war."[54]

In this, as in a score of other passages, Lee makes it perfectly evident that his idea of peace was an ample acknowledgment of Confederate independence. Yet it has been maintained, and with reliable testimony, that towards the close of the struggle he grew ready to accept some less radical basis of agreement. The apparent contradiction is perfectly explicable. Lee believed from first to last that the people of the South could get free, if they really wished to. They had the men, they had the resources, if they would endure and suffer and sacrifice. As late as February, 1865, he addressed to Governor Vance of North Carolina this most remarkable appeal,— remarkable for its earnestness and enthusiasm of conviction in the midst of despair: "So far as the despondency of the people occasions this sad condition of affairs, I know of no other means of removing it than by the counsel and exhortations of prominent citizens. If they would explain to the people that the cause is not hopeless; that the situation of affairs, though critical, is critical to the enemy as well as to ourselves; that he has drawn his troops from every other quarter to accomplish his designs against Richmond and that his defeat now would result in leaving nearly our whole territory open to us; that this great result can be accomplished if all will work diligently and zealously; and that his successes are far less valuable in fact than in appearance, I think our sorely tried people would be induced to bear their sufferings a little longer and regain some of the spirit that marked the first two years of the war. If they will, I feel confident that, with the blessing of God, our greatest danger will prove the means of deliverance and safety."[55]

But, alas, the spirit was crushed, the courage was broken, never to be reanimated again. Lee knew it, however much he fought the conviction. If the people were no longer behind him, what could he do? "General Lee says to the men who shirk duty," writes Mrs. Chesnut, "'This is the people's war: when they tire, I stop.'"[56] Or as he himself writes, more solemnly, "Our people have not been earnest enough, have thought too much of themselves and their ease, and instead of turning out to a man, have been content to nurse themselves and their dimes, and leave the protection of themselves and families to others."[57] It was this that made him so hopeless about obtaining supplies that in December, 1864, he is said to have told a committee of Congress that "he could devise no means of carrying on the war."[58] It was this that made him so despondent in his conversation with Hunter, about the same time that the above letter was written to Vance. "In the whole of this conversation he never said to me that he thought the chances were over; but the tone and tenor of his remarks made that impression on my mind."[59] It was this, finally, that made him say, as is reported, shortly after the war was over: "In my earnest belief peace was practicable two years ago and has been since that time, whenever the general government should see fit to give any reasonable chance for the country to escape the consequences which the exasperated North seemed ready to visit upon it."[60]

Yet here again, Lee was the soldier, not the president. So long as the civil government said fight, he fought, till fighting had become, in any reasonable sense, impossible. The distress of mind involved in this is nowhere more clearly indicated than in the words said to have been spoken to General Gordon. "General Gordon, I am a soldier. It is my duty to obey orders. It is enough to turn one's hair gray to spend one day in the Congress. The members are patriotic and earnest, but they will neither take the responsibility of action nor will they clothe me with authority to act for them. As for Mr. Davis, he is unwilling to do anything short of independence and feels that it is useless to try to treat on that basis."[61] But when at last Davis had left the capital and practically the control of affairs, the commander of the Army of Northern Virginia acted his final scene with the dignity, the sacrifice, the true patriotism which Mr. Adams has so nobly commemorated.[62] Instead of scattering the desperate remnant of his forces to carry on a murderous guerilla warfare, Lee recognized the inevitable, and surrendered his army on conditions certainly in no way hurtful to its lasting glory. With that surrender the government of the Confederate States in reality ceased to exist.

These studies of Lee in his relations to the civil government do not perhaps show him at his best or in the most splendid manifestation of his genius. Yet hardly anything in the man's character is grander than the way in which he instantly adapted himself to new circumstances and began to work as a loyal and devoted citizen, even when the United States still refused him the rights and privileges of citizenship. The importance of his influence in this regard, over his friends and family, over his old soldiers, over every Southern man and woman cannot be exaggerated. "When he said that the career of the Confederacy was ended; that the hope of an independent government must be abandoned; and that the duty of the future was to abandon the dream of a Confederacy and to render a new and cheerful allegiance to a reunited government,—his utterances were accepted as true as holy writ. No other human being upon earth, no other earthly power could have produced such acquiescence or could have compelled such prompt acceptance of the final and irreversible judgment."[63] There was no grudging, no holding back, no hiding of despair in dark corners, but an instant effort to do, and to urge others to do, everything possible to rebuild the fair edifice that had been overthrown.

"When I had the privilege, after his death, of examining his private letter-book, I found it literally crowded with letters advising old soldiers and others to submit to all authorities and become law-abiding citizens," writes his biographer.[64] "I am sorry," writes Lee himself, "to hear that our returned soldiers cannot obtain employment. Tell them they must all set to work, and if they cannot do what they prefer, do what they can. Virginia wants all their aid, all their support, and the presence of all her sons to sustain and recuperate her."[65] "To one who inquired what fate was in store for us poor Virginians, he replied, 'You can work for Virginia, to build her up again, to make her great again. You can teach your children to love and cherish her.'"[66]

If any one urges that this is still the old leaven, after all, Virginia, always Virginia, we answer, No, this man was great enough to forget and forget at once, to blend Virginia even then with a larger nationality. As a matter of policy he expresses this with clear insight: "The interests of the state are, therefore, the same as those of the United States. Its prosperity will rise or fall with the welfare of the country."[67] As a matter of feeling, he expresses it with profound and noble emotion, saying to a lady who cherished more bitterness than he, "Madam, don't bring up your sons to detest the United States Government. Recollect that we form one country now. Abandon all these local animosities and make your sons Americans."[68]

Abandon all these local animosities and make your sons Americans. What finer sentence could be inscribed on the pedestal of Lee's statue than that? Americans! All the local animosities forgiven and forgotten, can we not say that he, too, though dying only five years after the terrible struggle, died a loyal, a confident, a hopeful American, and one of the very greatest?

General Lee on Traveller

5

LEE AND HIS ARMY

W hat we have to study in Lee's relations with his army, as in other matters, is the character of the man, how he contrived to hold for three years—and long after—the absolute devotion of scores of thousands of soldiers. Other generals have led loyal and enthusiastic armies from victory to victory. This general held affection and confidence unshaken through defeat, disaster, and final ruin. And the army that loved him was an army to be proud of, "the best army," says one of its generous opponents, "which has existed on this continent."[1]

Lee built up his army before he commanded it. During the early months of the war he was busy at Richmond getting the troops ready for the field, and it was he more than any one else who transformed a chaotic afflux of volunteers into the semblance of an organized force which beat another semblance at the first battle of Bull Run. Even those who long doubted Lee's ability as a commander admitted his gift for extracting order out of confusion, his patient industry, his clear system, his tact in smoothing rough tempers and harmonizing wills that jarred. "In the space of two months," says Colonel Long, "he was able to equip for the field sixty regiments of infantry and cavalry, besides numerous batteries of artillery, making an aggregate of nearly fifty thousand men."

With this constructive experience behind him, Lee continued throughout the war to treat his army not as a mere fighting machine, but as a human body which must be fed and clothed, or ought to be, for even his efforts could not accomplish the impossible. He enjoins upon his subordinate officers care for the well-being of their men. "Do not let your troops run down, if it can possibly be avoided by attention to their wants, comforts, etc., by their respective commanders."[2] His constant appeals to the Richmond authorities for provisions, with graphic statement of the soldiers' sufferings, are pathetic in their earnestness. Submissive as he was to superior officials, he resented at once any indication that his men were being sacrificed to other commands elsewhere. "I have been mortified to find that when any scarcity existed, this was the only army in which it is found necessary to reduce the rations."[3] The best evidence of his care is that the soldiers trusted him and were willing to starve, if he bade them. It is recorded that a private once wrote saying that he could not do his work on his rations and asking if the general knew what they were, as, if he did, it must be that the scarcity was unavoidable and the men would do the best they could. Lee made no direct answer, but explained the situation in a general order. "After that there was not a murmur in the army."[4]

So with the less pressing but not less serious need of clothing. Near the end of the war Lee writes that the men "were greatly exposed in line of battle two days, had been without meat for three days, and in scanty clothing took the cold hail and sleet."[5] It was on a passage similar to this that Davis noted characteristically "these things are too sad to be patiently considered"; but I am not aware that he rose up in anger and made somebody consider them. Frequently Lee is obliged to allege the utter destitution of his troops as a reason for not making a forward movement, and in doing so he expresses his admiration for all they have been able to accomplish. "Nothing prevented my continuing in his front but the destitute condition of the men, thousands of whom are barefooted, a greater number partially shod, and nearly all without blankets, overcoats, or warm clothing. I think the sublimest sight of the war was the cheerfulness and alacrity exhibited by this army in the pursuit of the enemy under all the trials and privations to which it was exposed."[6] And it is with the grief of a mortified parent that he expresses his surprise at finding some of his followers ready to take advantage of the necessities of others. "It has also been reported that some men in this army have been so unmindful of their obligations to their comrades, and of their own characters, as to engage in the occupation of purchasing supplies of food and other things, for the purpose of selling them at exorbitant prices to their fellow soldiers."[7]

It was indeed always as a parent, not merely as a military superior, that Lee believed in controlling and disciplining his army. This attitude led to a certain freedom of discipline which did not wholly satisfy those accustomed to European methods. "Two defects as a general were ascribed to him personally," says a German critic, "an indifference to discipline and a too kindly consideration for incompetent officers."[8] And even Davis remarked that "his habit of avoiding any seeming harshness . . . was probably a defect."[9] Yet if the object of discipline is to make troops efficient and enthusiastic, it can hardly be said that Lee failed. An eye-witness, by no means uncritical and writing on the spot, says: "In Lee's army everything is reduced down to the smallest compass and the discipline and obedience of the officers and men is perfect."[10] While Hooker, an enemy who had felt the results, if he had not watched the processes, testified: "With a rank and file vastly inferior to our own, intellectually and physically, that army has, by discipline alone, acquired a character for steadiness and efficiency, unsurpassed, in my judgment, in ancient or modern times. We have not been able to rival it, nor has there been any near approximation to it in the other rebel armies."[11]

Some good observers, notably Mr. Eggleston, do not agree with Hooker as to the original quality of Lee's soldiers. Undoubtedly the best intelligence and education of the South went right into the ranks; but this element was naturally outbalanced by poverty and ignorance, and the average Southern soldier was less common-schooled than the Northern, because the same thing was true of the average Southern citizen. In any case, it was a popular army, composed of American freemen; and from the point of view of discipline, Lee, with his perfect human sympathy, at once seized this fact in all its bearings. "There is a great difference," he said to Colonel Long, "between mercenary armies and volunteer armies, and consequently there must be a difference in the mode of discipline. The volunteer army is more easily disciplined by encouraging a patriotic spirit than by a strict enforcement of the articles of war."[12] When Scheibert commended the bravery of Jackson's troops at Chancellorsville, Lee said: "Give me Prussian formations and Prussian discipline, and you would see very different results."[13]

This does not mean that Lee overlooked the absolute need of severity in dealing with refractory soldiers or was foolishly averse to it. "You must establish rigid discipline," he writes to a subordinate at the very beginning of the war.[14] He insisted everywhere on order and cleanliness. "Colonel," he said to an officer who begged for a visit, "a dirty camp gives me nausea. If you say your camps are clean, I will go."[15] He endeavored, as far as possible, to repress camp vices, especially gambling. "The general commanding is pained to learn that the vice of gambling exists and is becoming common in this army . . . it was not supposed that a habit so pernicious and demoralizing would be found among men engaged in a cause demanding the highest virtue and purest morality in its supporters."[16] The strictness of his orders in regard to pillage during his invasions of the North is well known; but they were not only strict in form, they were carried out in fact, as is proved by the testimony of his enemies, to the lasting glory of both army and commander. Violation of these orders provoked Lee's wrath more than anything except brutality,[17] and when he himself detected one soldier in theft, he ordered him shot immediately. He was equally ready to inflict the death penalty in cases of desertion, when they became too frequent, and had again and again to urge the necessity of rigor upon the Richmond authorities. "I hope I feel as acutely as any one the pain and sorrow that such events occasion, and I am sure that no one would more willingly dispense with them, if they could be avoided; but I am convinced that the only way to prevent them is to visit the offense, when committed, with the sternest punishment, and leave the offender without hope of escape, by making the penalty inevitable."[18]

Yet withal he was lenient, perhaps too lenient, and longed as a father would, to work by persuasion rather than by violence. "This is a case," he wrote in one instance, "where possible error is better than probable wrong";[19] and doubtless he applied the rule in many instances when an angry officer wanted to disband a whole company for cowardice, Lee defended them. "For the bad behavior of a few, it would not appear just to punish the whole."[20] And always his method was to get work done by kindly urgency, by playful rallying, by sympathetic encouragement, rather than by the spur or the lash: "General Lee, taking his daily ride about the lines, came on me while the working parties were digging and spading. His greeting was, 'Good-morning, my young friend, I feel sorry for you.' 'Why so, General?' 'Because you have so much to do,' answered the commander, the gleaming white teeth showing his pleasant humor, as he continued his ride. He generally had some such words to let one know he expected a lot of work out of him."[21]

Discipline of officers is a more delicate matter than discipline of soldiers and requires an even finer tact, sympathy, and divination of character. Here also Lee always remembered that he commanded an army of American freemen, accustomed to vote and to criticize everything and everybody. He let them say their say, asked their advice often, and occasionally followed it. Yet it is sometimes difficult to reconcile their free and easy ways with any idea of military subordination. Take, for example, that hard fighter and true-hearted gentleman, James Longstreet. I do not wish here to discuss his conduct at Gettysburg. But when I consider that conduct in the light of various passages in his letters to his chief, I feel myself more in a position to understand it. What would have happened to Ney or Soult, if he had addressed the first Napoleon in this wise: "I am pleased at all times to have any suggestions that you may make,"[22] or again, "There are several little points upon which you should be posted before the interview, and I do not see how I can well do this by writing."[23] Longstreet patronized his great commander as he would a budding subaltern. "I wrote a note to General Lee . . . and cautioned him to make his arrangements to return that night."[24] With men of this stamp discipline was not always a simple matter, as appears from some of the experiences of Jackson.

The summary methods of Jackson did not appeal to Lee, who, instead of the guardhouse, employed tact as soothing as it was inexhaustible. The hot-headed Stuart demands justification against some criticism. Lee writes to him: "I prefer your acts to speak for themselves, nor does your character or reputation require bolstering up by out-of-place expressions of my opinion."[25] It becomes necessary to dismiss Early from command, in spite of good service, because he has lost the confidence of his troops. Lee dismisses him, but states the facts so sympathetically that he loses no jot of Early's affection, who could say after the war, "It is difficult for those who did not know him personally to understand the wonderful magnanimity of character which induced General Lee often to take the chances of incurring censure himself rather than run the risk of doing possible injustice to another."[26]

Not that Lee could not rebuke, and sternly. When the Confederates were flying from Five Forks, he turned to a general officer and ordered him, with marked emphasis, to collect and put under guard "*all* the stragglers on the field,"[27] showing that he meant to include many of his officers as well as men. On another occasion he said to a dilatory commander: "General, I have sometimes to admonish General Stuart or General Gordon against being too fast, I shall never have occasion to find that fault with you."[28]

But usually he gave his criticism some turn of sympathetic suggestion or even of kindly laughter. It is to be noted that the success of this method depends upon the person who uses it, and there are times when one prefers a straight-out, sharp order, to a would-be pleasant insinuation. I confess that Lee's amiable reprimands sometimes suggest to me Xenophon's remark about Proxenus, that "he was fit to command the good; but he could not instill fear into the soldiers, and it seemed that he had more consideration for those he commanded than those he commanded had for him." Proxenus could not have won the battle of Chancellorsville, however; and it appears that Lee was feared, for all his mildness. "I believe all his officers feared him," says Major Ranson. "Their loved him as men are seldom loved, but they feared him too."[29] As to the reprimands, the best-known instance is that of the officer with the condition of whose lines Lee was far from satisfied. As they rode together, the general remarked, "That is a magnificent horse, General –, but I should not think him safe for Mrs. – to ride. He is entirely too spirited for a lady, and I would urge you by all means to take some of the mettle out of him before you suffer her to ride him again. And, by the way, General, I would suggest to you that the rough paths along these trenches would be admirable ground over which to tame him."[30] Another interesting case—made a little suspicious by the profanity—is that of the staff officer who took the liberty of altering orders to meet circumstances. Lee made no comment at the time, but later at dinner he told the story of General Twiggs, whose staff were always altering orders, until he finally remarked to one of them: "Captain, I know you can prove that you are right, and that my order was wrong, in fact you gentlemen always are right, but for God's sake, do wrong sometimes."[31]

Among Lee's greatest difficulties in dealing with his officers was, of course, the question of promotion. Apparently every man in the Army of Northern Virginia felt himself perfectly competent to be commander of it, except the man who had the honor of filling that office, and Stuart is said to have remarked sarcastically of the troops in general: "They are pretty good officers now and after a while will make excellent soldiers too. They only need reducing to the ranks."[32] "In an army," says Dumas in his rollicking fashion, "everybody, from the second in command to the rawest recruit, desires the death of somebody." This is quite legitimate. What is not so is to spend time and temper, not your own, in complaining, fretting, and repining. Too many high Confederate officers, J.E. Johnston among others, showed a sensitiveness and pettiness on the subject, which was as unbecoming as it was thoroughly human.

Lee himself at all times absolutely disclaimed any eagerness for advancement. "I think rank of trivial importance so that it is sufficient for the individual to exercise his command."[33] Again and again he offered to serve wherever and however his superiors thought he could be useful. To say this is easy. To convince others of the truth of it is less so. But I am not aware that any one has ever questioned Lee's sincerity. There was that about him, in manner and still more in action, which proved that he thought only of his country and his duty. Testimony is hardly needed, but Stiles offers a bit, which is impressive, if somewhat astounding. "I never but once heard of such a suggestion [that Lee acted from other than the purest motives], and then it so transported the hearers that military subordination was forgotten and the colonel who heard it rushed with drawn sword against the major-general who made it."[34]

Nor does there seem to be much disposition to accuse Lee of favoritism. He certainly had no hand in the advancement of his own sons, who rose steadily by their merit. He refuses a friend's application for a staff position, because "persons on my staff should have a knowledge of their duties and an experience of the wants of the service to enable me to attend to other matters."[35] It is indeed alleged that he was partial to Virginia, notably in the case of A.P. Hill; but the charge comes from sources too prejudiced to deserve much attention. Even those who complain bitterly of the jealousy and narrowness of the West Point tradition do not seem to include Lee in their animosity. Thus Tyler writes to Price: "I have found myself laboring under the odium of the little West Pointers in Richmond and their partisans. They oppose me in the War Office at all points in regard to any and every wish."[36] But in the same letter he says of Lee: "Without parade, haughtiness, or assumption, he is elevated in his thought and feeling, and is worthy of the cause he represents and the army he commands."[37]

One thing is beyond dispute, no personal consideration was allowed to enter into his decisions. When he urged the promotion of a certain officer, it was pointed out that that officer had been very free in criticizing the general. "The question is," Lee answered, "not what he thinks or is pleased to say about me, but what I think about him."[38]

It would be impossible to estimate the time, the strength, the nervous energy that must have been expended in counseling patience, in soothing injured vanity, in forestalling complaints, and in urging the sacrifice of personal gain, credit, and advantage to the cause which all were bound to serve. He writes to one officer—and the letter is typical: "Recognizing as fully as I do your merit, patriotism, and devotion to the state, I do not consider that either rank or position are necessary to bestow upon you honor, but believe that you will confer honor on the position. In the present crisis of affairs, I know that your own feelings, better than any words of mine, will point out the course for you to pursue to advance the cause in which you are engaged."[39] Without the power to make promotions himself, and obliged, even in suggesting, to exercise the utmost consideration towards a jealous and sensitive superior, Lee, like Washington, was forced to use infinite tact and sympathy in order to harmonize the claims that conflicted about him. But he seems to have been more fortunate than Washington in that at least his officers did not conspire and intrigue against himself.

If they did not quarrel with him, they sometimes quarreled with each other, however, and so added to his troubles. Jackson's repeated difficulties with A.P. Hill will call for more extended discussion in connection with Lee and Jackson. But among all these high-spirited young men dissensions and jealousies were almost inevitable and with little tradition of discipline to restrain them they were perpetually breaking out, to the detriment of the service and the extreme discomfort of the general. An officer of large experience writes: "I have myself heard a major-general send a message back to army headquarters by a staff officer of General Lee, that he didn't see why his division should be expected to abandon the position they had fought for just to accommodate General –, whose troops had fallen back where his had driven the enemy."[40] In Lee's early days of command he had to reconcile the animosities of Wise and Floyd. He did it in words as noble as they are simple: "You have spoken to me of want of consultation and concert; let that pass, till the enemy is driven back, and then, as far as I can, all shall be arranged. I expect this of your magnanimity."[41] Later the bellicose A.P. Hill quarreled with Longstreet over the praise accorded to their respective commands by newspaper correspondents and it is even said that a duel had been arranged; but Lee's patience and tact averted such an extremity.[42]

The most fruitful source of all these differences was the incurable human disposition to put the blame for one's failures on somebody else. No doubt Lee's noble example in constantly refusing to do this himself had a wide influence on others. It is reported that after the war he told a publisher that he could not write his memoirs, because to do it honestly would ruin too many reputations. This does not sound quite genuine; but we do know that after Gettysburg he wrote as follows to Pickett with reference to the latter's official report of the battle: "You and your men have crowned yourselves with glory, but we have the enemy to fight, and must carefully, at this critical moment, guard against dissensions which the reflections in your report will create. I will, therefore, suggest that you destroy both copy and original."[43] And Pickett did it.

As to his personal relations with his officers, I doubt if any of them ever felt entirely at ease with him. They were mostly younger men than he, but even in his early days he seems to have had few intimate associates, and age probably softened his natural dignity and gravity rather than increased it. Not that there was any stiffness about him or any pretense. I imagine that in his secret heart he envied the young fellows their careless ways, their idle jests, their trifling laughter. He liked Stuart's rollicking nonsense, liked to listen to the Irish banjo player, Sweeny. One night when the singing was unusually uproarious, he stepped out of his tent and noted with a smile a black jug perched on a boulder: "Gentlemen, am I to thank General Stuart or the jug for this fine music?"[44] He liked occasionally to pass a quiet joke himself. Still, he was no talker, no story-teller, knew nothing of the fine art of being idle; and even in the midst of a hundred thousand men who loved him I think he was very solitary.

This does not mean that he secluded himself, or kept apart, absorbed in his own thoughts. He discussed his plans freely with those in whom he had confidence and would ask a young officer's opinion of great questions with a frankness as winning as it was sincere. "Colonel Long," he said before Gettysburg, "do you think we had better attack without the cavalry? If we do, we will or not, if successful, be able to reap the fruits of victory."[45]

Also, he was constantly attentive to the comfort of those about him. On the retreat from Pennsylvania he rebuked his aide, Colonel Venable, for telling bad news too loudly. Venable was high-spirited and did not like it, nor did a kindly invitation to drink buttermilk entirely soothe him. Shortly afterwards the aide, worn out with running and watching, lay down to sleep in the mud and rain. When he awoke, he found that the general had spread his own oilskin over him.[46]

As to the ease of approaching the commander-in-chief on matters of business, accounts differ. Grant understood that he was "difficult of access to subordinates." Tyler, in his invaluable letter to Price, giving an account of Lee's army, says the commander is "almost unapproachable, and yet no man is more simple, or less ostentatious, hating all pretension."[47] Unapproachable—yet "the scouts compared him [Jackson] with Lee. The latter was so genial that it was a pleasure to report to him."[48] The explanation of these contradictions is simply that Lee mistrusted his good nature. He knew that a complainant, once admitted, would waste his time, his strength, his nerves; and he trained his aides to do needed snubbing vicariously. As Colonel Venable writes, "General Lee had certain wishes which his aides-de-camp knew well they must conform to. They did not allow any friend of a soldier condemned by a court martial to reach his tent for personal appeal.... He said that with the great responsibilities resting upon him he could not bear the pain and distress of such applications."[49] And when officers came to find fault in regard to their promotion, he would turn them over to an aide with the old-fashioned phrase, "Suage him, Colonel, suage him."[50]

By these methods Lee kept a certain remoteness, which did not hurt his popularity and helped his dignity. Men loved to gaze on him. "It is surprising to see how eager the men of this army are always to get a good view of General Lee, for though a person has seen him a hundred times, yet he never tires looking at him," is the charmingly naïve comment of a correspondent of the "Richmond Despatch" in 1863.[51] On the other hand, the element of distance is most happily suggested by the remark of an officer to Mrs. Pickett: "Lee was a great soldier and a good man, but I never wanted to put my arms round his neck, as I used to want to do to Joe Johnston."[52]

Yet when occasion brought him into close contact even with the common soldier, his manner was absolutely simple, as of equal to equal, of man to man. Once in a crowded car a wounded private was struggling to draw on his coat over a bandaged arm. An officer, seeing his difficulty, came forward and tenderly assisted him.[53] It was the commander-in-chief. At another time Lee had sat down to rest in the shade of a great tree. A busy surgeon wished to establish his headquarters there. "Old man, I have chosen that tree for my field hospital, and I want you to get out of the way." Then he discovered his mistake. But Lee gently relieved the embarrassment of the situation: "There is plenty of room for both of us, Doctor, until your wounded are brought."[54] Even when they knew him, the soldiers sometimes took incredible liberties. On the hottest of July days one of them left the ranks and approached the general. The staff tried to stop him, but Lee put them aside and asked what he wanted. "Please, General, I don't want much, but it's powerful wet marching this weather. I was looking for a rag or something to wipe the sweat out of my eyes." "Will this do?" said the general, handkerchief in hand. "Yes, my Lordy, that indeed!" "Well, then, take it with you, and back quick to ranks; no straggling this march, you know, my man."[55]

In more serious matters Lee was equally ready to show the most democratic feeling. A devout Christian himself, he thought of each man in his army as a soul to be saved and in every way he could encouraged the mission and revival work which went on all through the war with ever-increasing activity. Even in the midst of urgent duty he would stop and take part in a camp prayer-meeting, and listen to the exhortations of some ragged veteran, as a young convert might listen to an apostle.

One thing doubtless helped his hold on the soldiers, as it helped Napoleon's, an extraordinary memory for names, faces, and characters. The value of this in dealing with his officers was, of course, inestimable. "Lee knew his army man by man almost, and could judge of the probable results of the movement here announced by the name of the officer in command."[56] With the privates the advantage gained was less direct but quite as solid. "I have frequently seen him recognize at once some old soldier whom he had barely met during the war, and who would be as surprised as delighted that his loved commander had not forgotten him."[57] Lee himself is reported to have said that "he had never been introduced to a soldier of the Army of Northern Virginia whose face and name he could not instantly recall."[58] This I doubt, in view of his not too courteous remark to Grant, at the time of the surrender, that he had frequently endeavored to recall his features from their acquaintance in Mexico, but could never succeed in doing so, and from another anecdote to the effect that he was extremely annoyed at not recognizing a man who was introduced to him after the war. "I was really much ashamed at not knowing the gentleman yesterday; I ought to have recognized him at once. He spent at least an hour in my quarters in the City of Mexico just after its occupation by the American army [*twenty years previous*]; he made a very agreeable impression on me, and I ought not to have forgotten him."[59]

What is of most general interest in this matter of Lee's memory of individuals, is his own assertion that it was not a special gift, but purely a matter of attention, which recalls Lord Chesterfield's theory that attention is the most exquisite element of courtesy. "Want of attention, which is really want of thought, is either folly or madness. You should not only have attention to everything, but a quickness of attention, so as to observe, at once, all the people in the room, their motions, their looks, and their words, and yet without staring at them, and seeming to be an observer." Only, Lee would have completed Chesterfield's idea of courtesy by that other element of love, which Chesterfield knew nothing about.

Again, like some other great commanders, and unlike others, Lee won the hearts of his soldiers by living as they did. He managed the business of his position with as little fuss and parade as possible. Foreign officers were struck with the absolute simplicity of his arrangements. There were no guards or sentries around his headquarters, no idle aides-de-camp loitering about. His staff were crowded together, two and three in a tent, and none were allowed to carry more baggage than a small box each. Tyler writes to Price: "Your own headquarters are more numerous and bulky. He rides with only three members of his staff and never takes with him an extra horse or servant, although he is upon the lines usually from daylight until dark."[60] His dress was always of the simplest, though neat and tidy, no braid or gilding, nothing but the stars on the collar to indicate his rank. He was perfectly Spartan as to his abiding-place, almost never leaving his tent for solid walls; and he was especially particular that there should be no intrusion upon peaceful citizens for his comfort. On one occasion Colonel Long had established the headquarters in a yard, but the general insisted on moving, lest they should annoy the residents. Long, thereupon, rather vexed, picked out another spot that had little to recommend it; but Lee was perfectly contented: "This is better than the yard. We will not now disturb these good people."[61] At another time Colonel Taylor made everything as agreeable as possible, but sighed over his chief's indifference: "It was entirely too pleasant for him, for he is never so comfortable as when uncomfortable."[62] This same Colonel Taylor ventured to rally the general a little on the subject. It seems that Lee had the best bedroom, while his aide was obliged to put up with the parlor. "Ah, you are finely fixed," remarked the great soldier, as he looked in upon his subordinate. "Couldn't you find any other room?" "No, but this will do." "He was struck dumb with amazement at my impudence and vanished."[63]

The table was as simple as the dwelling-place. Neat tin camp dishes answered for the service and the food was plain as the tableware. Very frequently there was actual scarcity; for the general was not willing to have special effort made for him when the soldiers were starving. The dinner often consisted of cabbage boiled with a little salt. Sweet potatoes and buttermilk were deemed luxury and when the commander-in-chief offered his luncheon to a major-general, it was found to consist of two cold sweet potatoes of which Lee said he was very fond. Even when better was provided, the general refused it, sending delicacies to the hospitals, perhaps not always to the contentment of his young and hungry staff. On the last march to Appomattox Mrs. Guild writes: "When we would camp near a house, they would prepare their best for General Lee; but he would sleep in his tent or on the ground with his staff, and say that I must go and have what was prepared for him."[64]

That Lee was beloved by his army it is hardly necessary to say, immensely beloved, beloved as few generals have ever been. In the first place, officers and soldiers trusted him. They trusted him in victory, knew that he would spare their toil and spare their blood as much as was possible, would make no move for barren glory, but only for their good and his country's. What is far more, they trusted him in defeat, knew that he would do everything that could be done and would save them from further damage if human skill could contrive it. They trusted him after Gettysburg. "We've not lost confidence in the old man, this day's work won't do him any harm." "Uncle Robert will get us into Washington yet; you bet he will."[65] They trusted him in the dark days of the Wilderness, and in the darker days of Petersburg. If he could not help them, no one could. Even the hard-headed and critical Longstreet believed that Lee was the man. "We need some such great mind as General Lee's," he writes from Tennessee.[66] When the final disaster came, the universal trust in the general was still unshaken. What he decides is right, what he says is the thing to do must be done. One of the coolest of Confederate authors writes of the surrender: "Other men fairly raved with indignation, and declared their desire to escape or die in the attempt, but not a man was heard to blame General Lee. . . . On the contrary, all expressed the greatest sympathy for him and declared their willingness to submit at once, or fight to the last man, as he ordered."[67]

An army may trust their general without loving him, however. This army loved him. I have sought far and wide for expressions of jealousy, of hostility, of lukewarmness. They are rare indeed. In the early South Carolina days some disaffection appears. "I do not know if it prevails elsewhere in the army," writes Governor Pickens to the president, "but I take the liberty to inform you that I fear the feelings of General Ripley towards General Lee may do injury to the public service. His habit is to say extreme things even before junior officers, and this is well calculated to do injury to General Lee's command."[68] Occasionally an individual frets over some disappointment or hindrance, as G.W. Smith in North Carolina: "What I mean to say is that General Lee in command of an army at Fredericksburg is not in the same point of view and evidently does not see things precisely as they appeared to him when General Johnston commanded that army";[69] or the petulant A.P. Hill, near the close of the struggle: "It is arrant nonsense for Lee to say that Grant can't make a night march without his knowing it. Has not Grant slipped round him four times already?"[70]

But these mild and scattered notes of discordance are completely lost in the general chorus of love and loyalty. The officers, high and low, vie with each other in their expressions of enthusiasm, none being more complete and touching in pregnant brevity than that of Longstreet: "All that we have to be proud of has been accomplished under your eye and under your orders. Our affections for you are stronger, if it is possible for them to be stronger, than our admiration for you."[71] But to me the simple and almost inarticulate devotion of the common soldiers is even more beautiful than that of their superiors. The loving, familiar nicknames, the quaint anecdotes, the eagerness to see, and to hear, and to obey, mean more than volumes of eulogy. Curious testimony to the quality of the feeling the soldiers had is furnished by several independent observers: "When he appeared in the presence of the troops, he was sometimes cheered vociferously, but far more frequently his coming was greeted with a profound silence which expressed more truly than cheers could have done the well-nigh religious reverence with which the men regarded his person."[72] This is, I think, a phenomenon somewhat rare in the psychology of crowds. Another interesting bit of out-of-the way evidence is furnished by a writer in the "Richmond Examiner" in August, 1864. It had been proposed to offer a one hundred dollar bond to all old soldiers who had served faithfully, but this correspondent, writing from the army, says: "The soldiers would prefer a strip of parchment in the shape of a certificate, setting forth their good conduct and soldierly qualities, signed by General R.E. Lee. This would be indeed a treasure to keep in after years."[73] Finally, one who knew both general and army well sums up the matter as follows: "Such was the love and veneration of the men for him that they came to look upon the cause as General Lee's cause, and they fought for it because they loved him. To them he represented cause, country, and all."[74]

If we seek the origin of this extraordinary personal devotion, we shall be told that it was magnetism. Doubtless there was some intangible element in the matter, something in the man's bearing, something in his words, something in his lofty and passionate appeals, which won hearts and held them. A concrete instance of this power appears in General Alexander's account of his desire to persuade Lee into keeping up a guerrilla warfare at the time of the surrender and of the effect of Lee's answer: "I had not a single word to say in reply. He had answered my suggestion from a moral plane so far above it that I was ashamed of having made it. With several friends I had planned to make an escape on seeing a flag of truce, but that idea was at once abandoned by all of them on hearing my report."[75]

I think, however, the general explanation of the soldier's love for Lee is much simpler, elementary, in fact, and is contained in the nursery rhyme recording the adventures of Mary and her little lamb.

Lee loved his men and trusted them. It is curious to read Wellington's expressions of disgust and contempt for his Peninsular army,–the soldiers "were detestable for anything but fighting and the officers were as culpable as the men,"–[76] and then to turn to the words, ever varied, in which Lee declares over and over his confidence in his followers and affection for them. After Gettysburg he says to them: "You have fought a fierce and sanguinary battle, which, if not attended with the success that has hitherto crowned your efforts, was marked by the same heroic spirit which has commanded the respect of your enemies, the gratitude of your country, and the admiration of mankind."[77] Without rhetoric, writing privately, he says of them, "I need not say to you that the material of which this army is composed is the best in the world and if properly disciplined and instructed, would be able successfully to resist any force that could be brought against it. Nothing can surpass the gallantry and intelligence of the main body."[78] And again, "There never were such men in an army before. They will go anywhere and do anything, if properly led."[79] His soldiers were his children, and he mourned their loss with a parental passion of grief: "The loss of our gallant officers and men throughout the army causes me to weep tears of blood, and to wish that I could never hear the sound of a gun again."[80]

Is it any wonder that his men loved him, or that their love grew with the years and after the war they haunted him with offers of service, offers of protection, offers of actual food, touching and pathetic, even when they were mixed with ill-timed drollery. Of all the numerous anecdotes bearing on this point, one especially is full of tragic significance. Lee was riding alone through the woods on his beloved Traveler, when he met an old Confederate. "Oh, General," said the fellow, "it does me so much good to see you that I'm going to cheer." The general protested the utter inappropriateness. But the man cheered just the same. And as the great soldier passed slowly out of hearing through the Virginia forest, it seems to me that his heart and his eyes must have overflowed at the thought of a great cause lost, of fidelity in ruin, and of the thousands and thousands and thousands who had cheered him once and in spirit would go on cheering him forever.

Stonewall Jackson

6

LEE AND JACKSON

J ackson was a born fighter. In his youth he fought poverty. He fought for an education at West Point. There he fought his way through against prejudice and every disadvantage. Fighting in Mexico, he thoroughly enjoyed himself. As a professor at the Virginia Military Institute he probably did not. When the war came, it was a godsend to him; and he fought with every nerve in his body till he fell, shot by his own soldiers, at Chancellorsville.

For pure intellectual power he does not seem to have been remarkable. He learned what he set out to learn, by sheer effort. What interested him he mastered. Without doubt his restless, active mind would have fought abstract problems, if it had found nothing else to fight. But I do not imagine he loved thought for itself or had the calm breadth to study impersonally the great questions of the world and flash sudden, sharp illumination on them, as did Napoleon.

And Jackson had no personal charm. He was courteous, but with a labored courtesy; he was shy, abrupt, ungainly, forgetful, and apt to be withdrawn into himself. His fellow students admired him, but shrank from him This pupils laughed at his odd ways and did not always profit by his teaching. This, before his star shone out. And it is strange to contrast such neglect with the adoration that pressed close about his later glory. In Martinsburg the ladies "cut every button off his coat, commenced on his pants, and at one time threatened to leave him in the uniform of a Georgia colonel—shirt-collar and spurs."[1] Nothing similar is recorded of Lee—even humorously.

It must not be supposed that, though unsuccessful in general society, Jackson lacked warmth or human kindness. He was sensitive, emotional, susceptible. He felt the charm of art in all its forms. He read Shakespeare, and quoted him in a military dispatch,–"we must burn no more daylight,"[2]–as I cannot imagine Lee doing. When he was in Europe, he keenly enjoyed painting, and architecture, and loved to talk of them after his return, entertaining the "Times" correspondent with a long discussion of English cathedrals, partly, to be sure, to avoid talk on things military. When in Mexico, he was charmed by the Mexican girls, so much so that he fled them, as Dr. Johnson fled Garrick's ballets.[3] In his youth he was even a dancer. When age and religion came upon him, he used still to indulge for exercise in an occasional polka, "but," as Mrs. Jackson remarks, deliciously, "no eye but that of his wife was ever permitted to witness this recreation."[4] In his family he was tender, affectionate, playful, sympathetic. He adored his little daughter and all children. "His abandon was beautiful to see, provided there were only one or two people to see it."[5] His letters to his wife are ardent and devoted, full of an outpouring and self-revelation which one never finds in the printed letters of Lee.

In short, he was a man with a soul of fire. Action was his life. To do something, to do high, heroic things, to do them with set lip and strained nerve and unflinching determination,–to him this was all the splendor of existence. In his youth he had not learned Latin well and it was questioned whether he could do it in age. He said he could. He was set to teach matters that were strange to him and some doubted whether he could do it. He said he could. Extempore prayer came to him with difficulty, and his pastor advised his not attempting it, if he could not do it. He said he could. "As to the rest, I knew that what I willed to do, I could do."[6] Such a statement has its foolish side and takes us back to what I said above about Jackson's intelligence. Pure intelligence sees insurmountable difficulties, too many and too plain. Jackson, if ever any man, came near to being pure will.

It seems that his courage, flawless as it was, was courage of will rather than of stolid temperament. "He has told me," says his sister-in-law, "that his first sight of a mangled and swollen corpse on a Mexican battlefield filled him with as much sickening dismay as if he had been a woman."[7] And Dabney writes: "It was not unusual to see him pale and trembling with excitement at the firing of the first gun of an opening battle."[8] Yet his power of concentration was so enormous that when he was thinking out a military problem he forgot bullet and shell and wounds and death. "This was the true explanation of that seeming recklessness with which he sometimes exposed himself on the field of battle."[9]

Also he had the magnetic faculty of extending to others his own furious determination. He could demand the impossible of them because he performed it himself. "Come on," he cried in Mexico, "you see there is no danger."[10] And a shot passed between his legs spread wide apart. His soldiers marched to death, when he bade them. What was even worse, they marched at the double through Virginia mud, without shoes, without food, without sleep. "Did you order me to advance over that field, sir?" said an officer to him. "Yes," said Jackson. "Impossible, sir! My men will be annihilated! Nothing can live there! They will be annihilated!" "General —," said Jackson, "I always endeavor to take care of my wounded and to bury my dead. You have heard my order—obey it."[11]

What was there back of this magnificent, untiring, inexhaustible will and energy, what long dream of glory, what splendid hope of imperishable renown? Or was it a blind energy, a mere restless thirst for action and adventure, unceasing, unquenchable? Something of the latter there was in it doubtless, of the love of danger for its pure nerve-thrill, its unrivaled magic of oblivion. "Nothing is more certain than that this love of action, movement, danger, and adventure was a prominent trait in his organization," says one of his earlier biographers.[12] "I envy you men who have been in battle. How I should like to be in one battle," he remarked in Mexico;[13] and he confessed that to be under fire filled him with a "delicious excitement."[14]

Nevertheless, he was far enough from being a mere common sworder, or even the gay, careless fighter who does the day's work and never looks beyond it. In his youth there can be no doubt that he dreamed dreams of immense advancement, of endless conquest, of triumph and admiration and success. During the war some one expressed the belief that Jackson was not ambitious. "Ambitious!" was the answer. "He is the most ambitious man in the Confederacy." We have his own reported words for his feelings at an earlier date. "The only anxiety I was conscious of during the engagement was a fear lest I should not meet danger enough to make my conduct conspicuous."[15] Most striking of all is Mrs. Preston's picture of him before Wolfe's monument at Quebec. He "swept his arm with a passionate movement around the plain and exclaimed, quoting Wolfe's dying words, 'I die content,—'to die as he died, who would not be content?'"[16]

Very little things often throw a fine light on character and difference of character. On one occasion, as the troops were marching by, they had been forbidden to cheer, lest the noise might betray them to the enemy. When Jackson's own brigade passed their general, however, their enthusiasm was too much for any prohibition, and they cheered loud and long. Jackson smiled as he listened, and turning to those beside him murmured, "You see, I can't stop them."[17] Whether Lee had any ambition or not, it is difficult to imagine him betrayed into such a naïve expression as this. The smile might have been possible for him, the words never.

So in Jackson's younger days his devouring ardor fed on worldly hopes. Then religion took possession of him, not suddenly, but with a gradual, fierce encroachment that in the end grasped every fibre of his being. Like a very similar nature in a different sphere, John Donne, he examined all creeds first, notably the Catholic, but finally settled in an austere and sturdy Calvinism. Not that his religion was gloomy or bitterly ascetic; for it had great depths of love in it and sunny possibilities of joy. But it was all-absorbing and he fought the fight of God with the same fury that he gave to the battles of this world. There must be no weakness, no trifling, no inconsistency. "He weighed his lightest utterance in the balance of the sanctuary," writes one who knew him well.[18] Christians are enjoined to pray. Therefore Jackson prayed always, even in association with the lightest act. "I never raise a glass of water to my lips without lifting my heart to God in thanks and prayer for the water of life."[19] They must remember the Sabbath day to keep holy. Therefore Jackson not only refrained from writing letters on Sunday: he would not read a letter on Sunday; he even timed the sending of his own letters so that they should not encumber the mails on Sunday.[20] It was the same with a scrupulous regard for truth. Every statement, even indifferent, must be exact, or, if inexact, corrected. And Jackson walked a mile in the rain to set right an error of inadvertence.[21] The wonder is that a man of such a temper accomplished anything in the world at all. I confess that I feel an unsanctified satisfaction in seeing the exigencies of war override and wither this dainty scrupulousness. It is true they cannot do it always. "Had I fought the battle on Sunday instead of on Monday I fear our cause would have suffered."[22] But then again, the Puritan Lee writes to the Puritan Jackson (italics mine): "I had hoped her own [Maryland's] citizens would have relieved us of that question, and *you must endeavor to give to the course you may find it necessary to pursue the appearance of its being the act of her own citizens.*"[23] How many leagues the praying Jackson should have walked in the rain to correct the fighting Jackson's peccadilloes.

And now how did Jackson's ambition and his religion keep house together? His admirers maintain that religion devoured the other motive completely. "Duty alone constrained him to forego the happiness and comforts of his beloved home for the daily hardships of a soldier's life."[24] But certain of his reported words in the very closing scene make me think that the thirst for glory was as ardent as ever, even if it had a little shifted its form. "I would not agree to the slightest diminution of my glory there [in heaven], no, not for all the fame which I have acquired or shall ever win in this world."[25] It does not sound quite like the chastened spirit of a son of peace, does it?

No, the early Jackson and the late Jackson were the same Jackson. The blare of trumpets, the crash of guns, the cheers of an adoring army, were a passionate delight to him and would have been as long as he walked this fighting world. Only that will, which by itself was mighty force enough, was doubled and tripled in power when it got the will of God behind it. To gratify personal ambition the man might have hesitated at destruction and slaughter. But to do his duty, to carry out the designs of Providence,—that mission must override all obstacles and subdue all scruples. In face of it human agony counted simply as nothing. Henderson, who is reluctant to find shadows in his idol, questions the authenticity of Jackson's interview with his brother-in-law, as reported by Mrs. Jackson; but I am perfectly ready to believe that the hero of the Valley declared for hoisting the black flag and giving "no quarter to the violators of our homes and firesides."[26] Certainly it is not denied that when he was asked how to dispose of the overwhelming numbers of the enemy, his answer was, "Kill them, sir! kill every man!"[27] And again, when some one deplored the necessity of destroying so many brave men, "No, shoot them all; I do not wish them to be brave."[28]

Such a tremendous instrument as this might have gone anywhere and done anything, and if Jackson had lived, his future defies prevision. "No man had so magnificent a prospect before him as General Jackson," wrote Lawley, the correspondent of the "London Times." "Whether he desired it or not, he could not have escaped being Governor of Virginia, and also, in the opinion of many competent judges, sooner or later President of the Confederacy."[29] But this regular method of ascent would have been slow. When things went wrong, when politicians intrigued and triumphed, when the needs of the army were slighted and forgotten for petty jealousies, Jackson would have been just the one to have cried out, "Here is man's will, where is God's will?"—just the one to have felt God's strength in his own right arm, to have purged war offices, and turned out congresses, and made incompetent presidents feel that they must give up to those who saw more clearly and judged more wisely. There would have been no selfishness in all this, no personal ambition, because it would have been just doing the will of God. And I can perfectly imagine Jackson riding such a career and overwhelming every obstacle in his way except one—Robert E. Lee.

When Jackson and Lee first met does not appear. Jackson said early in the war that he had known Lee for twenty-five years. They may have seen something of each other in Mexico. If so, there seems to be no record of it. At any rate, Jackson thought well of Lee from the first, and said of him when he was appointed to command the Virginia forces, "His services I regard as of more value to us than General Scott could render as a commander. . . . It is understood that General Lee is to be commander-in-chief. I regard him as a better officer than General Scott."[30]

From the beginning the lieutenant's loyalty to his chief grew steadily; not only his loyalty but his personal admiration and affection. I like the elementary expression of it, showing unconsciously Jackson's sense of some of his own deficiencies, in his remark to McGuire, after visiting Lee in the hospital: "General Lee is the most perfect animal form I ever saw."[31] But illustrations on a somewhat broader plane are abundant enough. "General Lee has always been very kind to me and I thank him," said Jackson simply, as he lay on his deathbed.[32] The enthusiasm of that ardent nature was ever ready to show itself in an almost over-zealous devotion. Lee once sent word that he should be glad to talk with his subordinate at his convenience on some matter of no great urgency. Jackson instantly rode to headquarters through the most inclement weather. When Lee expressed surprise at seeing him, the other answered: "General Lee's lightest wish is a supreme command to me, and I always take pleasure in prompt obedience."[33] If we consider what Jackson's nature was, it is manifest that he gave the highest possible proof of loyalty, when it was suggested that he should return to an individual command in the Valley, and he answered that he did not desire it, but in every way preferred a subordinate position near General Lee.[34]

Jackson's personal affection for Lee was, of course, intimately bound up with confidence in his military ability. Even in the early days, when Jackson had been in vain demanding reinforcements and word was brought of Lee's appointment to supreme command, Jackson's comment was, "Well, madam, I am reinforced at last."[35] On various occasions, when others doubted Lee's judgment or questioned his decisions, Jackson was entirely in agreement with his chief. For instance, Longstreet disapproved Lee's determination to fight at Sharpsburg, and Ropes and other critics have since condemned it. Jackson, however, though he had no part in it, gave it his entire and hearty approval.

I do not find anywhere, even in the most private letters, a disposition in Jackson to quarrel with Lee's plans or criticize his arrangements. On the contrary, when objections are made, he is ready to answer them, and eagerly, and heartily. "General Lee is equal to any emergency that may arise. I trust implicitly in his great ability and superior wisdom."[36] Jackson had plans of his own and sometimes talked of them. He was asked why he did not urge them upon Lee. "I have done so," was his answer. "And what does he say to them?" "He says nothing. But do not understand that I complain of this silence; it is proper that General Lee should observe it. He is wise and prudent. He feels that he bears a fearful responsibility and he is right in declining a hasty expression of his purpose to a subordinate like me."[37] Again, some one found fault with Lee's slowness. Jackson contradicted warmly: "General Lee is not slow. No one knows the weight upon his heart, his great responsibility. He is commander-in-chief and he knows that if an army is lost, it cannot be replaced. No! There may be some persons whose good opinion of me will make them attach some weight to my views, and if you ever hear that said of General Lee, I beg you will contradict it in my name. I have known General Lee for twenty-five years; he is cautious; he ought to be. But he is not slow."[38] And he concluded with one of the finest expressions of loyalty ever uttered by a subordinate, and such a subordinate: "Lee is a phenomenon. He is the only man I could follow blindfold."[39] After this, who can question the sincerity of the words spoken on his deathbed: "Better that ten Jacksons should fall than one Lee?"[40]

And what did Lee think of Jackson? As always, Lee's judgments are more difficult to get at. In spite of all respect and all affection, I cannot but think that his large humanity shrank a little from Jackson's ardors. When he told a lady, with gentle playfulness, that General Jackson, "who was smiling so pleasantly near her, was the most cruel and inhuman man she had ever seen,"[41] I have no doubt it was ninety-nine parts playfulness, but perhaps there was one part, one little part, earnest. Even after Antietam his military commendation of Jackson was very restrained, to say the least. "My opinion of the merits of General Jackson has been greatly enhanced during this expedition. He is true, honest, and brave, has a single eye to the good of the service, and spares no exertions to accomplish his object."[42] No superlatives here. Sharp words of criticism, even, are reported, which, inexplicable as they sound, seem to come with excellent authority. "Jackson was by no means so rapid a marcher as Longstreet and had an unfortunate habit of never being on time."[43]

Yet Lee's deep affection for his great lieutenant and perfect confidence in him are beyond question. It has been well pointed out that this was proved practically by the fact that the commander-in-chief always himself remained with Longstreet and left Jackson to operate independently, as if the former were more in need of personal supervision. Lee's own written words to Jackson are also—for Lee—very enthusiastic: "Your recent successes have been the cause of the liveliest joy in this army as well as in the country. The admiration excited by your skill and boldness has been constantly mingled with solicitude for your situation."[44] Jackson's wound and death and the realization of his loss produced expressions of a warmth so unusual as to be almost startling. "If I had had Stonewall Jackson at Gettysburg, I should have won that battle."[45] "Such an executive officer the sun never shone on. I have but to show him my design, and I know that if it can be done it will be done."[46] The messages sent to the dying general are as appreciative as they are tender. "You are better off than I am, for while you have only lost your left, I have lost my right arm."[47] "Tell him that I wrestled in prayer for him last night, as I never prayed, I believe, for myself."[48] (Yet if the words are correctly reported, note even here the most characteristic Lee-like modification, *I believe*.) And only those who are familiar with Lee can appreciate the agony of the parting outcry, "'Jackson will not—he cannot die!' General Lee exclaimed, in a broken voice and waving every one from him with his hand, 'he cannot die.'"[49]

The study of the practical military relations of the two great commanders is of extreme interest. Lee does not hesitate to advise Jackson as freely as he would any other subordinate. "It was to save you the abundance of hard fighting that I ventured to suggest for your consideration not to attack the enemy's strong points, but to turn his positions at Warrenton, etc., so as to draw him out of them. I would rather you should have easy fighting and heavy victories. I must leave the matter to your reflection and cool judgment."[50] He even frequently gives a sharp order which approaches sternness: "You must use your discretion and judgment in these matters, and be careful to husband the strength of your command as much as possible."[51] And again: "Do not let your troops run down, if it can possibly be avoided by attention to their wants, comforts, etc., by their respective commanders. This will require your personal attention."[52]

Jackson seems usually to have accepted all this with unquestioning submission. It is true that Longstreet is said once to have accused him of disrespect because he groaned audibly at one of Lee's decisions.[53] But Longstreet was a little too watchful for those groans. Also, on one occasion, when Lee proposed some redistribution of artillery, Jackson protested, rather for his soldiers than for himself: "General D.H. Hill's artillery wants existed at the time he was assigned to my command, and it is hoped that artillery which belonged to the Army of the Valley will not be taken to supply his wants."[54] But, for the most part, the lieutenant writes in the respectful, affectionate, and trustful tone which he adopted at the very beginning of the war and maintained until the end: "I would be more than grateful, could you spare the time for a short visit here to give me the benefit of your wisdom and experience in laying out the works, especially those on the heights."[55]

Jackson's complete submission to Lee is the more striking because, though a theoretical believer in subordination, he was not by nature peculiarly adapted to working under the orders of others. Some, who knew him well, have gone so far as to say that "his genius never shone under command of another."[56] This is absurd enough considering his later battles; but it seems to me that some such explanation may be sought for his comparative inefficiency on the Peninsula, as to which almost all critics are agreed. It was physical exhaustion, says Dabney. It was poor staff service, says Henderson. Is it not possible that, accustomed hitherto to working with an absolutely free hand, his very desire to be only an executive and carry out Lee's orders may, for the time, to some extent, have paralyzed his own initiative?

However that may be, there is no doubt that Jackson did not take kindly to dictation from Richmond. It is said that on one occasion he wrote to the War Office requesting that he might have fewer orders and more men.[57] It is certain that he complained bitterly to Lee of the custom of sending him officers without previous consultation. "I have had much trouble resulting from incompetent officers being assigned to duty with me, regardless of my wishes. Those who have assigned them have never taken the responsibility of incurring the odium which results from such incompetence."[58] And very early in his career he had a sharp clash with Secretary Benjamin, who had attempted to interfere in the detail of military arrangements. Jackson sent in his resignation at once, explaining that his services could be of no use, if he was to be hampered by remote and ill-informed control. The fact of the resignation, which was withdrawn by the kindly offices of Johnston and Governor Letcher, is of less interest than the spirit in which Jackson offered it. When it was represented to him that the Government had proceeded without understanding the circumstances, he replied: "Certainly they have; but they must be taught not to act so hastily without a full knowledge of the facts. I can teach them this lesson now by my resignation and the country will be no loser by it."[59] Was I wrong in saying that this man would have ridden over anything and anybody, if he had thought it his duty? Such summary methods may have been wise, they may have been effective: they were certainly very unlike Lee's.

Now let us turn from Jackson's superiors to his inferiors. The common soldier loved him. It was not for any jolly comradeship, not for any fascinating magnetism of personal charm or heroic eloquence. He was a hard taskmaster, exacting and severe. "Whatever of personal magnetism existed in Stonewall Jackson," says his partial biographer, "found no utterance in words. Whilst his soldiers struggled painfully towards Romney in the teeth of the winter storm, his lips were never opened save for sharp rebuke or peremptory order."[60] But the men had confidence in him. He had got them out of many a difficulty and something in his manner told them that he would get them out of any difficulty. The sight of his old uniform and scrawny sorrel horse stirred all their nerves and made them march and fight as they could not have done for another man. And then they knew that though he was harsh, he was just. He expected great things of them, but he would do great things for them. He would slaughter them mercilessly to win a victory; but when it was won he would give them the glory, under God, and would cherish the survivors with a parent's tenderness. "We do not regard him as a severe disciplinarian," writes one of them, "as a politician, as a man seeking popularity,–but as a Christian, a brave man who appreciates the condition of a common soldier, as a fatherly protector, as one who endures all hardship in common with his followers, who never commands others to face danger without putting himself in the van."[61]

But with his officers it was somewhat different. They did indeed trust his leadership and admire his genius. How could they help it? It is said that all the staff officers of the army at large liked him.[62] And Mrs. Jackson declares that his own staff were devoted to him, as they probably were. Yet even she admits that they resented his rigid punctuality and early hours. And there is no doubt that in these particulars and in many others he asked all that men were capable of and sometimes a little more. "General Jackson," says one of his staff, "demanded of his subordinates implicit obedience. He gave orders in his own peculiar, terse, rapid fashion, and he did not permit them to be questioned."[63] General Ewell is said to have remarked that he never "saw one of Jackson's couriers approach him without expecting an order to assault the North Pole."[64] On one occasion he had given his staff directions to breakfast at dawn and to be in the saddle immediately after. The general appeared at daybreak–and one officer. Jackson lost his temper. "Major, how is it that this staff never will be punctual?" When the major attempted some apology for the others, his chief turned to the servant in a rage. "Put back that food into the chest, have that chest in the wagon, and that wagon moving in two minutes."[65]

Also Jackson had a habit of keeping everything to himself. This may have been a great military advantage. It was a source of constant amusement to the soldiers. Jackson met one of them one day in some place where he should not have been. "What are you doing here?" "I don't know." "Where do you come from ?" "I don't know." When asked the meaning of this extraordinary ignorance, the man explained, "Orders were that we shouldn't know anything till after the next fight." Jackson laughed and passed on.[66]

But the officers did not like it. Jackson made his own plans and took care of his own responsibilities. Even his most trusted subordinates were often told to go to this or that place with no explanation of the object of their going. They went, but they sometimes went without enthusiasm. And Jackson was no man for councils of war. Others' judgment might be as good as his, but only one judgment must settle matters, and his was for the time to be that one.

Hence his officers fretted and he quarreled with some of the best of them. And when things did not go right, with him it was the guardhouse instantly. All five regimental commanders of the Stonewall Brigade were once under arrest at the same time.[67] The gallant Ashby, just before his last charge and death, had a sharp bit of friction with his superior. When Gregg lay dying, he sent to the general to apologize for a letter recently written "in which he used words that he is now sorry for . . . He hopes you will forgive him."[68] Jackson forgave him heartily; but he could not have deathbed reconciliations with all of them.

In some of these cases Lee was obliged to interfere, notably in that of A.P. Hill. Hill was a splendid soldier. Lee loved him. By a strange coincidence his name was on the dying lips of Lee and Jackson both. But he was fiery and impetuous and did not hesitate to criticize even the commander-in-chief with hearty freedom. He chafed sorely under Jackson's arbitrary methods. Lee, in recommending him, foresaw this, and tried to insinuate a little caution. "A.P. Hill you will, I think, find a good officer, with whom you can consult, and, by advising with your division commanders as to your movements,

Lee The American

much trouble will be saved you in arranging details, and they can aid more intelligently."[69]

It was quite useless. The two fiery tempers clashed immediately. Jackson put his subordinate under arrest more than once In the "Official Records" we may read the painful but very curious correspondence in which the two laid their grievances before Lee and Lee with patient tact tried to do justice to both. "If," says Hill, "the charges preferred against me by General Jackson are true, I do not deserve to command a division in this army; if they are untrue, then General Jackson deserves a rebuke as notorious as the arrest."[70] It is said that Lee at last brought the two together, and, "after hearing their several statements, walking gravely to and fro, said, 'He who has been the most aggrieved can be the most magnanimous and make the first overture of peace.' This wise verdict forever settled their differences."[71] Forever is a long word, but surely no judgment of Solomon or Sancho Panza could be neater.

Lee's relations with Jackson as to strategy and tactics are no less interesting than the disciplinary. Some of Jackson's admirers seem inclined to credit him with Lee's best generalship, especially with the brilliant and successful movements which resulted in the victories of the Second Bull Run and of Chancellorsville. Just how far each general was responsible for those movements can never be exactly determined. The conception of flank attacks would appear to be an elementary device to any military mind. Lee certainly was sufficiently prone to them and urged them upon Jackson at an early stage, as is shown by a passage quoted above.[72] It is in nice and perfect execution that the difficulty lies, and in the delicate adjustment of that execution to the handling of the army as a whole; and in this Lee and Jackson probably formed as wonderful a pair of military geniuses as ever existed.

As to Lee's initiative, it can be easily shown that even in the first Valley campaign he had, to say the least, a most sympathetic and prophetic comprehension of Jackson's action. If Jackson may possibly have conceived the plan of the Second Bull Run campaign, it was Lee who designed the tactics of Gaines's Mill, that Jackson failed to carry out. At a later date, just before Fredericksburg, when Jackson was again operating in the Valley, Henderson, in the absence of authentic data, assumes that the lieutenant was anxious to realize some flanking conception of his own and that Lee assented to it. This may be so, but a few weeks later still, when the battle was imminent, Lee expresses himself to a very different effect. "In previous letters I suggested the advantages that might be derived by your taking position at Warrenton or Culpeper, with a view to threaten the rear of the enemy at Fredericksburg.... As my previous suggestions to you were left to be executed or not at your discretion, you are still at liberty to follow or reject them."[73]

The case that has aroused most controversy, one of those delightful problems that can be always discussed and never settled, is that of Chancellorsville. The facts, so far as they can be gathered from conflicting accounts, seem to be as follows. On the night of May 1, Hooker had withdrawn to Chancellorsville. Lee end Jackson met and talked over the state of things. Examination had shown that to attack Hooker's left and centre was out of the question. On the other hand, reports received from the cavalry made it appear that the right might be assailed with advantage. Lee decided on this and ordered Jackson to make the movement. Jackson then secured further information, elaborated his plans accordingly, and acted on them with Lee's approval.

Evidently this statement leaves many loopholes, but it is impossible to be more definite, or to say just where Lee's conception ended and Jackson's began. If we turn for information to the two principal actors, we shall not progress much. "I congratulate you upon the victory which is due to your skill and energy,"[74] says Lee; but this passing of compliments means no more than Jackson's general acknowledgment: "All the credit of my successes belongs to General Lee; they were his plans and I only executed his orders."[75] Jackson's special comment is not more helpful: "Our movement was a great success; I think the most successful military movement of my life. But I expect to receive more credit for it than I deserve. Most men will think that I planned it all from the first, but it was not so."[76]–"Ah," we interrupt, "this is magnanimous. He is going to give the credit to Lee."–Not at all; he is only going to give it to God. Nor does Lee's letter to Mrs. Jackson make matters much clearer. "I decided against it [front attack] and stated to General Jackson we must move on our left as soon as practicable; and the necessary movement of troops began immediately. In consequence of a report received about this time from General Fitzhugh Lee, . . . General Jackson, after some inquiry, undertook to throw his command entirely in Hooker's rear."[77]

What interests me in the controversy is not the debated point, which cannot seriously affect the greatness of either party concerned, but the characteristic reserve of Lee, as shown in the last sentence above quoted, and far more in the letter to Dr. Bledsoe, written, says Jones, in answer to a "direct question whether the flank movement at

Chancellorsville originated with Jackson or with himself." Lee's reply is so curious that I quote the important part of it entire.

> I have learned from others that the various authors of the life of Jackson award to him the credit of the success gained by the Army of Northern Virginia where he was present, and describe the movements of his corps or command as independent of the general plan of operations and undertaken at his own suggestion and upon his own responsibility.
>
> I have the greatest reluctance to say anything that might be considered as detracting from his well-deserved fame, for I believe no one was more convinced of his worth or appreciated him more highly than myself; yet your knowledge of military affairs, if you have none of the events themselves, will teach you that this could not have been so. Every movement of an army must be well considered and properly ordered, and every one who knew General Jackson must know that he was too good a soldier to violate this fundamental principle. In the operations around Chancellorsville, I overtook General Jackson, who had been placed in command of the advance, as the skirmishers of the approaching armies met, advanced with the troops to the Federal line of defenses, and was on the field until their whole army recrossed the Rappahannock.
>
> There is no question as to who was responsible for the operations of the Confederates, or to whom any failure would have been charged.[78]

The more I read this letter, the less I understand it. It does not answer Bledsoe's question at all, makes no attempt to answer it. Instead, it tells us that Jackson did not rob Lee of the command, or the responsibility, or the glory. Who ever supposed he did? And why did Lee write so? Did he wish to leave Jackson the credit of initiative in the matter? It sounds as if he wished the precise contrary, which is quite impossible. Or did he miss the whole point, which seems equally impossible? This letter, like many others, goes far to reconcile me to the loss of the memoirs that Lee did not write. I feel sure that with the best intentions in the world he would have left untold a great deal that we desire to know.

It is hardly necessary to say that in a comparison of Lee and Jackson the question of just how far either one originated the military designs which covered both with glory is not really very essential. I hope that I have already indicated the difference between them.

Perhaps in their religion it is as significant as in anything. To both religion was the main issue of life; but in Lee religion never tyrannized; in Jackson I think it did. Lee said that "duty was the sublimest" word in the language. Nevertheless, if he had heard Mrs. Jackson's remark that her husband "ate, as he did everything else, from a sense of duty,"[79] I think he would have smiled and observed that it might be well occasionally to eat for pure pleasure. It would be most unjust to say that Jackson's was a religion of hell; but it would be nobly true to say that Lee's was a religion of heaven. It would be fairer to both to speak of Jackson's as a devouring fire, of Lee's as a pure and vivifying light. Indeed, especially in comparison with Jackson, this idea of light satisfies me better for Lee than anything else. His soul was tranquil and serene and broadly luminous, with no dark corner in it for violence or hate.

And, although I speak with humility in such a matter, may we not say that the military difference between the two was something the same? It is possible that Jackson could strike harder, possible even that he could see as deeply and as justly as his great commander. I think that Lee had the advantage in breadth, in just that one quality of sweet luminousness. He could draw all men unto him. What a splendid mastery it must have been that kept, on the one hand, the perfect friendship and confidence of the high-strung, sensitive, and jealous Davis, and on the other, the unquestioning loyalty, affection, and admiration of a soul so swift and haughty and violent as that of Jackson!

Robert E. Lee (from the painting by Pioto)

7

LEE IN BATTLE

Any study of Lee would be incomplete without portrayal of him in the greatest crises of all. For my purpose it would have been convenient if some keen-sighted journalist could have accompanied the general in his various battles and left a stenographic report of where he went and what he said and what he did. Unfortunately the many memoir writers who were in a good position to observe were at the time, for the most part, excellently occupied with their own affairs. Therefore I ask in vain as to Lee's whereabouts and action at certain very critical moments.

We like to imagine the master mind in a great conflict controlling everything, down to the minutest detail. But with vast modern armies this is far from being the case, even with the elaborate electrical facilities of today; and in Lee's time those facilities were much less complete. Lee himself indicated this humorously when he was remonstrated with for running unnecessary risk and answered: "I wish some one would tell me my proper place in battle. I am always told I should not be where I am."[1] And he expressed it with entire seriousness when he said, in words in part already quoted: "My interference in battle would do more harm than good. I have, then, to rely on my brigade and division commanders. I think and work with all my power to bring the troops to the right place at the right time; then I have done my duty. As soon as I order them forward into battle, I leave my army in the hands of God."[2] Some critics hold that Lee was inclined to carry the principle too far. What impresses me in this, as in other things, is the nice balance of his gifts. Persons by nature disposed to direct others almost always seek to direct in everything. How wise and constant Lee's guidance was, where he thought it needed, is shown by his son's remark: "We were always fully instructed as to the best way to get to Lexington, and, indeed, all the roads of life were carefully marked out for us by him."[3] Yet the moment he reached the limit of what he thought was his province, he drew back and left decision to others whom he felt to be, by nature or training, better qualified.

The amount of Lee's direction and influence seems to have varied greatly in different battles. At Fredericksburg he adopted a central position whence he could survey the whole field. Colonel Long's remarks in describing this must have given Longstreet exquisite pleasure. "In the battle Longstreet had his headquarters at the same place, so that Lee was able to keep his hand on the rein of his 'old war-horse' and to direct him where to apply his strength."[4] At Antietam critics are agreed that Lee's management of things was perfect. "He utilized every available soldier: throughout the day he controlled the Confederate operations over the whole field."[5] On the other hand, in the Peninsular battles, owing perhaps, to imperfect organization and staff arrangements, his hold on the machine was much less complete; and at Gettysburg the vast extension of his lines made immediate personal direction almost impossible, with results that were disastrous.

It is at Gettysburg that we get one of the most vivid of the few pictures left us of Lee in the very midst of the crash and tumult of conflict. This is from the excellent pen of General Alexander, who says that the commander-in-chief rode up entirely alone, just after Pickett's charge, "and remained with me for a long time. He then probably first appreciated the extent of the disaster, as the disorganized stragglers made their way back past us. . . . It was certainly a momentous thing to him to see that superb attack end in such a bloody repulse. But, whatever his emotions, there was no trace of them in his calm and self-possessed bearing. I thought at that time his coming there very imprudent and the absence of all his staff officers and couriers strange. It could only have happened by his express intention. I have since thought it possible that he came, thinking the enemy might follow in pursuit of Pickett, personally to rally stragglers about our guns and make a desperate defense. He had the instincts of a soldier within him as strongly as any man. . . . No soldier could have looked on at Pickett's charge and not burned to be in it. To have a personal part in a close and desperate fight at that moment, would, I believe, have been at heart a great pleasure to General Lee and possibly he was looking for one."[6]

And I ask myself how much of that born soldier's lust for battle, keen enjoyment of danger and struggle and combat, Lee really had. Certainly there is little record of his speaking of any such feeling. At various times he expressed a deep sense of all the horrors of war. "You have no idea of what a horrible sight a battlefield is."[7] And again: "What a cruel thing is war; to separate and destroy families and friends, and mar the purest joys and happiness God has granted us in this world; to fill our hearts with hatred instead of love for our neighbors, and to devastate the fair face of this beautiful world."[8] Yet we must remember that at the time of his great military glory Lee was an old man and the fury of hot blood was tempered in him. I imagine that he found an intense delight in Mexico, "when the musket balls and grape were whistling over my head in a perfect shower,"[9] and when he was threading his way alone in night and solitude through the murky pitfalls of the Pedregal. Even at a later time one vivid sentence, spoken in the midst of the slaughter of Fredericksburg, lights the man's true instincts, like a flash: "It is well that war is so terrible, or else we might grow too fond of it."[10]

As to Lee's personal courage, of course the only point to be discussed is the peculiar quality of it. Judging from his character generally and from all that is recorded of him, I should not take it to be a temperamental indifference to danger, a stolid disregard of its very existence, such as we find perhaps in Grant or Wellington. Though far from being a highly nervous organization, Lee was sensitive, imaginative; and he probably had to accustom himself to being under fire and was always perfectly aware of any elements of peril there might be about him. By the time the war broke out, however, he was doubtless as indifferent to bullets as to raindrops, and went where duty took him without a moment's thought of the result.

Testimony to his entire coolness in battle is abundant enough. I do not know of any more striking statement than Scheibert's. "During the battle of Chancellorsville, at the very crisis of the struggle, I happened to be standing beside the general under fire and in full view of a very interesting episode of the fight. I was astonished when, in spite of the excitement natural to such a scene, he . . . began to converse with me about popular education."[11] A vivid concrete instance of self-possession in the midst of turmoil is narrated by a Union soldier: "A prisoner walked up to him and told him a rebel had stolen his hat. In the midst of his orders he stopped and told the rebel to give back the hat and saw that he done it, too."[12]

I am not aware that Lee was wounded at any time during the war, or indeed in his life, except slightly at Chapultepec. His hands were

Lee The American

severely injured just before Antietam, but this was by the falling of his horse. He was, however, constantly under fire. At Antietam A.P. Hill, who was close to the general, had his horse's forelegs shot off. On another occasion, when Lee was sitting with Stuart and his staff, "a shell fell plump in their midst, burying in the earth with itself one of General Lee's gauntlets, which lay on the ground only a few feet from the general himself."[13] In 1864 Lee was inspecting the lines below Richmond and the number of soldiers gathered about him drew the enemy's fire rather heavily. The general ordered the men back out of range and himself followed at his leisure; but it was observed that he stopped to pick up something. A fledgling sparrow had fallen out of its nest and he took it from the ground and tenderly replaced it, with the bullets whistling around him.[14]

As in this case, Lee was always extremely solicitous about the unnecessary exposure of his men. Once, when he was watching the effect of the fire from an advanced battery, a staff officer rode up to him by the approach which was least protected. The general reprimanded him for his carelessness, and when the young man urged that he could not seek cover himself while his chief was in the open, Lee answered sharply: "It is my duty to be here. Go back the way I told you, sir."[15] At another time Lee had placed himself in a very exposed position, to the horror of all his officers. They could not prevail upon him to come down, so finally General Gracie stepped forward and interposed himself between his commander and the enemy. "Why, Gracie," protested Lee, "you will certainly be killed." "It is better, General, that I should be killed than you. When you get down, I will." Lee smiled and got down.[16]

No protest and no entreaty, however, could make the commander-in-chief protect himself as much as his officers wished. Perhaps the most amusing instance of this is an experience of Lee and Davis together in the early days on the Peninsula. They were riding side by side under fire when Davis realized the danger and urged his companion to withdraw. Lee returned the compliment. Then they both forgot all about it, till A.P. Hill rode up and begged them to go back. They withdrew a few feet, without mending matters much, till finally Hill reappeared and insisted that they should betake themselves to some position out of range.[17]

When matters became really critical, Lee completely threw aside all caution. In the terrific battles of the Wilderness, where at times it seemed as if Grant would succeed in effecting a permanent break, the Confederate general repeatedly (on three separate occasions, as it appears) rushed to the front to rally his men and charge, like Ney or

Murat, at the head of them. "Go back, General Lee, go back," shouted the soldiers. But he would not go back till they had promised to do as much for him as they could have done with him. And they did as much. No men could have done more.[18]

It was this occasional fury of combativeness which made Longstreet assert that the general was sometimes unbalanced, not by any personal exposure or excitement, but by critical situations affecting the army as a whole. Longstreet, defending his own conduct at Gettysburg, urges that Lee was particularly overwrought at the time of that battle. In what is, to say the least, peculiar phraseology, the lieutenant writes of his commander: "That he was excited and off his balance was evident on the afternoon of the first, and that he labored under that oppression till blood enough was shed to appease him."[19] The suggestion that Lee required blood to appease him is grotesque and his loyal admirers ridicule the idea that at Gettysburg he was unbalanced. But there is evidence beside Longstreet's that, once in a fight, he hated to give it up and perhaps occasionally allowed his ardor to overcome his discretion. The Prussian officer Scheibert remarks that, while at Chancellorsville Lee was admirably calm, at Gettysburg he was restless and uneasy.[20] General Anderson bears witness that at Gettysburg his chief was "very much disturbed and depressed."[21] Curious independent testimony to a relation between Lee and Longstreet just before the final surrender, precisely similar to what Longstreet depicts at Gettysburg, is furnished by Captain Ranson in "Harper's Magazine," though I confess I cannot quite adjust it to Longstreet's own narrative. The captain involuntarily overheard a conversation between the two generals. "I must have slept for an hour at least when again I was awakened by the loud, almost fierce tones of General Lee, saying, 'I tell you, General Longstreet, I will strike that man [Grant] a blow in the morning.' General Longstreet again recounted the difficulties, ending as before, 'General, you know you have only to give the order and the attack will be made, but I must tell you that I think it a useless waste of brave lives.'"[22] Also that excellent critic Colonel T.L. Livermore proposes to solve the difficult question, why Lee did not earlier abandon Petersburg, by accepting Davis's suggestion that the general's too combative temperament made him reluctant to retire from an enemy.[23]

The most heroic picture that is left us of Lee, high-wrought by the excitement of battle and determined to fight to the end, is the account, received by Henderson from a reliable eye-witness, of the chief's decision to remain north of the Potomac after Antietam. General after general rode up to the commander's headquarters, all with the same tale of discouragement and counsel of retreat. Hood was quite unmanned. "My God!" cried Lee to him, with unwonted vehemence, "where is the splendid division you had this morning?" "They are lying on the field where you sent them," answered Hood. Even Jackson did not venture to suggest anything but withdrawal. There were a few moments of oppressive silence. Then Lee rose in his stirrups and said: "Gentlemen, we will not cross the Potomac to-night. You will go to your respective commands, strengthen your lines; send two officers from each brigade towards the ford to collect your stragglers and bring them up. Many have come in. I have had the proper steps taken to collect all the men who are in the rear. If McClellan wants to fight in the morning, I will give him battle. Go!"[24] They went, and in this case at least Lee's glorious audacity was justified; for he proved to all the world that McClellan did not dare attack him again.

However Lee's judgment may have been affected by the excitement of battle, it made little alteration in his bearing or manner. Fremantle tells us that the general's dress was always neat and clean, and adds: "I observed this during the three days' fight at Gettysburg, when every one else looked and was extremely dirty."[25] Stress of conflict sometimes seems to alter men's natures. Odd stories are told in the war-books of officers quite saintly in common converse who in battle would swear like reprobates. Conversely, it is said of the great Condé that in his daily dealings with his soldiers his tongue was incredibly rough, but the moment he got under fire he addressed everybody about him with exquisite politeness. Lee's politeness was always exquisite. It was only very, very rarely that some untoward incident stirred either his temper or his speech. "Probably no man ever commanded an army and, at the same time, so entirely commanded himself as Lee," says the cool-blooded Alexander. "This morning [after Chancellorsville] was almost the only occasion on which I ever saw him out of humor."[26]

Nor was it only a question of mere politeness. Lee was as tender and sympathetic to man and beast in the fury of combat, in the chaos of defeat, as he could have been in his own domain at Arlington. After the great charge on the third day at Gettysburg, an officer rode up to him lashing an unwilling horse. "Don't whip him, Captain, don't whip him," protested the general, "I have just such another foolish beast myself and whipping doesn't do any good."[27] And as the tumult of disaster increased, the sympathy took larger forms of magnanimity than mere prevention of cruelty to animals. There was no fault-finding, no shifting of perhaps deserved blame to others, nothing but calmness, comfort, cheerfulness, and confidence. "All this will come right in the end; we'll talk of it afterwards; but in the mean time all good men must rally."[28] "Never mind, General. All this has been my fault. It is I that have lost this fight, and you must help me out of it the best way you can."[29]

So, with incomparable patience, tact, and energy, the great soldier held his army together after defeat and kept it in a temper and condition which went far to justify Meade's reluctance to follow up his success. Only, to complete the picture, one should turn to General Imboden's brief sketch, taken after the work was done and natural human exhaustion and despair claimed some little right over even a hero's nerve and brain. It must be remembered that this was a man fifty-six years old. Towards midnight Lee rode up to Imboden's command. "When he approached and saw us, he spoke, reined up his horse and endeavored to dismount. The effort to do so betrayed so much physical exhaustion that I stepped forward to assist him, but before I reached him, he had alighted. He threw his arm across his saddle to rest himself and, fixing his eyes upon the ground, leaned in silence upon his equally weary horse: the two formed a striking group, as motionless as a statue. After some expressions as to Pickett's charge, etc., he added in a tone almost of agony, 'Too bad! Too bad! Oh, too bad!'"[30]

With the portrait of Lee himself in the shock of battle we should put a background of his soldiers and their feeling as he came among them. We have already heard their passionate cry when he rushed to put himself at their head and charge into the thickest of the fight. "Go back, General Lee! Go back!" General Gordon, who loved to throw a high-light of eloquence on all such scenes, describes this one with peculiar vividness, his own remonstrance, "These men are Georgians, Virginians, and Carolinians. They have never failed you on any field. They will not fail you now. Will you, boys?" and the enthusiastic answer, "No, no, no!"[31] Those who like the quiet truth of history, even when it chills, will be interested in an eye-witness's simple comment on this picturesque narrative. "Gordon says, 'We need no such encouragement.' At this some of our soldiers called out, 'No, no!' Gordon continuing, said, 'There is not a soldier in the Confederate army who would not gladly lay down his life to save you from harm'; but the men did not respond to this last proposition."[32]

It cannot be doubted, however, that Lee's personal influence in critical moments was immense. On one occasion just before battle there was heard to pass from mouth to mouth as a sort of watchword the simple comment, "Remember, General Lee is looking at us."[33] Mr. Page describes a scene which is very effective as showing how little the general relied on words and how little he needed to. Lee was riding through the ranks before a conflict. He "uttered no word. He simply removed his hat and passed bareheaded along the line. I had it from one who witnessed the act. 'It was,' said he, 'the most eloquent address ever delivered.' And a few minutes later, as the men advanced to the charge, he heard a youth, as he ran forward, crying and reloading his musket, shout through his tears that 'any man who would not fight after what General Lee said was a – coward.'"[34]

Perhaps the most splendid battle-piece of Lee in the midst of his fighting soldiers is Colonel Marshall's account of the triumphant advance on the third day at Chancellorsville. The enemy were retiring and the troops swept forward through the tumult of battle and the smoke of woods and dwellings burning about them. Everywhere the field was strewn with the wounded and dying of both armies. "In the midst of this scene General Lee, mounted upon that horse which we all remember so well, rode to the front of his advancing battalions. His presence was the signal for one of those uncontrollable outbursts of enthusiasm which none can appreciate who have not witnessed them. The fierce soldiers, with their faces blackened with the smoke of battle, the wounded, crawling with feeble limbs from the fury of the devouring flames, all seemed possessed with a common impulse. One long, unbroken cheer, in which the feeble cry of those who lay helpless on the earth blended with the strong voices of those who still fought, rose high above the roar of battle, and hailed the presence of the victorious chief. He sat in the full realization of all that soldiers dream of–triumph."[35]

This was victory. But there came a day of defeat, when the Army of Northern Virginia, after four years of fighting and triumphing and suffering, shrunk almost to nothing, saw its great commander ride away to make his submission to a generous conqueror. Their love, their loyalty, their confidence were no less than they had ever been. If he said further fighting was useless and inhuman, it must be so.

But this very absolute confidence increased the weight of the terrible decision. All these thousands trusted him to decide for them. He must decide right. What the burden was we can only imagine, never know. But through the noble serenity maintained by habitual effort good observers detected signs of the struggle that was going on. "His face was still calm, but his carriage was no longer erect, as his soldiers had been used to see it. The trouble of those last days had already ploughed great furrows in his forehead. His eyes were red as if with weeping; his cheeks sunken and haggard; his face colorless. No one who looked upon him then, as he stood there in full view of the disastrous end, can ever forget the intense agony written upon his features. And yet he was calm, self-possessed, and deliberate."[36] So great was his anguish that it wrung a wish to end it all, even from a natural self-control complete as his. "How easily I could get rid of this and be at rest. I have only to ride along the lines and all will be over. But," he quickly added, "it is our duty to live, for what will become of the women and children of the South if we are not here to support and protect them?"[37]

So the decision had to be made. And he made it. "Then there is nothing left me but to go and see General Grant, and I would rather die a thousand deaths."[38] His officers protested passionately. "O General, what will history say of the surrender of the army in the field?" "Yes, I know, they will say hard things of us; they will not understand how we were overwhelmed by numbers; but that is not the question, Colonel; the question is, is it right to surrender this army? If it is right, then I will take all the responsibility."[39]

The scene that ensued has been described often: the plain farmhouse room, the officers, curious, yet sympathetic, the formal conversation, as always painfully unequal to the huge event it covered, the short, ungainly, ill-dressed man, as dignified in his awkwardness almost as the royal, perfectly appointed figure that conferred with him. Lee bore himself nobly, say his admirers, nobly, but a little coldly, say his opponents. And who shall blame him? Then it was over. One moment he paused at the door, as he went out, waiting for his horse; and as he paused, looking far into the tragic future, or the tragic past, he struck his hands together in a gesture of immense despair, profoundly significant for so self-contained a man.[40] Then he rode away, back to his children, back to the Army of Northern Virginia, who had seen him daily for three years and now would never see him any more.

In all this scene two figures stand out beyond every other, the man who succeeded and the man who failed. In some respects there are remarkable resemblances between them. Though one had old family traditions behind him and the other had not, both were absolutely simple, democratic, and indifferent to fuss, parade, or show. Both were frank and straightforward, yet both were men of extreme reticence, using as few words as possible and only for the deliberate conveyance of their purposes. Both, under a calm if not frigid exterior, covered tender human sympathy and warm human kindness.

Lee The American

But one was a man of the eighteenth century, the other of the nineteenth, one of the old America, the other of the new. Grant stands for our modern world, with its rough, business habits, its practical energy, its desire to do things no matter how, its indifference to the sweet grace of ceremony and dignity and courtesy. Lee had the traditions of an older day, not only its high beliefs, but its grave stateliness, its feeling that the way of doing things was almost as much as the thing done. In short, Grant's America was the America of Lincoln, Lee's the America of Washington. It is in part because of this difference and because I would fain believe that without loss of the one we may some day regain something of the other that I have given so much thought to the portrayal of Lee's character and life.

Long ago Milton said that he who would be a great poet must make his own life a true poem. Lee had certainly no care for being a great poet, but if ever man made his own life a true poem, it was he. Grant's career has the vigor, the abruptness, the patness, the roughness of a terse military dispatch. It fits its place and fills it, and all is said. Lee's has the breadth, the dignity, the majesty, the round and full completeness of a Miltonic epic, none the less inspiring because it had a tragic end. It was indeed a life lived in the grand style.

8

LEE AS A GENERAL

I n the year 1901 I was invited to attend a meeting called to discuss the question, who was the greatest man of the nineteenth century. I accepted with pleasure. As all those present were citizens of the Northern portion of the United States they happily arrived at unanimous agreement upon Abraham Lincoln, just as they would have agreed upon Napoleon, if they had been French, or, if they had been Germans, upon Bismarck.

What interested me most was that no one seemed disposed to inquire very carefully into the essential or comparative elements of greatness. How was it about the great artists, painters, sculptors, and musicians? How about the poets, or the novelists, who, like Scott, had brought delight to millions? How about the great discoverers in science? Or the great philanthropists? Was the greatest man he who had shown the highest development of human power and genius, as perhaps Napoleon? Or he who had pushed the standard of pure truth some steps further into outer darkness, as perhaps Darwin? Or he who—and I know not even whom to instance without too much begging of the question—had been simply of the greatest use and service to humanity? And I could not but be reminded of Edward FitzGerald's caustic sentence: "It is wonderful how Macaulay, Hallam, and Mackintosh could roar and bawl at one another over such questions as which is the Greatest Poet? Which is the greatest work of that Greatest Poet? etc., like Boys at some Debating Society?"[1]

FitzGerald, too, here narrows the discussion to a particular field. And with a poem or a picture we can at least say, this I prefer, this the majority of men seem to prefer, though Heaven knows that even such decision is difficult enough. But in more complicated lines of human activity the problem is far more puzzling, and in none more than in that of soldiership. When I see the readiness with which persons whom I should not suppose especially competent grade, classify, and adjust, setting A above B, B above C, D above B and C but below A, with the nicest accuracy of discrimination, I can only wonder and be forcibly reminded of FitzGerald's little quip.

There are so many things to be taken into account. Lord Roberts quotes Napoleon's remark that "the first quality of a general is that he shall have a cool head," and, as Wellington had a supremely cool head, infers that he was equal, if not superior to Napoleon. But surely a general may use a few other qualities besides coolness. Ropes admirably suggests the difficulties in the discussion in his comparison of Joseph E. Johnston with Lee. "Johnston," he says, "possessed as good a military mind as any general on either side; but in that fortunate combination of qualities—physical, mental, and moral—which go to make up a great commander, General Lee was unquestionably more favored than any of the leaders in the Civil War."[2] Yet even here—"physical, mental, and moral"—how much room there is for question and distinction.

After which, it must be admitted that humanity will go on forever grading and ranking, like the great schoolboys that we all are. And the instinct that impels us to do so is a right instinct. We can never settle which is the greatest man, or what is true greatness. Yet we must be always trying to settle it. Only so can we choose our models and examples. Only so can we establish the standard by which, however shifting, and uncertain, and imperfect, we must guide our lives.

A series of studies of Lee which did not include "Lee as a General" would be absurd. Yet it cannot be expected that a civilian should attempt any scientific analysis of military genius. Some civilians have attempted it, which does not encourage me in the least. Even professional men would do well to remember Lee's own reply, when he was asked to review a book on the Austro-Prussian war in 1866: "At the time of the occurrence I thought I saw the mistakes committed by the Austrians; but I did not know the facts, and you are aware that, though it is easy to write on such subjects, it is difficult to elucidate the truth."[3] If we were all as modest as this, I fear nothing would be written about anything. Fortunately we are not. And on the topic of Lee's soldiership volumes have been filled. I shall endeavor as briefly as possible to illustrate the different points of view and then to state some conclusions, not as to comparative rank but as to particular qualities. But first we should have a rapid summary of the unquestioned facts of Lee's military career during the war.

When Virginia seceded, he was made commander-in-chief of all her forces. When she joined the Confederacy, he was appointed to organize the Southern troops as they arrived in Richmond. In the autumn of 1861 he conducted an inconspicuous and unsuccessful campaign in West Virginia. Towards the end of the same year he was sent to take charge of the seacoast defenses of South Carolina and Georgia. Early in 1862 he was called to Richmond and made military adviser to the president. On the first of June, in consequence of the wounding of Johnston, Lee took command of the Army of Northern Virginia. He then fought the series of Peninsular battles, which resulted in the retreat of McClellan and the relief of Richmond. In the autumn he and Jackson defeated Pope in the second battle of Bull Run, invaded the North, captured Harper's Ferry, but were checked by McClellan at Antietam, and forced to withdraw again into Virginia. In December they defeated Burnside at Fredericksburg, and in May, Hooker at Chancellorsville, the latter victory being dearly bought by Jackson's death. Lee then invaded Pennsylvania, but was severely repulsed by Meade at Gettysburg, and once more recrossed the Potomac. In the autumn and winter of 1863 and 1864 the two armies confronted each other at different points in Virginia without any very decisive contact. In the spring Grant took control of all the Northern forces and, with Meade under him in immediate command of the Army of the Potomac, made his plans to destroy Lee's army and push straight for Richmond. Lee met him at point after point, however; and Grant finally took his army across the James to Petersburg. Here he was at first no more successful than in the Wilderness. But a winter of privation and starvation, together with the failure of Southern resources consequent upon Sherman's and other movements in the South and West, greatly reduced Lee's strength and efficiency; and when Grant and Sheridan closed in upon him in March and April, they very speedily brought about the final surrender at Appomattox.

Starting with this indisputable statements of events, let us examine the various estimates of Lee's generalship. Let us take first the eulogies of his Southern admirers, premising, however, that not by any means all Southern writing is unreasonable or extravagant. The sane and discriminating spirit of Allan or Alexander, for example, is but little removed from the moderate tone of equally cool heads on the Northern side. But the usual strain of Confederate rhapsody is quite different. Listen to B. H. Hill's comparison of the Southern leader with other great commanders: "He was a Cæsar without his ambition: a Frederick without his tyranny; a Napoleon without his selfishness; and a Washington without his reward."[4] Or to General Gordon's masterly rhetoric, which is more specifically military: "Compare this, my friends, the condition of France, with the condition of the United States, in the freshness of her strength, in the luxuriance of her resources, in the lustihood of her gigantic youth, and tell me where belongs the chaplet of military superiority, with Lee, or with Marlborough or Wellington? Even the greatest of captains, in his Italian campaigns, flashing his fame, in lightning splendor, over the world, even Bonaparte met and crushed in battle but three or four (I think) Austrian armies; while our Lee, with one army, badly equipped, and in time incredibly short, met and hurled back, in broken and shattered fragments, five admirably prepared and most magnificently appointed invasions.... Lee was never really beaten. Lee could not be beaten! Overpowered, foiled in his efforts, he might be, but never defeated until the props which supported him gave away.... On that most melancholy of pages, the downfall of the Confederacy, no Leipsic, no Waterloo, no Sedan can ever be recorded."[5] One is reminded of Matthew Arnold's remark about Macaulay's essay on Milton: "Truly, with what a heavy brush does this man lay on his colors." Reverend J. William Jones, however, manages to produce as great an effect with much simpler means. "I think I put it very conservatively when I say that he had proven himself the greatest soldier of the war, if not of history."[6] What would the reverend gentleman have said, if he had not wished to be conservative?

Now let us turn to those who are as evidently prejudiced against Lee as these eulogists in his favor. The fault-finders are not all Northerners. In the early days, before the general's reputation was established, there was plenty of criticism in the South. Thus Pollard, who afterwards became an enthusiastic admirer, could say in regard to the West Virginia campaign, "a general who had never fought a battle, who had a pious horror of guerrillas, and whose extreme tenderness of blood inclined him to depend exclusively upon the resources of strategy";[7] and even after the Peninsula, "Lee, who by no fault of his own was followed by toadies, flatterers, and newspaper sneaks in epaulets who made him ridiculous by their servile obeisances and excess of praise."[8] Longstreet, who loved Lee personally, was goaded by the attacks of Lee's admirers on his own record into a frankness of comment which sounds far different from the ecstasies quoted above. "On the defensive Lee was absolutely perfect . . . but of the art of war, more particularly of that of giving battle, I do not think General Lee was a master. In science and military learning he was greatly the superior of General Grant, or any other commander on either side. But in the art of war I have no doubt that Grant and several others were his equals. In the field his characteristic fault was headlong combativeness."[9]

Longstreet's strictures, as indeed those of most critics, are chiefly connected with Gettysburg, in Longstreet's case not unnaturally, since the responsibility for the failure of that battle has usually been made to rest either with Longstreet or with Lee. Longstreet had his own ideas beforehand of what should be done. He tried to persuade Lee to accept them. Lee declined, and told Longstreet what he himself wished. Longstreet either would not or could not carry out the general's wishes, and the battle was lost. The following are a few of Longstreet's remarks. "The cause of the battle was simply General Lee's determination to fight it out from the position in which he was at that time."[10] "He seemed under a subdued excitement, which took possession of him when 'the hunt was up' and threatened his superb poise."[11] "There is no doubt that General Lee during the crisis of that campaign lost the matchless equipoise that usually characterized him."[12] And the lieutenant supports himself by a quotation which it takes all the authority of his character as a soldier and a gentleman to make us accept. He says that when he was in Tennessee Lee wrote him, "If I only had taken your counsel even on the 3d, and had moved around the Federal left, how different all might have been."[13] Lee's own quiet comment elsewhere on the battle does not sound to me entirely consistent with this: "It would have been gained, could one determined and united blow have been delivered by our whole line."[14]

If we wish to get the extreme Northern partisan view of Lee's generalship, we must come down a little later than Gettysburg, to the Wilderness, and listen to Badeau. Badeau had, of course, but one object, to exalt Grant; and it is extremely curious to see how his disposition to do this directly by depreciating Lee is constantly checked by his realization that since Grant finally won, the more able Lee can be shown to have been, the greater is the glory of having beaten him. Some reserves are, therefore, made in favor of Lee's defensive generalship. But for the most part, he is unequal to his opportunities and much overrated. In the first place, he is morally not all he should be: "The fact is that Lee was often disingenuous in his reports. He did not absolutely falsify, but he colored and concealed so as to convey a very incorrect impression."[15] Militarily, his genius served for little more than to be a foil to Grant's. "The genius of the leader as well as the valor of his men was reserved for negative

117

displays."[16] His was the "natural policy of a second-rate commander."[17] "Grant himself, in Lee's situation, would never have been content with a negative defense."[18] "And whether his spirit was cowed and acknowledged its master, or whether Grant's skill was so absolute as to allow no opportunity, the rebel general never again [after the Wilderness] assumed a completely offensive attitude."[19]

This sort of thing would appear quite as hyperbolical as the Southern praise, were it not that so great an authority as Grant himself uses very much the same expressions. During his trip around the world he said to Young: "I never ranked Lee so high as some others in the army, that is to say, I never had so much anxiety when he was in my front as when Joe Johnston was in front. [Yet Grant said to Meade in the Wilderness, "Joe Johnston would have retired after two days' such punishment."[20] Lee was a good man, a fair commander, who had everything in his favor. He was a man who needed sunshine. ... Lee was of a slow, cautious nature, without imagination or humor, always the same, with grave dignity. I never could see in his achievements what justified his reputation. The illusion that heavy odds beat him will not stand the ultimate light of history. I know it is not true. Lee was a good deal of a headquarters general, from what I can hear and from what his officers say. He was almost too old for active service—the best service in the field."[21] Grant's written words in his "Memoirs," though more guarded, are to the same effect. I am not aware that he ever said anything in commendation of Lee's military ability. Lee is reported—to be sure, on rather circuitous authority—to have remarked after the war: "I have carefully searched the military records of both ancient and modern history, and have never found Grant's superior as a general."[22]

With the flight of years and the cooling of passion, Northern judgment has come to take an attitude very different from Badeau's.[23] To begin with, Lee's immense difficulties are better appreciated. Grant says he needed sunshine and support. It may be so, but he did not always get them. Often he was obliged to relinquish his own plans for those of others, and even in carrying out his own he was so hampered by superior authority that the results could not properly be said to be his. And the limitation of authority was less serious than the limitation of resources. Grant had men, money, means of all sorts at his back. Lee's numbers shrank daily and could not be replaced, and the men he had could not be armed or shod or clothed or fed. The pitifulness of his disabilities in this respect can only be appreciated by wide reading of his correspondence and that of others. He was not a man to complain, yet passage after passage like the following occurs:

"I can do nothing for want of proper supplies. With these and effective horses I think I could disturb the quiet of the enemy and drive him to the Potomac."[24] When he was asked, after the war, why he did not advance upon Washington after the Second Bull Run, he answered, "Because my men had nothing to eat. I could not tell my men to take that fort [pointing to Fort Wade] when they had had nothing to eat for three days. I went to Maryland to feed my army."[25] Palfrey's comment on this sort of thing, though not well taken in the South, has a good deal of force in it. He says, in substance, that one reason the Army of Northern Virginia fought so splendidly was that victory meant a square meal at last.

The Northern critics who are most favorable to Lee of course all admit that he made mistakes. He himself would have been the first to recognize this, as in his well-known humorous comment on the newspaper editors: "Even as poor a soldier as I am can generally discover mistakes after it is all over. But if I could only induce these wise gentlemen who see them so clearly beforehand to communicate with me in advance, it would be far better for my reputation and—what is of more consequence—far better for the cause."[26]

In regard to Gettysburg, Northern writers generally feel that Lee was wrong. He did not mean to fight there and never should have fought there, as he did. They hold that he violated Jomini's fundamental principle: "These two bloody days [of Eylau] prove how dubious must be the success of an attack which is directed at the front and centre of a well-concentrated enemy: even if victory is won, it is too dearly bought to be of any use."[27] "He [Lee] could easily have manœuvred Meade out of his strong position on the heights and should have done so," says Doubleday,[28] though he remarks a little later that "the great effort of Wilcox and Wright would have been ruinous, if followed up,"[29] which surely shows that the second day might have proved successful for the South. Ropes and Colonel W.R. Livermore go further, holding that Gettysburg was merely the culmination of a series of unjustifiable audacities. Ropes maintained that the risk of the Second Bull Run campaign was greater than was justified by the chance of advantage. "The rules of war allow of no such dangerous movement as Jackson's, unless the object is far more important than the one which on this occasion he proposed to himself."[30] Elsewhere he says that Lee "showed on several occasions a singular lack of caution."[31] And although he contrasts Jackson's flank attack at Chancellorsville with others as a case where the risk was worth running for the great results to be obtained, he agrees in the main with Colonel Livermore that Gettysburg may be regarded as the last act of a drama that began long before.[32] "It is certainly a mistake," writes Ropes, "for a general to overestimate his adversary's strength and prowess; it is no less a mistake, however, to underrate them. But this was, as we know, the habit of General Lee's mind; and his subsequent successes confirmed him in it. It was not until the disastrous assault on the heights of Gettysburg that he found out his mistake."[33]

Nor do the Northern critics confine their strictures to Gettysburg and its immediate antecedents. They insist that in the earlier Peninsula campaign, important as the results were, they might have been much greater, and that Malvern Hill was almost as ill-managed as Gettysburg. And they recognize that the failure to anticipate Grant's crossing of the James, was a very serious and unfortunate oversight.

Yet, in spite of all this, it would be difficult for intelligent enthusiasm to be warmer or more generous than that of many of these Northern writers for their ancient adversary. Some of them by no means agree in condemning even Gettysburg. General Hunt thought that "a battle was necessary to Lee and a defeat would be more disastrous to Meade, and less so to himself, at Gettysburg than at any other point east of it."[34] Ropes cannot refuse his admiration to the very rashness which he blames. "One hardly knows which is the more remarkable–General Lee's sagacity in estimating the inertia of his antagonist [before Fredericksburg], or his temerity in confronting him so long with a force only one third as strong, and actually for a time refusing the aid which Jackson was bringing to him."[35] As to the conduct of the Wilderness campaign there is a general concord of commendation. Instead of agreeing with Badeau that Lee was cowed out of all initiative, Colonel Dodge says: "Grant's method was just what Lee preferred. He was right in not coming out of his intrenchments to fight."[36] "Grant had been thoroughly defeated in his attempt to walk past General Lee on his way to Richmond," writes General Webb.[37] And Colonel W.R. Livermore, the latest authority on the subject, declares (in answer to a frequent comment on the Wilderness battles) that "it was due to Lee's skill that he fought behind breastworks,"[38] that "if Grant in the spring of 1864 had come to the Army of Northern Virginia and Lee to the Army of the Potomac, it is not impossible that the war would have ended then and there,"[39] and that "this campaign alone would entitle him to the high place he justly holds among the great commanders of the world."[40]

Nor is Northern eulogy of Lee confined to the conduct of special campaigns. Mr. Bache, in his "Life of Meade," writes, "He had not, like most successful generals, as Tacitus says, become insolent with success, but had never failed in gentle courtesy to his officers, in boundless tenderness to his men, in humanity to all, and in word and deed had proved himself the rarest type of soldier and gentleman."[41] Colonel W.R. Livermore calls him "the greatest general of the day."[42] Ropes says that the feeling in the army towards the commander was "one of entire confidence and enthusiastic devotion. This was not because it was a Southern army, but because the Army of Northern Virginia was so fortunate as to have in Lee a man who was head and shoulders above his colleagues."[43] And Colonel Roosevelt has added his testimony to all the rest: "As a mere military man Washington himself cannot rank with the wonderful war-chief who for four years led the Army of Northern Virginia."[44] And again: Lee "will undoubtedly rank as without any exception the greatest of all the great captains that the English-speaking people have brought forth—and this, although the last and chief of his antagonists may claim to stand as the full equal of Marlborough and Wellington."[45]

Now let us turn to the opinion of foreign military experts and critics, which should be more impartial than that of any American. As a matter of fact, in the early days the foreigners who wrote about the war were certainly not impartial. The Comte de Paris, excellent as his history is, was distinctly Northern in his sympathies. Fremantle and Scheibert were even more distinctly Southern. And when Lord Wolseley said of Lee, "He was the ablest general, and to me seemed the greatest man I had ever conversed with; and yet I have had the privilege of meeting Von Moltke and Prince Bismarck, . . . General Lee was one of the few men who ever seriously impressed and awed me with their natural and their inherent greatness,"[46] he was probably somewhat influenced by personal sympathy with the Southern leader and the cause he served.

Within the last ten or fifteen years, however, there has come up a generation of English critics whose interest in our Civil War seems to be almost purely impersonal and scientific. They are perfectly ready to find ability and military genius on the Northern side as well as on the Southern. Indeed, I think they are generally inclined to estimate Grant's soldiership more highly than is usual with many of the more rigorous Northern writers. The judgments of these Englishmen in regard to Lee have, therefore, a peculiar interest and suggestiveness.

Here again, there is of course no attempt to overlook or belittle Lee's errors. Henderson is inclined, in many cases, to criticize Lee's use of his cavalry, especially during the early part of the war. As to the sequel, or lack of sequel, to Malvern Hill, Captain Battine remarks, "It can now be said that Lee missed a grand opportunity;"[47] and the same writer says of the movements against Meade in the autumn of 1863, "It cannot be denied that Lee, great strategist as he was, on this occasion, as on the march to Gettysburg, clung too long to his preconceived scheme of how the campaign should develop, nor did he watch as narrowly as he should have done for the first good chance to strike."[48] As to the great crux of Gettysburg I think the English critics are a little more lenient than the American, and Battine even declares that the decision to attack was "sound and wise, the failure lay in faults of execution which were caused, to some extent, at any rate, by the want of sympathetic coöperation of the corps commanders,"[49] while Wood and Edmunds hold that Jackson in Longstreet's place would have "annihilated the greater part of Meade's army and forced the remainder to retreat on Washington."[50] Beside this it is well to place Henderson's quiet comment, substantially in accord with Ropes and Colonel Livermore: "I am forced to the conclusion that at Gettysburg Lee's whole army suffered from overconfidence."[51] Henderson is also decidedly critical as to Lee's failure to keep track of Grant's crossing of the James. "Grant certainly outmanœuvred Lee. It was only the slackness of one of his subordinates that saved the Confederate army not indeed from defeat, but from being driven back into Richmond itself."[52]

On the other hand, these critics unite in the warmest admiration for Lee's greatness and genius. This appears in the remarks on individual operations. Henderson says, speaking of the Second Bull Run, "If, as Von Moltke avers, the junction of two armies in the field of battle is the highest achievement of military genius, the campaign against Pope has seldom been surpassed. . . . Tried by this test alone, Lee stands out as one of the greatest soldiers of all times."[53] In regard to the Wilderness campaign Captain Vaughan-Sawyer writes: "In this [Lee's not taking the offensive] only a few of his detractors have seen evidence of failing courage. Actually, it is only another exhibition of his genius, which enabled him to see that the day for those tactics was passed. His unerring perception told him that his only chance lay in wearing out his enemy and he would not be tempted into a false move."[54] And Captain Battine's verdict is even more favorable: "Lee had emerged triumphant from a campaign which is surpassed by no other in gallant fighting and skillful direction. Even the glories of the campaign of France in 1814, and Frederick's wonderful defiance of his enemies in the Seven Years' War, pale before Lee's astonishing performance; for neither Napoleon till he met Wellington, nor Frederick at any time, was opposed to such a dangerous enemy as Grant."[55]

The general summaries as to Lee's ability are in the same enthusiastic tone. Henderson, like Colonel Roosevelt, improved on Von Moltke's reported dictum that the Southern commander was in all respects the equal of Wellington by calling him "undoubtedly one of the greatest if not the greatest soldier who ever spoke the English tongue."[56] And Captain Battine, concluding his estimate of the general's character, says: "In the tact and diplomatic skill with which he softened the jealousies of his people and tightened the combination of the different states he is only to be compared with the great Duke of Marlborough. In the boldness and sagacity of his strategy and in the affectionate devotion he inspired in his troops he resembled Napoleon himself. He enjoyed alike the confidence of the nation, government, and army, which he never lost for an instant in the darkest days of misfortune. . . . Such as he was, brave, chivalrous, and conscientious to a fault, he will remain the most attractive personality among American heroes and one of the most famous of the world's great generals."[57]

For the eulogy of Lee which is at once the most enthusiastic and the most discriminating we must, however, return to the United States. Colonel Eben Swift, in his paper read before the American Historical Society in 1910, reviews the Wilderness battles in the light of the military equipment and conditions of to-day, and incidentally discusses Lee's handling of the material and resources that he had. Colonel Swift is a member of the United States General Staff, and his opinion should, therefore, represent the latest and most scientific military judgment. He writes as follows: "All great soldiers before him inherited a ready-made army, but Lee made his own army. None of the others probably encountered as dangerous an adversary as Grant, and none of them except Hannibal, and Napoleon in the last two years, were opposed to soldiers as good as their own. The odds of numbers were greater against Lee in the Wilderness campaign than they were against Napoleon in the Waterloo campaign. But Lee had his army at the end and Napoleon's disaster was complete. In the Wilderness campaign Lee inflicted losses in killed and wounded almost as great as the army he commanded. Lee made five campaigns in a single year; no other man and no other army ever did so much. . . . Lee practiced his own theory of the art of war. Although indebted to Napoleon, he treated each problem as a concrete case, which he solved according to circumstances, and he had his greatest success when he departed furthest from established rules. Napoleon formulated the principle at St. Helena that you must never uncover your line of retreat or fight a battle with a front to a flank. Lee's violation of that rule placed Grant's plans in the Wilderness in greater danger than they ever were at any period of the campaign. But Lee's art seems to have died with him. Up to the present he has taught no pupil and he has inspired no successor."[58]

After feasting on this luxury of comparative estimates of Lee's military greatness, the reader certainly has no desire to hear mine. It will now, however, be profitable to dwell for a moment on some special elements of his character which are particularly significant in connection with his soldiership.

In the first place, there is his organizing, systematizing ability. As Colonel Swift says, "All great soldiers before him inherited a ready-made army, but he made his own army." So far as the civil authorities would allow, he built it up from its component elements and made it one of the finest fighting machines in the world. As a little minor instance of his thoughtfulness, it is interesting to note that he is credited with having suggested the gray uniform on account of its protective quality.[59] But in a thousand details, large and small, he was always caring for the effectiveness of his soldiers and for their comfort. This talent for organization is apt to go, as it did in McClellan's case, with too great deliberation, a constitutional reluctance to give up plans and depart from programmes. What is remarkable about Lee is that he instantly responded to the demands of the occasion and strode right out of all rules and right over them.

Then there is his boldness—or rashness. Some of his detractors assert that he failed in offense. Others that he was too aggressive. These charges contradict each other, say his friends. They do not. Nothing requires a cool head and perfect calm, so much as a vigorous and daring system of attack. And if Lee's offensive really failed, it was because a too great combativeness hurled him for the moment off his balance. As Sainte-Beuve says of Napoleon, there were times when he broke loose from the world of men into the world of Titans. When Lee first took command of the army, General Alexander asked General Ives whether he had audacity enough. "Alexander," said Ives, "if there is one man in either army, Confederate or Federal, head and shoulders above every other in audacity, it is General Lee. His name might be Audacity. He will take more desperate chances and take them quicker than any other man in this country, North or South."[60] At the same time, it should be remembered that Jackson felt obliged to defend Lee against the charge of excessive caution and to point out that he had the responsibility of a great army on his hands and felt it.

In regard to this matter of taking chances, Lee should be heard in his own defense. He recognized perfectly again and again that he ran enormous risks; but he felt that in his situation it was absolutely necessary. "If you can accomplish the object, any risk would be justifiable,"[61] he writes to D.H. Hill, early in the war. Again, "There is always hazard in military movements, but we must decide between the possible loss of inaction and the risk of action."[62] And after all was over, his cool observation on the matter was that criticism of his rashness was obvious, but that the disparity between the forces rendered such risks unavoidable.[63] It may at least be observed that when a man thrice in succession takes the apparently fearful chances of the Second Bull Run of Antietam, of Chancellorsville, and comes out whole, if not triumphant, there may be something more in it than the mere luck of the successful gambler.

Another quality of Lee's, and one that will hardly be disputed, is energy and rapidity of action. Napoleon said, "In the art of war, as in mechanics, time is the great element that balances the force and the resistance."[64] The promptness with which Lee drew Jackson to himself before the Peninsular battles and before Fredericksburg, the vigor and swiftness of the retreat from Gettysburg, above all, the instant preparedness which met Grant at point after point as he circled about Richmond, would surely have won the approval of Napoleon himself.

As to energy, and especially as to independence, of decision there is more dispute. It is sometimes asserted that Lee deferred too much to the judgment of his officers. I feel that there may be some misapprehension here. Lee, when he chose, could be as secret as Jackson. He liked to consult his subordinates because they liked it. He was genuinely interested in their opinions. I doubt if he ever felt the need of any one's support for his own judgment or, at any rate, the desire to divide his responsibility. As to the great latitude he gave his division commanders in the field, Henderson believes that he was simply anticipating the latest developments of modern war, which prescribe "first, that an army cannot be effectively controlled from headquarters; second, that the man on the spot is the best judge of the situation; third, that intelligent coöperation is of more value than mechanical obedience."[65] It can hardly be denied, however, that Lee was too considerate, not of the opinions but of the feelings of his subordinates. As his nephew said of him, "He had a reluctance to oppose the wishes of others or to order anything that would be disagreeable or to which they would not consent."[66]

Among the foremost of Lee's military qualities we must put his knowledge of human nature. I have already dwelt upon the importance of this in his dealings with his own army. It was quite as useful to him in his dealings with the enemy. Possibly his divination of actual plans and movements may have been somewhat exaggerated. Sir Edward Hamley gives us an excellent caution in this regard. "Historians," he says, "are fond of ascribing to successful generals such endowments as 'prescience,' 'intuitive divination of their enemy's designs.' There will be evidence in subsequent pages that these gifts, in the preternatural extent implied, exist only in the imagination of the chroniclers, and in this campaign [Jena] Napoleon had in three days made three erroneous calculations of the Prussian doings."[67]

But although Lee may not always have foreseen the actual plan, he had the keenest appreciation of the man who made it and the way in which he was likely to carry it out. Certainly no one could say of him what Lord Wolseley, rather surprisingly, says of Napoleon: "Although I believe Napoleon to have been by far the greatest of all great men, he has always struck me as having been a bad judge of character."[68] Lee's comments on McClellan, on Pope, on Hooker, on Meade, on Grant, still more his conduct when confronted with each of them, show how watchful and how careful his judgment was with regard to them all. And, as always with him, this results not merely from intuition, but from profound study. Polybius said, two thousand years ago, "It is to be ignorant or blind in the science of commanding armies to think that a general has anything more important than to apply himself to learn the inclinations and character of his adversary." Lee so understood his business. He made use of every bit of information that could possibly be acquired. He read the Northern papers systematically. And, on learning that McClellan was superseded, he is said to have expressed with much humor the difficulty of his task: "I am sorry to part with McClellan. We understood one another so well." While he remarked to a Northern general after the war: "You people changed your commanders in front of me so frequently that it was no small labor to study them and it was a work constantly to be renewed."[69]

In short, what impresses me perhaps more than anything else in Lee's purely military success is the splendid triumph of intelligence, of brains, and I do not find any really more satisfying eulogy than Henderson's simple phrase, "He was the clearest-sighted soldier in America."[70]

It is hardly necessary to say, however, that it is not Lee's excellence as a general that has led one to these extensive studies of his life. Modest as he was, if it had not been for the necessities of war, he might have left no mark on the history of his country. But the mark he has left is far deeper and more permanent than a merely military one.

Perhaps he is as often compared with Wellington as with any other great leader. Wellington loved his country and saved England. Yet Lord Roberts says of him, "That he was honest, straightforward, resolute, and patriotic, none can deny; but there appears to be no instance in his military career of his adopting a course where his duty was opposed to his own interest."[71] How different is the record of Lee! Emerson says of Napoleon: "His soldiers called him *Cent Mille.* Add honesty to him and they might have called him hundred million." To military qualities not unlike Napoleon's how much did Lee add besides honesty!

Mrs. Robert E. Lee

9

LEE'S SOCIAL AND DOMESTIC LIFE

There is a curious conflict of testimony about Lee's manner in general society. Was he cold and distant? Was he genial, merry, cordial, and ready to meet others in an open, confiding spirit? Pendleton, writing of old West Point days, tries, with the ingenuity of a biographer, to reconcile the two points of view: "There was always about him a dignity which repelled improper familiarity, and yet a genial courtesy and joyous humor, often passing into and creating delightful merriment, that rendered him a charming companion. . . . The possessor of these excellences could not but be a universal favorite. No other feeling toward him was ever experienced, I believe, by any one of his several hundred fellow students from all parts of the United States."[1] On the other hand, Charles Anderson, who knew him before the war, speaks of his "grave, cold dignity of bearing and the prudent reserve of his manners which rather chilled over-early or over-much intercourse,"[2] and Grant, from acquaintance in Mexico, says that he was "a large, austere man and, I judge, difficult of approach to his subordinates."[3]

All this evidence—in fact all the evidence—comes from decided friends or enemies, speaking in view of Lee's later glory. I have sought in vain for an illuminating word written in the thirties. The wonderful charm which so impressed Pendleton and others, as they looked back, does not seem to have forced contemporaries to report it. In the war period Mrs. Chesnut, an admirer, but a shrewd, keen woman, gives us a glimpse which is well worth noting: "All the same, I like Smith Lee better, and I like his looks too. I know Smith Lee well. Can anybody say they know his brother? I doubt it. He looks so cold, quiet, and grand."[4] Long, in disputing Grant's opinion of his great

Lee The American

adversary, says that he was not austere, but that "he was clothed with a natural dignity which could either repel or invite, as occasion might require,"[5] and that he had "that just degree of reserve that suited his high and responsible position."[6] Here we have an interesting clue. I imagine that Lee had the reserve before he had the responsible position, that in the early days he held a little aloof, not in the least from haughtiness, but rather from the unwillingness of a deep, strong nature to yield itself too readily. As grandeur came upon him, he did not change his manner in the least, but what had before seemed coldness, seemed now dignity, and the austerity of the lieutenant appeared only a proper self-respect in the commanding general.

In other words, he was not, in the expressive slang of to-day, "a good mixer." He did not smoke, he did not drink, and his attitude toward smoking and drinking shows that he hardly cared for the social exhilaration they bring with them. Mrs. Davis deduces from his playful remark, "'My cups in camp are thicker, but this is thinner than the coffee,' the intense realization that he had of the coarse ways and uncomfortable concomitants of a camp."[7] But this is Mrs. Davis, not Lee. I think that, either by nature or by stoical self-discipline, he liked work, and cared little for the lighter pursuits of life, liked the soldier's hardships, the soldier's toil, even the soldier's fare, as well as the soldier's glory. "He rarely relaxed his energy in anything calculated to amuse him," says one of his biographers, "but, when not riding along his lines, or among the camps, to see in person that the troops were properly cared for, generally passed his time in close attention to official duties."[8]

Yet we know that he cherished to the full all the large traditions of Virginia hospitality. Whenever he mingled with his fellows in social relations, there was, at any rate in later years, a sweet, spontaneous courtesy about him, a ready tact, a kindly interest and sympathy, which won the affection of every one. "Could anybody know him?" asks Mrs. Chesnut. Perhaps not. But people could and did love him.

Women seem to have attracted him much and he had a singular charm for them. If he had love affairs in his youth, they have escaped record. He was young when he married Miss Custis, he was much younger when he fell in love with her. She made him a most worthy and devoted wife and no shade of any other affection seems ever to have interfered between them. Nevertheless, from youth to age, Lee loved a pretty girl, loved to chat with her, and jest with her, and write her gay trifles even in the midst of war. "Fond of the company of ladies," says one of his officers, "he had a good memory for pretty girls. . . . While in Savannah and calling on my father, one of my sisters sang for him. Afterwards, in Virginia, almost as soon as he saw me, he asked after his 'little singing bird.'"[9] His letters to his daughters-in-law have a peculiar grace, vivacity, and charm. In the midwinter of 1863, with a load of care upon him that would have crushed most men, he finds time to write to a girl, of other girls, in this gay and sprightly fashion: "I caught glimpses of sweet Carrie, but she was so surrounded by her little beaux that little could be got from her. But there was one tall one with her, a signalman of that voracious family of Randolphs, whom I threatened with Castle Thunder. I did not see her look at Rob once. But you know he is to take her home on certain conditions. I hope your mother has given her consent and that the cakes are baking. I also saw happy Mrs. Ada. Her face was luminous with content and she looked as if she thought there was but one person in the world."[10]

And it was not only the pretty girls; Lee had, in its finest form, that Old-World courtesy and chivalry, honoring a woman as a woman, which it is something the fashion to sneer at now, perhaps because so many women are bent on considering themselves as men. In the very height of the war, when the general was incontestably the most prominent man in the South, it was noted that he was the first to rise in a crowded car and offer his seat to a lady.[11] During the last desperate movement to Appomattox one woman, the wife of Dr. Guild, the surgeon, accompanied the headquarters of the army. Even in that crisis Mrs. Guild says that the general "would come to my ambulance early in the morning with a cup of coffee, depriving himself for the only woman who was on that sorrowful, hopeless march."[12]

The letter above quoted shows that Lee's dignity and gravity did not prevent him from making and enjoying a jest. He had not, indeed, Lincoln's wild inspiration of the comic spirit; but he had a twinkle of quiet fun, which made social life more gay and toil more easy. "He was not exactly witty, nor was he very humorous, though he gave a light turn to table talk, and enjoyed exceedingly any pleasantry or fun even. He often made a quaint or slightly caustic remark, but he took care that it should not be too trenchant."[13]

One would not suspect him of practical jokes, yet it is recorded that in the early days he rode double down Pennsylvania Avenue past the White House and a Secretary of the Treasury gaping with astonishment.[14] He loved to tease his young officers, one day assembling them all for a social treat around a most promising demijohn, from which he finally drew bumpers of his favorite stimulant—buttermilk;[15] another sending an aide at a grand review to "tell a young lady that such and such a battery was coming." "I rode up," says the officer, "and saluted the young lady. There was great surprise shown by the entire party, as I was not known to any of them, and when I came out with my message, there was a universal shout, while the general looked on with a merry twinkle in his eye."[16]

The same turn of gentle raillery was often given to much more serious matters, as when some one wrote that a stolen Bible was in possession of a Northern lady and Lee answered that if she made the use of it he hoped she would, it would before long be restored to its rightful owner.

Finally, Lee was by no means deficient in that most useful function of humor, the gift of laughing at one's self. "You know she is like her papa," he writes of one of his daughters,—"always wanting something."[17] And to Mrs. Chesnut he defined his wants. "He remonstrated and said his tastes 'were of the simplest.' He only wanted 'a Virginia farm, no end of cream, fresh butter, and fried chicken,—not one fried chicken, or two, but unlimited fried chicken.'"[18] It takes a considerable sense of the comic to laugh at those who find one's social manner charming. "Last night," writes Lee, "there was a cadet hop. Night before, a party at Colonel Johnston's. The night preceding, a college *conversazione* at your mother's. . . . You know how agreeable I am on such occasions, but on this, I am told, I surpassed myself."[19]

The same gracious and quiet courtesy which distinguished Lee in the lighter forms of social intercourse was also unfailingly apparent in all business transactions. "General Lee had but one manner in his intercourse with men. It was the same to the peasant as to the prince, and the student was received with the same easy courtesy that would have been bestowed on the greatest imperial dignitary of Europe."[20] Note, however, that in such cases the manner almost always is a manner and that the man who has it rarely gives himself.

The substance of too much of our conversation, perhaps of the most brilliant part of it, is the faults and follies of our neighbors. Lack of this high seasoning may have made Lee less calculated to shine in general society. "It can always be said of him that he was never heard to speak disparagingly of any one, and when any one was heard so to speak in his presence, he would always recall some trait of excellence in the absent one."[21] On the other hand, what charms us most in talk is that some one older, wiser, whom we admire and respect, should defer to our opinions, as if they were really worth something. It appears that this attractive quality Lee had in the highest degree, and that in him it was not only tact, not only courtesy, but real humility by which the charm is always doubled. One of his subordinates in the college, during the years after the war, writes,

"We all thought he deferred entirely too much to the expression of opinion on the part of the faculty, when we would have preferred that he should simply indicate his own views or desire."[22] This is surely an interesting trait in a great and successful general and it shows in Lee's military as well as in his civil relations. When he crossed the Potomac in June, 1863, he said to a mere staff officer, "What do you think should be our treatment of the people in Pennsylvania?"[23]

Respect for the opinions of one's friends and sympathy with all of them naturally breed the desire to reconcile them when they jar. Here lay one of the greatest secrets of Lee's value to his country. Even in the early days in Mexico it was said of him: "I remember nothing special in those visits except his desire to heal the differences between General Scott and some of his subordinate officers and the efforts he was making in that direction, about which he conversed with me. He was a peacemaker by nature."[24] Could there be a nobler eulogy for a mighty man of war?

So much for Lee's relations with the world at large. Had he near and intimate friends? To return to Mrs. Chesnut, "Could anybody say they knew him?" With her I am inclined to answer, "I doubt it." It is true that Davis said, "He was my friend"; but Davis was a master of figures of speech. That Lee loved many men, I know, that he gave them kindness and sympathy in unstinted measure, sometimes speaking in terms of glowing warmth and tenderness, as when he wrote to Beauregard, after Bull Run, "I cannot express the joy I feel at the brilliant victory of the 21st. The skill, courage, and endurance displayed by yourself and others excite my highest admiration;"[25] and to Joseph E. Johnston on the same occasion, "I almost wept with joy at the glorious victory achieved by our brave troops. The feelings of my heart could hardly be repressed on learning the brilliant share you had in the achievement."[26] Nevertheless, I find no word to indicate that he ever gave himself.

Of all the friendships that he had, that with J.E Johnston is undoubtedly the most interesting. They were the two foremost generals of the Confederacy, rivals in position, rivals in power, rivals in the affection of their soldiers, far unequal only in the support and favor of their government. But in spite of all that tended to estrange them, they seem to have cherished to the end an affection which, if we are to believe one who knew them well, made them "meet after separation with the demonstrativeness of two schoolboys."[27] A knowledge of the character of each lends a double charm to the beautiful words written by Johnston after his friend's death: "We had the same associates, who thought, as I did, that no other youth or man so united the qualities that win warm friendship and command respect. For he was full of sympathy and kindness, genial, and fond of gay conversation and even of fun, that made him the most agreeable of companions, while his correctness of demeanor and language and attention to all duties, both personal and official, and a dignity as much a part of himself as the elegance of his person, gave him a superiority that every one acknowledged in his heart."[28]

Johnston follows this eulogy with a curious comment: "He was the only one of all the men I have known who could laugh at the faults and follies of his friends in such a manner as to make them ashamed without touching their affection." Surely this is a rare tribute, rarely deserved, still more rarely bestowed. Is it ever deserved? Can any man laugh at our faults and follies and not touch our affection a little? Without accepting entirely the cynical French saying, "Ce sont nos faiblesses qui nous font des amis, et non pas nos vertus," it is permitted to doubt whether friendship in all its comfortable ease, its large, unbuttoned relaxation, would be quite possible with one who was too ready to play the mentor, felt bound to play it, even under a smile.

There are one or two anecdotes of Lee, many in fact, but one or two especially, full of the most fascinating significance, when read in connection with this remark of Johnston's. In his very early youth Lee went to visit an old friend who lived in the ample, careless style of Virginia hospitality, hunting by day and drinking by night, with an idle dissipation which the earnest boy could not approve. "The old man shrunk before the unspoken rebuke of the youthful hero. Coming to his bedside the night before his departure, he lamented the idle and useless life into which he had fallen, excusing himself upon the score of loneliness, and the sorrow which weighed upon him in the loss of those most dear. In the most impressive manner he besought his young guest to be warned by his example; prayed him to cherish the good habits he had already acquired, *and promised to listen to his entreaties that he would change his own life, and thereby secure more entirely his respect and affection*" (italics mine).[29] I read this, and even allowing for the biographer's embroidery, I say to myself that Lee was remarkable in other ways besides being commander of the Army of Northern Virginia.

Let us take another incident showing not the biographer's point of view, but the friend's who got the rebuke. It bears very closely on my doubts as to the intimacy of Lee's friendships. General Wise had damned an intruding civilian out of camp. A few days after, Lee visited Wise, made himself delightfully agreeable at dinner to Mrs.

Wise and other ladies who happened to be there, and then suggested to his subordinate that they should take a walk together: "I knew what was coming," said Wise, narrating the story. "After telling me of the complaint made of my treatment of the Richmond man, and hearing my account of the affair, not omitting the apology and broadside, he laid his hand upon my arm, and with that graceful cordiality, which, at such times, tempered his stately dignity, he said, 'Wise, you know as well as I do what the army regulations say about profanity. As an old friend, let me ask you if that dreadful habit cannot be broken—and remind you that we have both passed the meridian of life, etc.' Seeing that he was in for a sermon, and one that I could not answer, I replied, 'General Lee, you certainly play the part of Washington to perfection, and your whole life is a constant reproach to me. Now, I am perfectly willing that Jackson and yourself shall do the praying for the whole Army of Northern Virginia, but, in Heaven's name, let me do the cussin' for one small brigade.' Lee laughed and said, 'Wise, you are incorrigible,' and then rejoined the ladies."[30] "The only man," writes Johnston, "the only man." And again I say to myself, "Ce sont nos faiblesses qui nous font des amis, et non pas nos vertus."

But let us get still closer to Lee in his home. As to his dealings with those who were subordinate to him here, what record there is is favorable. The few slaves whom he himself inherited, he disposed of long before the war. Those who came into his charge by Mr. Custis's will, under stipulation of manumission at a fixed date, he took the most watchful care of till the appointed time arrived and then set free. In the thickest of his military duties he writes to his son with deep concern as to their welfare: "As regards Leanthe and Jim, I presume they had better remain with Mrs. D. this year, and at the end of it devote their earnings to their own benefit. But what can be done with poor little Jim? It would be cruel to turn him out on the world. He could not take care of himself."[31]

At the same time, it is curious to observe how the general curse of slavery could involve even a man like Lee in slander and reproach. A correspondent writes to the "New York Tribune," on June 24, 1859, saying that three slaves, two men and a woman, escaped from Lee's plantation, had been captured and brought back. "Colonel Lee ordered them whipped. The officer whipped the men and said he would not whip the woman, and Colonel Lee stripped her and whipped her himself. These are facts, as I learn from near relatives of the men whipped." We who know Lee's character know that they are not facts, and hardly require the indignant repudiation of another correspondent (June 28), who writes as an opponent of slavery, but with a thorough knowledge of the Lees, and shows not only the injustice of the attack, but its probable motive. But such things cannot have been agreeable.

Lee's own reference to this affair, in a letter to his son, is, "I do not know that you have been told that George Wesley and Mary Norris absconded some months ago, were captured in Maryland, making their way to Pennsylvania, brought back, and are now hired out in lower Virginia. . . . The 'New York Tribune' has attacked me for my treatment of your grandfather's slaves, but I shall not reply. He has left me an unpleasant legacy."[32]

Writing to a Western correspondent, after the war, Lee makes a still more explicit statement, doubtless in this same connection: "I am very much obliged to you for your bold defense of me in the New York papers, at a time when many were willing to believe any enormity charged against me. This same slander, which you at the time denounced as false, was nevertheless circulated at the North, and since the termination of hostilities has been renewed in Europe. Yet there is not a word of truth in it, or any ground for its origin. No servant, soldier, or citizen, that was ever employed by me, can with truth charge me with bad treatment."[33]

In the more personal domestic relations also Lee appears to advantage. Of his father he saw little; but his devotion to his mother is as attractive in its delicacy and tact as in its completeness. Even in his early years she was a great invalid and he tended her as a woman might have done, "carrying her in his arms to the carriage, and arranging her cushions with the gentleness of an experienced nurse."[34] As he drove with her, he would make every effort to entertain her, "assuring her with the gravity of an old man that unless she was cheerful, the drive would not benefit her. When she complained of cold or drafts, he would pull from his pocket a great jack-knife and newspaper and make her laugh with his efforts to improvise curtains, and shut out the intrusive wind which whistled through the crevices of the old family coach."[35] On his departure for West Point, his mother said, "How can I live without Robert? He is both son and daughter to me."[36]

As a father, Lee is better known to us than in any other aspect; for a very large number of his letters to his sons and daughters has been printed. In one of these Lee himself remarks: "It has been said that our letters are good representations of our minds. They certainly present a good criterion for judgment of the character of the individual. You must be careful that yours make as favorable an impression of you as I hope you will deserve."[37] It is not fair, however, to judge Lee's own character too much by the tone of these paternal letters. A man may tell his near friends, with a smile, what Lee once told of his boy's following him in the snow, imitating his every movement and stepping exactly in his footprints. "'When I saw this,' said the general, 'I said to myself, "It behooves me to walk very straight, when this fellow is already following in my tracks.""'[38] But such a thing in cold print sounds priggish. We know the stiltedness of Chesterfield's letters to his son. Flaubert, too, wrote pages of inspiration to Mademoiselle X, pages of limitation to his beloved niece. It is well to turn occasionally from some of Lee's letters to his family to his more sprightly correspondence with outside friends or more distant relatives.

These reserves as to the paternal epistolary relation once accepted, no father's attitude could be finer. His discipline was always steady. There was no injudicious relaxation, no spoiling. "My mother I could sometimes circumvent, and at times took liberties with her orders, construing them to suit myself," writes his youngest son; "but exact obedience to every mandate of my father was a part of my life and being at that time."[39] In public and military matters Lee was absolutely stoical in his avoidance of all family favoritism. Foreign visitors could not conceal their astonishment at finding the son of the commander-in-chief serving in the ranks as a dirty and begrimed artilleryman. Another son lay wounded in a Union prison; his wife was dying at home. A Union officer imprisoned in Richmond begged that a letter might be written to Lee asking him to bring about an exchange. Lee wrote back that he would not ask any favor for his own son that could not be asked for the humblest soldier in the army.[40]

Lee's letters to his children are full of advice and admonition, sometimes more or less conventional, but often expressed with touching sweetness and simplicity. Good evidence of this is the fact that they were counterfeited at a very early date. One expects forged documents after a great man's death. But in the middle of the war a letter was widely circulated, purporting to be from Lee to one of his sons, but in reality manufactured by a clever newspaper man on a basis of fragments of real correspondence. There is enough authentic material, however, without resorting to forgery, and in this material there is a passionate sincerity of interest which it would be difficult to forge: "You see I am following my old habit of giving advice, which I dare say you neither need nor require. But you must pardon a fault which proceeds from my great love and burning desire for your welfare and happiness. When I think of your youth, impulsiveness, and many temptations, your distance from me, and the ease (and even innocence) with which you might commence an erroneous course, my heart quails within me, and my whole frame and being trembles at the possible result. May Almighty God have you in his holy keeping."[41]

We see here what there was back of discipline and advice; a devoted tenderness, a watchful care founded not only on parental duty, but on deep and abiding affection. "Oh, what pleasure I lose in being separated from my children. Nothing can compensate me for that."[42] "I wish I could see you," he writes to his daughter, "be with you, and never again part from you. God only can give me that happiness. I pray for it night and day."[43] And elsewhere, "I long to see you through the dilatory nights. At dawn when I rise, and all day, my thoughts revert to you in expressions that you cannot hear or I repeat. I hope you will always appear to me as you are now painted on my heart."[44]

Nor was the affection a matter of feeling only; it was constantly taking practical forms of care and sacrifice. Lee was a good manager, exact in every detail of domestic economy, frugal and thrifty in the little affairs of daily life. I like to think of the rival of Frederick and Napoleon writing to his son, four months before Gettysburg, "If my pants are done, will you give them to Mr. Thomas, the bearer, who will bring them up to-morrow? If they are not, keep them. I am on my last pair, and very sensitive, fearful of an accident."[45] He cautions his family repeatedly as to care in money matters: "I wish you to save all your money, and invest it in some safe and lucrative way, that you may have the means to build up old Arlington, and make it all we would wish to see it. The necessity I daily have for money has, I fear, made me parsimonious."[46] But it was that noble parsimony, which pinches self to comfort others; and page after page of Lee's life records his readiness in giving. All his care for Arlington was not for his own possession, for the place was his son's, left him by his mother's father; and when the son begged the father to accept it, Lee refused, "not from any unwillingness to receive from you a gift you may think proper to bestow, or to be indebted to you for any benefit great or small. But simply because it would not be right to do so."[47] After the war he showed himself in every way most anxious to aid his sons in establishing themselves, and he had that crowning grace of giving, the abstinence from all dictation as to the use of the gift. "Will that suit you? If it does not, let me know what will, and you shall have that too."[48] Also, he was as indulgent in trifles as in farms and barns. One Christmas season his youngest, pet daughter "enumerated, just in fun, all the presents she wished—a long list. To her great surprise, when Christmas morning came she found each article at her place at the breakfast table—not one omitted."[49] One hardly knows which to admire most, the father's generosity or the daughterly simple desires. This was she of whom her father said, "She is always wanting something." Apparently, with Lee-like moderation, she did not want much.

As this incident shows, Lee not only loved his children, but enjoyed them. The two do not always go together by any means. In fact, just before the war he wrote, "I have no enjoyment in life but what I derive from my children."[50] And he enjoyed them in their childishness, their sports, their gayety. It is true that he did not quite approve of too much festivity in the midst of national disaster. "There are too many Lees on the ball committee. I like them all to be present at battles, but can excuse them at balls."[51] Into all the harmless home laughter, however, he was ready to enter at any time. He was full of pleasant jests and kindly teasing. "We all enjoyed that attention from him. He never teased any one whom he did not especially like."[52] "Kiss your sisters for me. Tell them they must keep well, not talk too much, and go to bed early."[53] "The girls are well and have as many opinions with as few acts as ever."[54] "We are all as usual—the women of the family very fierce and the men very mild."[55]

In Captain R.E. Lee's charming volume, from which these natural touches are mainly drawn, we get many pictures of the great soldier with his children about him, and nothing shows him in a simpler, more attractive, more geninely human aspect. "He was very fond of having his hands tickled, and, what was still more curious, it pleased and delighted him to take off his slippers and place his feet in our laps in order to have them tickled. . . . He would often tell us the most delightful stories, and then there was no nodding. Sometimes, however, our interest in his wonderful tales became so engrossing that we would forget to do our duty, when he would declare, 'No tickling, no story.'"[56] Some persons may perhaps think the hero of Chancellorsville too dignified for such unslippered ease. But it strikes me that this matter of tickling reduces Lee more sweetly than almost anything else to the common level of mortality. Was there ever a more charming picture of Jove unparadised than this drawn by a Virginia girl after the war (italics mine)? "I can only remember the great dignity and kindness of General Lee's bearing, how lovely he was to all of us girls, that he gave us his photographs and wrote his name on them. He liked to have us tickle his hands, but when Cousin Agnes sat by him, that seemed to be her privilege. We regarded him with the greatest veneration. *We had heard of God, but here was General Lee.*"[57] That last touch a great poet might envy.

In the most intimate of all human relations we naturally see Lee but very dimly. We know that Mrs. Lee was a charming wife and mother, always careful of the welfare of her family and always beloved by them, and that her husband's devotion was unfailing. Brief glimpses come to us of those little rubs which should always properly occur in the best adjusted wedlock between differing characters, and we see that they were taken in the light, sweet spirit in which they should be taken. "My father, as I remember, always in full uniform, always ready and waiting for my mother, who was generally late. He would chide her gently, in a playful way and with a bright smile."[58] "The *Mim*, the dear *Mim*, considers herself a great financier; consult her about the expenditure of money, but do not let her take it shopping, or you will have to furnish her with an equal amount to complete her purchases. She has such a fine eye for a bargain."[59] But none of these rubs interfered with the husband's constant affection and devotion, as tender in the long years of sickness and confinement as in the early glow of young love and perfect health. "To my mother, who was a great invalid from rheumatism for more than ten years, he was the most faithful attendant and tender nurse. Every want of hers that he could supply he anticipated. . . . During the war he constantly wrote to her, even when on the march and amidst the most pressing duties."[60]

Yet as I turn to the limited number of these letters that have been printed, I find in them positive traces of the same limitations I have before noted. Lee lectures,–oh, so sweetly, and so kindly, and so gently,–but lectures. On his children: "You must not let him run wild in my absence, and will have to exercise firm authority over all of them. . . . Mildness and forbearance, tempered by firmness and judgment, will strengthen their affection for you, while it will maintain your control over them."[61] On the care of her own health: "System-atically pursue the best course to recover your lost health. . . . Do not worry yourself about things you cannot help, but be content to do what you can for the well-being of what properly belongs to you. . . . Lay nothing too much to heart. Desire nothing too eagerly, nor think that all things can be perfectly accomplished according to our own notions."[62] This is playing the role of Marcus Aurelius, or, as General Wise would say, of Washington, to perfection. But–but–More than ever, I am forced to return to Mrs. Chesnut's comment, "Can anybody say they know him?"[63]

The truth is, there are three motives which lead us to seek the society of others. First, we grow weary of ourselves. We wish to share our joys and sorrows, we wish others to help and strengthen us, above all, we wish others to fill the great void which is neither joy nor sorrow, but just the blank monotony of every day. With most of us the motive of social life is not that you are so charming, but that I am so dull. "Why," said the wife of the Harvard professor, "when there is no one else about, I go into the kitchen and talk to the cook." Lee did not prefer the cook's society to Robert E. Lee's. He could fill his own void, desired no help or strength from others, or, at least, none that others could give him. It is only at the rarest moments that he expresses any sense of solitude or loneliness. "I wish you were with me, for always solitary, I am sometimes lonely, and long for the reunion of my family once again. But I will not speak of myself but of you."[64] Note even here the characteristic touch by which he turns instantly from discussion of his own affairs to discussion of others!

The second motive that leads us to go out among men is but a modification of the first, a desire to lead, to guide and manage and regulate the affairs of others. This makes the soldier and the states-man. It also makes the petty village official and the woman who advises the neighborhood, often most kindly and usefully. As it happened, few men have had wider cure of souls and bodies than fell to Lee and no one can say he shunned what came to him. Yet I do not think he sought it or loved it. I do not think he desired either public or private responsibility. Certainly he had no wish to dictate or control. And few can have been moved less than he to seek the society of others for the pleasure that comes from asserting our own power over them.

There remains a third social motive, kindness, tenderness, sympa-thy, the sense of human kinship. And surely in no one was this element at least ever more present than in Lee. Perhaps its sweetest manifestation was his love of children. In one sense children ask everything and give nothing. In another sense they ask nothing and give all. They ask all your time and effort and attention. They do not ask yourself. This suited Lee exactly. Hence he loved children—and children loved him, which is surely the most flattering and conclusive evidence as to character. I cannot quote the multitude of charming anecdotes which support me here. "On one occasion [after the war], calling at Colonel Preston's he missed two little boys in the family circle, who were great favorites of his, and on asking for them he was told that they were confined to the nursery by croup. The next day, though the weather was of the worst description, he went trudging back to their house, carrying in one hand a basket of pecan nuts, and in the other a toy, which he left for his sick friends."[65] At another time a small girl, who had charge of her baby sister, saw the general come riding by. "'General Lee, won't you please make this child come home to her mother?' The general immediately rode over to where Fannie sat, leaned over from his saddle, and drew her up into his lap. There she sat in royal contentment, and was thus grandly escorted home. When Mrs. Letcher inquired of Jennie why she had given General Lee so much trouble, she received the naïve reply: 'I couldn't make Fan go home, and I thought he could do anything.'"[66]

With animals it was something as with children. Lee loved them and they him. "Everybody and everything—his family, his friends, his horse, and his dog—loves Colonel Lee," was said of him before the war.[67] His letters are full of tender and humorous allusions to his cats and his horses. In his last years the old war-horse, Traveler, seemed to be almost as near to him as any living thing. "General Lee was more demonstrative toward that old companion in battle than seemed to be in his nature in his intercourse with men. I have often seen him, as he would enter his front gate, leave the walk, approach the old horse and caress him for a minute or two before entering his front door, as though they bore a common grief in their memory of the past."[68] And Lee himself admits the same thing. "Traveler is my only companion; I may also say my only pleasure. He and I, whenever practicable, wander out in the mountains and enjoy sweet confidence."[69]

What was the nature of that confidence? Among the vast regrets for a lost cause and a nation ruined, did Lee also wish at moments that there was some human soul to which he could really unburden himself? "All are gay, and only I solitary. I am all alone."[70] "You must make friends while you are young, that you may enjoy them when old. You will find when you become old, it will then be too late. I see my own delinquencies now when too late to mend, and point them out to you, that you may avoid them."[71] Were these only the slight expressions of a temporary lack, or were they the true outcry of a longing for something never attained, perhaps impossible? We do not know. Lee had, however, one intimate friend,—God. But that requires a separate chapter.

10

LEE'S SPIRITUAL LIFE

L ee had, of course, a liberal education, though we do not know much of his early studies. Those pursued at West Point were largely technical; but before going to that institution he must have had a good grounding in the classics, for long after, when he was president of Washington College, he used to visit the Greek classes and astonish the students by his familiarity with that language. His general ideas as to educational matters were both broad and solid. During his college presidency, while sustaining as far as possible the old traditions of culture, he seems to have taken decided steps in modern directions,–that is, towards practical training and individual development,–steps which meant far more in the South than in the North. "Nothing," he wrote after the war, "will compensate us for the depression of the standard of our moral and intellectual culture."[1] And again, "The education of a man or woman is never completed till they die."[2]

If Lee had written his proposed memoirs, we should be better able to judge whether he had literary gifts. As it is, his only bit of formal writing is the brief sketch prefixed to his father's "Memoirs." Here, as in so many other matters, we see curiously the inheritance of the eighteenth century, its dignified finish, its determination to clothe even common things in lofty phraseology. The elder Lee takes cold because "a slight, but driving snow, which was falling, insinuated itself among the wrappings encircling his throat."[3] Where it is more appropriate, this breadth of expression often attains real beauty and grandeur, as in some of the addresses and general orders to the army. "Soldiers! You tread with no unequal step the road by which your fathers marched through sufferings, privations, and blood to independence. Continue to emulate, in the future, as you have in the past, their valor in arms, their patient endurance of hardships, their high resolve to be free, which no trial could shake, no bribe seduce, no danger appall, and be assured the just God who crowned their efforts with success will, in His own good time, send down his blessing upon yours."[4]

The reports, and especially the dispatches written in the field, contain no such literary effort. They are terse, and clear, saying what is needed and only what is needed. The familiar letters are less successful as mere writing. They are loose and hasty and not always correct in grammar and syntax. They are charming, however, so far as they show the intimate character of the man.

In spite of his deep respect for education, I do not find that Lee had any great love for books or for things purely intellectual. In later years he expressed "his lifelong regret that he had not completed his classical education (in which, however, he had a respectable scholarship) before going to West Point";[5] and he thanks Worsley for the translation of the "Odyssey" in terms which indicate pleasure in the perusal of the original. Judge Tyler tells us that he could talk "in the most interesting manner about the beauty of the tongue and the richness of the literature of Spain."[6] Among English authors he is said to have been partial to Macaulay, especially the essays, which can hardly be considered the sign of a literary temperament, and in writing of his father he once quotes Burke. But it is really remarkable that in so varied and extensive a correspondence there should be so little reference to literature, even in its historical aspects. This seems the more curious when we turn to the letters of Harry Lee,—surely as much a man of action as his son,—and find a spirit keenly alive to literary questions, ready to criticize Racine and to delight in Sophocles.

So with science. In Lee's army the soldiers discussed Darwin and concluded that "Marse Robert" was sufficient proof that man was not descended from apes. But I find no evidence that Lee himself ever gave a thought to the vast speculations that were unhinging the world. Perhaps it is worth while to refer in this connection to Mrs. Putnam's shrewd remark that the Southern slaveholding planter was almost obliged in self-defense to adopt this attitude towards all modern thought.

Even as to his profession there is no record of Lee's making it a passionate study. He stood well at West Point, and results would certainly indicate that he did more. But nothing is said of his ever spending feverish days and nights, as did Jackson, over the campaigns of Frederick and the battles of Napoleon.

Nor do I see that he was in any way sensitive to æsthetic pleasures. While one child assiduously tickled his toes and another narrated the story of the "Lady of the Lake," he would occasionally break in with the recitation of long passages of the poem, disconcerting the narratress and boring the tickler. This shows that he liked the poetry of Scott. (Mark Twain, by the way, believed that Scott's false chivalry was largely responsible for the Civil War.) But of other poetry no mention and no trace. I do not remember that the name of Shakespeare occurs once in all he wrote. Novels he disapproved of, as many of us do—for others. "Read history, works of truth, not novels and romances. Get correct views of life, and learn to see the world in its true light. It will enable you to live pleasantly, to do good, and, when summoned away, to leave without regret."[7] The world would, indeed, be much less regrettable, if there were no novels in it. With painting and with music it is as with poetry. Lee may have enjoyed such things, but he makes no mention of his enjoyment.

The nineteenth century had one æsthetic delight peculiarly its own, appreciation of the beauty of nature. This seems to have made somewhat more appeal to Lee; yet even here his language certainly gives no indication of ecstasy. A quiet Virginia farm life, in the fields and woods rather than in cities, pleased him best—that is all. "You do not know how much I have missed you and the children, my dear Mary. To be alone in a crowd is very solitary. In the woods I feel sympathy with the trees and birds, in whose company I take delight, but experience no pleasure in a strange crowd."[8] "I enjoyed the mountains as I rode along. The views are magnificent and the valleys so beautiful, the scenery so peaceful. What a glorious world Almighty God has given us. How thankless and ungrateful we are, and how we labor to mar his gifts."[9]

In short, the bent of Lee's character was absolutely moral and practical. It is not to be inferred from this, however, that he was a man of no passions or that his staid decorum resulted from a lack of sensibility. We have seen that Longstreet thought his weakness as a general was an excessive fury of combat. At any rate, there is plenty of evidence that he had a good hot temper, which came to the surface on provocation. Colonel Venable, of his staff, says: "No man could see the flush come over that grand forehead and the temple veins swell on occasions of great trial of patience and doubt that Lee had the high, strong temper of a Washington."[10] He disliked very much to have officers with a grievance allowed to make their way to him. At times this would happen. Immediately after one such occurrence, "General Lee came to the adjutant's tent with flushed face, and said warmly, 'Why did you permit that man to come to my tent and make me show my temper?'"[11] In the same way he had a great dislike to "reviewing army communications" and his aides spared him when they could. On one occasion Colonel Taylor had made matters as easy as possible; but the general "was not in a very pleasant mood; something irritated him and he manifested his ill-humor by a little nervous twist or jerk of the neck and head, accompanied by some harshness of manner." Taylor became impatient and showed it; whereupon the general said, "Colonel Taylor, when I lose my temper, don't let it make you angry."[12]

It is a curious coincidence that one of Lee's few violent explosions of wrath occurred when he found an artilleryman brutally abusing a horse and that one of the rare recorded outbreaks of Grant was owing to the same cause. Apropos of Grant also, Lee is said to have once spoken sharply after the war, though not in the connection we should expect. One of his university faculty had been criticizing the Union general with some harshness. "Sir," said Lee, "if you ever presume again to speak disrespectfully of General Grant in my presence, either you or I will sever his connection with this university."[13]

A particularly interesting example of Lee's indignation, because we see it, as it were, bursting forth and passing at once under control, is his reference to the desecration of Arlington: "Your old home, if not destroyed by our enemies, has been so desecrated that I cannot bear to think of it. I should have preferred it to have been wiped from the earth, its beautiful hill sunk, its sacred trees buried, rather than to have been degraded by those who revel in the ill they do for their own selfish purposes. You see what a poor sinner I am, and how unworthy to possess what was given me; for that reason it has been taken away."[14]

It was by considerations of this nature that Lee dominated his passions and secured the high temperance and triumphant control which were among his most marked characteristics. His temperance, however, was no less a spiritual grace than a moral victory. Here again the resemblance to Grant is striking. Every one knows Grant's quiet remark when some one prefaced a dubious story with the familiar "I believe there are no ladies present": "No, but there are gentlemen." It is said of Lee also, "I dare say no man ever offered to relate a story of questionable delicacy in his presence. His very bearing and presence produced an atmosphere of purity that would have repelled the attempt."[15]

Evidence of Lee's supreme self-control in other directions is hardly needed. The final disaster, surely as overwhelming as could befall a man, hardly broke his calm or wrung from him a complaint except for others. In good and evil fortune alike he strove to maintain the same stoical–or no, I should say, as he would have wished, Christian–fortitude. A striking instance of this is narrated by Taylor. Doubtless it could be paralleled in many other lives. Something similar is told of Stuart, of Cox on the Union side, and may remain untold of many a private soldier in the armies of the Potomac and of Northern Virginia. It is none the less noble and beautiful in Lee. The general had just received and read his mail, when Colonel Taylor appeared with the usual list of matters of army routine as to which the commander's judgment was desired. "The papers containing a few such cases were presented to him; he reviewed and gave his orders in regard to them. I then left him, but for some cause returned in a few moments, and with accustomed freedom entered his tent without announcement or ceremony, when I was startled and shocked to see him overcome with grief, an open letter on his knees. That letter contained the sad intelligence of his daughter's death. . . . His army demanded his first thought and care; to his men, to their needs, he must first attend; and then he could surrender himself to his private, personal affliction."[16]

The force of will which appeared as self-control in great matters showed in little as exactness, system, accuracy. It is said that in his youth his mother taught him rigid economy; and throughout life he continued to exercise it. He was as scrupulously punctual as Washington, for himself and for others. When young men called on his daughters, he began his locking up exactly at ten o'clock and the callers were expected to conform.[17] A member of his faculty once came to his office and asked for a certain paper. Lee told him where it could be found. Afterwards he said to him, "Did you find the paper?" "Yes, General." "Did you return it to the place where you found it?" "Yes, General."[18] Mrs. Lee said of her husband that "he could go, in the dark, and lay his hand on any article of his clothing, or upon any particular paper, after he had once arranged them."[19]

This minuteness seems to have been inborn. At any rate it appeared in early youth. "His specialty was finishing up. . . . He drew the diagrams on a slate; and although he well knew that the one he was drawing would have to be removed to make room for another, he drew each one with as much accuracy and finish, lettering and all, as if it were to be engraved or printed."[20] The biographer quotes this as an admirable trait; but I have my doubts. A high authority has said, "Never finish a thing after it is done." And I am inclined to think that a prime attribute of greatness is disregarding the unnecessary. In commanding the Army of Northern Virginia for three years Lee must have sacrificed a world of intellectual if not moral scruples, and it is the more remarkable in him, since—like Jackson, if in less degree –he certainly had the germs of what is sarcastically termed the New England conscience. Imagine Cromwell or Napoleon, shortly after such a battle as Gettysburg, writing the following: "I have been much exercised as to how I can pay my taxes. I have looked out for assessors and gatherers in vain. I have sent to find collectors in the counties where I have been, without success. I wish to pay the amount as a matter of right and conscience, and for the benefit of the State, but can not accomplish it. . . . In addition, I own three horses, a watch, my apparel, and camp equipage. . . . See if you can find some one that can enlighten me as to what I am to pay."[21]

The same self-control, precision, economy of resource marked Lee in speech as in other things. There is no abandon in his letters, no freedom, no outpouring; and this unquestionably makes them some-what colorless. So with his reports. He avoids the first person, wherever possible, and says, "It was decided," "It was thought best." How different this from the vivacity of Hooker or Sherman. Very rarely does he use brusque expressions, "It may be only a Yankee trick,"[22] or criticize his opponents freely: "His [Grant's] talent and strategy consists in accumulating overwhelming numbers."[23] Even his recorded conversations contain little that seems like unrestrained confidence. Thus, one is startled when one finds him supposed to have said, "I have never understood why General Sherman has been commended for that march, when the only question was whether he could feed his army by consuming all the people had to eat"; [24] and the tone of his remarks to Badeau is even more unusual: "He spoke very bitterly of the course of England and France during the war and said that the South had as much cause to resent it as the North; that England especially had acted from no regard to either portion of the Union, but from a jealousy of the united nation and a desire to see it fall to pieces. England, he said, had led the South to believe she would assist them, and then deserted them when they most needed aid."[25]

Bancroft speaks admirably of "the wonderful power of secrecy of Washington in which he excelled even Franklin; for Franklin some-times left the impression that he knew more than he was willing to utter, but Washington seemed to have said all that the occasion required."[26] Lee, I think, resembled Washington in this and had an excellent faculty, when he was interrogated, of seeming to say much and saying little. Thus he answered a question about McClellan, "I have always entertained a high opinion of his capacity, and have no reason to think that he omitted to do anything that was in his power."[27] And when one of his officers tried to draw him out by speaking somewhat freely about another, Lee answered, "Well, sir, if that is your opinion of General –, I can only say that you differ very widely from the general himself."[28]

Reserve of this character is always liable to be misinterpreted, and so we get what foundation there is for Badeau's charge of duplicity. His complaint of this in reference to Lee's reports seems rather absurd, for the unhappy necessities of war always involve some departure from candor if not from veracity. But Badeau also criticizes Lee's last correspondence with Grant, probably read and reread as much as any letters ever written in the world. To accuse Lee of intentional deception in any of these is preposterous; but the letter especially singled out by Badeau, that of April 8, 1865, is certainly not direct, simple, and straightforward, any more than is the other important letter in which Lee discusses Jackson's share in the tactics of Chancellorsville.

So far as Lee's reserve is concerned, however, it must not in any way be attributed to haughtiness or aristocratic superiority. It is true that he, like Washington, found it difficult to throw off his dignity, to mingle freely with his fellows in common intercourse; but there never was a man who believed more heartily in American liberty, in the absolute equality of all men before the law and before God, who would have more entirely accepted Mr. H.D. Sedgwick's noble definition of democracy–noble especially because it levels by exalting instead of lowering: "The fundamental truth of democracy is the belief that the real pleasures of life are increased by sharing them."[29] Lee hated parade, display, and ceremony, hated above all things being made an object of public gaze and adulation. His idea of high position was high responsibility, a superior was one who had larger duties as well as larger privileges, and the mark of a gentleman was a keen sense of the feelings and susceptibilities of others.

This attitude has rarely been expressed more delicately than by Lee himself in a memorandum found among his papers after his death (italics mine): "The forbearing use of power does not only form a touchstone, but the manner in which an individual enjoys certain advantages over others is a test of a true gentleman. The power which the strong have over the weak, the magistrate over the citizen, the employer over the employed, the educated over the unlettered, the experienced over the confiding, even the clever over the silly–the forbearing or inoffensive use of all this power or authority, or a total abstinence from it when the case admits it, will show the gentleman in a plain light. The gentleman does not needlessly and unnecessarily remind an offender of a wrong he may have committed against him. He can not only forgive, he can forget; and he strives for that nobleness of self and mildness of character which impart sufficient strength to let the past be but the past. *A true man of honor feels humbled himself when he cannot help humbling others.*"[30] It reminds one of Dekker's

"First true gentleman that ever breathed."

The thing that puzzles me, as it has doubtless puzzled many, is how much personal ambition had Lee under this august reserve, this firm moderation, this constant sacrifice of self to duty. What led him into the army first? He is reported to have said in later years: "The great mistake of my life was taking a military education."[31] Why did he make that mistake? Was it merely the desire to follow his father's profession? Had he a love of adventure and excitement? Did he—like Jackson—in his early days cherish dreams of distant glory? Glimpses of such a passion may be caught in Washington's youthful letters. I find no trace of it in Lee's. When his friends display anxiety for his advancement, he discourages them. "I hope my friends will give themselves no annoyance on my account, or any concern about the distribution of favors. I know how those things are awarded at Washington, and how the President will be besieged by clamorous claimants, I do not wish to be numbered among them."[32] And again: "Do not give yourself any anxiety about the appointment of the brigadier. If it is on my account that you feel an interest in it, I beg that you will discard it from your thoughts."[33]

By the time the Civil War came, this indifference to honors had grown to be a fixed habit. No one can doubt the sincerity of Lee's repeated expressions of willingness to serve in any capacity where he could be useful. It is said that when Virginia first joined the Confederacy, he made arrangements to enlist as a private in a company of cavalry.[34] Later he observed to a restless subordinate, "What do you care about rank? I would serve under a corporal if necessary."[35] And to Davis he wrote, after Gettysburg: "I am as willing to serve now as in the beginning in any capacity and at any post where I can do good. The lower in position, the more suited to my ability and the more agreeable to my feelings."[36]

But there is a harder test of self-sacrifice in these matters than even the willingness to forego rank; and that is patience under criticism. Here, too, Lee is conspicuous. To be sure, Grant asserts that his great rival was not criticized. Less than some others, perhaps, but enough. And I think his immunity from it was partly due to the temper in which it was received. One of the finest passages in all his letters relates to this. "My whole time is occupied, and all my thoughts and strength are given to the cause to which my life, be it long or short, will be devoted. Tell her not to mind the reports she sees in the papers. They are made to injure and occasion distrust. Those that know me will not believe them. Those that do not will not care for them. I laugh at them."[37] And laughing at them, in his own sunny, kindly fashion, he told B.H. Hill that the great mistake of the war was in making all the best generals editors of newspapers. "I am willing to serve in any capacity to which the authorities may assign me. I have done the best I could in the field and have not succeeded as I could wish. I am willing to yield my place to these best generals, and I will do my best for the cause editing a newspaper."[38]

The more widely one reads in the literature of the war, the more one appreciates the greatness of Lee's indifference to glory, his absolute freedom from jealousy and self-justification. Doubtless there were other eminent examples of this on both sides; but one grows heartsick over the petty disputes, the ignominious wrangling which identifies a grand cause with a little man. In many cases injured merit is only trying to get its rights and perhaps does not deserve blame. But here is precisely the hardest lesson of all. To abstain from justifying one's self at the expense of others when one is wrong is not always easy. To abstain when one feels one's self to have been right— that is the labor and the difficulty indeed. Even in this Lee succeeded, when so many failed.

As to his love of adventure and excitement, we have seen in a previous chapter how rarely it appears. Beside the significant Fredericksburg phrase, "It is well that war is so terrible, or else we might grow too fond of it," I like to put the quiet words, written after the war and very different from what we should expect from a soldier homesick for far-off battle and glory, "I much enjoy the charms of civil life."[39] Altogether, a man to whom the ambitions of this world meant very little. Yet it was he who wrote of his daughter, "She is like her papa—always wanting something." I wonder what he wanted.

It is said that Darwin confessed that all he required for happiness in life was his scientific pursuits and the family affections. It might equally well be said that all Lee needed was the family affections and religion. And now, what about his religion?

Assuredly it was not a religion of sect. It was broad enough to go even beyond the bounds of Christianity and recognize earnestness of intention in those of a different creed altogether. "An application of a Jew soldier for permission to attend certain ceremonies of his synagogue in Richmond was indorsed by his captain: 'Disapproved. If such applications were granted, the whole army would turn Jews or shaking Quakers.' When the paper came to General Lee, he indorsed on it, 'Approved, and respectfully returned to Captain –, with the advice that he should always respect the religious views and feelings of others.'"[40] Lee was an Episcopalian, but he had no narrow belief in the power of rituals or formulas. One of his friendly enemies, General Hunt, records that at the time of the excitement over Pussyism, efforts were made in the parish to which Lee belonged to enlist him on one side or the other of the controversy. He resisted these steadily, and on some public occasion, when the appeals were urgent, he remarked audibly to Hunt: "I am glad to see that you keep aloof from the dispute that is disturbing our little parish. That is right and we must not get mixed up in it; we must support each other in that. But I must give you some advice about it, in order that we may understand each other: Beware of Pussyism! Pussyism is always bad, and may lead to unchristian feeling; therefore beware of Pussyism!"[41] He seems to have had ready always in controversy, whether religious or military, some pleasant turn of this kind, which assuaged bitterness and broadened bigotry. Thus, when a lady once complained to him that little Lenten food–fish, oysters, etc.,–was obtainable in Lexington, he said to her, "Mrs.–, I would not trouble myself about special dishes; I suppose if we try to abstain from special sins, that is all that will be expected of us."[42]

Nor was Lee's religion a matter of dogma or theology. Some speculative doubts appear, indeed, to have beset him in his earlier years, and it is extremely curious to find the shadow of Unitarianism hinted at by one of his devout biographers as keeping him for a long time from the church (italics mine): "Although at that time, and for a score of years thereafter, his estimate of his own unworthiness, and *some mistaken view of Christ, perhaps*, prevented his making an avowal of the Christian faith and becoming a communicant of the church, he was, nevertheless, all the while guided and restrained by belief in the Bible, reverence for its Author as revealed therein, reliance *more or less* implicit upon the Saviour, and prayer secret, but sincere."[43] When once these difficulties were overcome, his acceptance seems to have been complete and unquestioning. He liked sermons to be simple and practical. "It was a noble sermon, one of the best I ever heard– and the beauty of it was that the preacher gave our young men the very marrow of the Gospel."[44] He liked prayers to be brief and to the point. "You know our friend – is accustomed to make his prayers too long. He prays for the Jews, the Turks, the heathen, the Chinese, and everybody else, and makes his prayers run into the regular hour for our college recitations. Would it be wrong for me to suggest to Mr. – that he confine his morning prayers to us poor sinners at the college, and pray for the Turks, the Jews, the Chinese, and the other heathens some other time?"[45] He avoided the discussion of speculative points, whenever possible. Some one asked him once whether he believed in the apostolic succession. He said he had never thought of it, and on another, similar occasion, "I never trouble myself about such questions; my chief concern is to try to be a humble, sincere Christian myself."[46]

That humility is the key to this as to many other problems in Lee's character is indisputable, a genuine humility. Others might explain the universe and probe the mysteries of God. Surely he need not. Indeed, it is recorded that he was reluctant to commit himself on any general matter of intellectual interest. "He studiously avoided giving opinions upon subjects which it had not been his calling or training to investigate; and sometimes I thought he carried this great virtue too far."[47] Too far, perhaps. But there are so many in these days, in all days, who do not carry it far enough. I think it is this entire and unconscious humility of Lee's that saves him more than anything else from the wild doings of some of his biographers. He has no thought of his own excellences, nor of intruding them upon us. No one would have shrunk more than he from being held up as a model of perfection.

Even in military affairs, where he knew his ground, the humility is always obvious. "I could not have done as well as has been done, but I could have helped and taken part in a struggle for my home and neighborhood. So the work is done, I care not by whom it is done."[48] But in matters of the soul the great warrior's self-abasement is as touching as it is manifestly sincere. "As we were about to leave his tent, Mr. Lacy said: 'I think it is right that I should say to you, General, that the chaplains of the army have a deep interest in your welfare and some of the most fervent prayers we offer are in your behalf.' The old hero's face flushed, tears started in his eyes, and he replied with choked utterance and deep emotion: 'Please thank them for that, sir– I warmly appreciate it. And I can only say that I am nothing but a poor sinner, trusting in Christ for salvation, and need all of the prayers they can offer for me.'"[49]

Lee's religion was, therefore, mainly practical. He was most devout and constant in all religious observances, though his son does not conceal a human propensity to slumber during sermon time. He was ardent in worship both private and public. Such a curious religious democracy as prevailed in his army has probably not been seen in the world since the days of Cromwell. On one occasion he was hurrying with his staff to battle. The firing had begun and the shells were flying. But the cavalcade happened to pass a camp meeting where some ragged veteran was holding forth in prayer. At once the commander-in-chief dismounted and he and all his officers, with bared heads, reverently took part in the simple worship.[50] Again, as the army was being moved rapidly across the James in 1864 to meet Grant at Petersburg, Lee, with a thousand cares and duties on his shoulders, turned out from the road and knelt in the dust beside a minister, to ask for guidance and blessing.[51]

All that I have written of Lee has indeed been written in vain, if it is necessary to point out that his religion was practical not only in form and observance but in the deeper touching and moulding of the heart. Perhaps the final test of this is utter and complete forgiveness of those who have injured or are trying to injure us, not the forgiveness of the lips ("I forgive you as a Christian," said Rowena; "which means," said Wamba, "that she does not forgive him at all"), but the forgiveness of broad tolerance, of perfect understanding and sympathy, that is, of love. After the war a minister expressed himself rather bitterly as to the conduct of the North. "Doctor," said Lee to him, "there is a good old book which says, 'Love your enemies.' . . . Do you think your remarks this evening were quite in the spirit of that teaching?"[52] On another occasion a general exclaimed, "I wish those people were all dead!" "How can you say so?" answered his chief. "Now, I wish they were all at home attending to their own business, and leaving us to do the same."[53] And he summed up the whole matter more generally: "I have fought against the people of the North because I believed they were seeking to wrest from the South dearest rights. But I have never cherished bitter or vindictive feelings, and have never seen the day when I did not pray for them."[54]

The belief that "the real pleasures of life are increased by sharing them" certainly finds application more completely in religion than in anything else. No missionary ever had more ardent zeal than Lee for bringing the knowledge of God to all about him. Not that he had any air of being holier than others, of that reaching down a saving hand from vast heights of perfection which evokes a perverse desire not to be saved. Here as else where his sweet humility averts any charge of too aggressive saintliness. "He one day said to a friend in speaking of the duty of laboring for the good of others: 'Ah, Mrs. P–, I find it so hard to try to keep one poor sinner's heart in the right way, that it seems presumptuous to try to help others.'"[55] Nevertheless, one almost feels as if he cared more for winning souls than battles and for supplying his army with Bibles than with bullets and powder. Even this solemn aspect of things he could color occasionally with the gentle sunshine of his humor, as when he remarked, on hearing that many of his soldiers were taking part in a revival, "I am delighted. I wish that all of them would become Christians, for it is about all that is left them now."[56] But under the smile there was a passionate earnestness which appears not only in his private talk, but in his public orders. "The commanding general . . . directs that none but duties strictly necessary shall be required to be performed on Sunday, and that all labor, both of men and animals, which it is practicable to anticipate or postpone, or the immediate performance of which is not essential to the safety, health, or comfort of the army, shall be suspended on that day. Commanding officers . . . will give their attention to the maintenance of order and quiet around the places of worship, and prohibit anything that may tend to disturb or interrupt religious exercises."[57] These might be general orders of Cromwell or of Moses.

When it came to the guidance of the young at Washington College in later years, Lee's fervor grew even more marked. "We had been conversing for some time respecting the religious welfare of the students. General Lee's feelings soon became so intense that for a time his utterance was choked; but, recovering himself, with his eyes overflowed with tears, his lips quivering with emotion, and both hands raised, he exclaimed: 'Oh, Doctor! If I could only know that all the young men in this college were good Christians, I should have nothing more to desire.'"[58] You will remember that this man surrendered a great army and saw a nation sink to dust without a tear.

The central fact of all religion is the personal relation to God, prayer. And it is here that I have followed Lee with the deepest interest. In our modern busy life most of us set God so far apart that we are in danger of losing sight of Him entirely. This springs in great part from reverence. We are afraid of soiling sacred things with the dust of every day. The mediæval Christian had no such timidity. God was his companion, his friend, to be called on every hour, every moment, if needed. Go back two thousand years to the sweet, simple piety of an Athenian gentleman, Xenophon,–some call it degrading superstition,–and see how he summons the divine to direct his comings and goings, to cast down his enemies and support his friends. Just so Lee. God gives the victory. God permits the defeat.

God sends rain to mire the Virginia roads. He sends his sunshine to make them passable again. If God is appealed to passionately enough, devoutly enough, humbly enough, we win. If we lose, it is because we have not honored God sufficiently. But—but—what if your cause is wrong and the other right? What if millions on the other side are praying, as honestly, as humbly, as zealously as you are? To set out to kill, to pray God to help you kill, those who are devoutly praying God to help them kill you—it inevitably recalls the eternal contradiction put with such vividness by the poet,—

> "For prayer the ocean is where diversely
>   Men steer their course, each to a several coast;
> Where all our interests so discordant be
>   That half beg winds by which the rest are lost."[59]

These are old difficulties, but war always gives them a fierce and startling significance. I trust it will be believed that I do not bring them up in any spirit of mockery. My one interest is to know what Lee thought of them. Did he meet them? Did he consider them? Or did he put them aside with the simple concreteness of his practical temperament? "I had taken every precaution to insure success and counted on it. But the Ruler of the Universe willed otherwise and sent a storm to disconcert a well-laid plan, and to destroy my hopes."[60] Does he never ask why? "I hope we will yet be able to damage our adversaries when they meet us. That it should be so, we must implore the forgiveness of God for our sins, and the continuance of his blessings."[61] Does this never sound strange? Apparently not. Since he repeats it and repeats it with an inexhaustible and, I cannot help adding, an at times exasperating piety.

As to prayer on its more spiritual side, Lee's use of it is naturally less revealed to us. That a relation to God so constant and so intimate as his should be turned to only for worldly advantage and material benefit is wholly unworthy of a nature so finely touched, and we must believe that the sweetest part of his religion lay in the high rapture and forgetfulness of spiritual communion. He was not one to speak of such experience, however, or to write of it. And we are only told that "he was emphatically a man of prayer and was accustomed to pray in his family and to have his seasons of secret prayer which he allowed nothing else—however pressing—to interrupt";[62] and again, "I shall never forget the emphasis with which he grasped my hand as, with voice and eye that betrayed deep emotion, he assured me that it [knowledge of prayer] was not only his comfort, but his only comfort, and declared the simple and absolute trust that he had in God and God alone."[63]

So I think we may conclude that the cardinal fact of Lee's life was God. Schleiermacher said that Spinoza was God-intoxicated. It would be indecorous to speak of Lee as intoxicated with anything. But everywhere and always he had God in his heart, not so much the God of power, or the God of justice, or even the God of beauty, but the God of love, tempering the austerity of virtue, sweetening the bitterness of failure, above all, breathing loving kindness into the intolerable hell of war. There have been fierce saints who were fighters. There have been gentle saints who were martyrs. It is rare to find a soldier making war—stern war—with the pity, the tenderness, the sympathy of a true follower of Christ.

Facsimile of Lee's letter accepting the Presidency of Washington College

11

LEE AFTER THE WAR

Immediately after the surrender Lee, a paroled prisoner of war, withdrew into private life and took no further official part in the affairs of his country. What he personally desired, above all, was rest, quiet, solitude. "I am looking for some little, quiet home in the woods, where I can procure shelter and my daily bread, if permitted by the victor."[1] In all the remaining five years of his life he never complained, never discouraged or disheartened others, never quarreled with the doom of fortune; but those who watched him closely saw something of the burden from which his heart could not get free. "I never saw a sadder expression than General Lee carried during the entire time I was at Washington College. It looked as if the sorrow of a whole nation had collected in his countenance, and as if he was bearing the grief of his whole people. It never left his face, but was ever there to keep company with the kindly smile."[2]

Lee's attitude towards the United States Government was from the first one of loyal recognition and submission. In June, 1865, he applied for amnesty under the President's proclamation, and though his request was never formally granted, he acted in every way as if he considered himself a citizen of the united country. To a friend he wrote, "I believe it to be the duty of every one to unite in the restoration of the country, and the reëstablishment of peace and harmony."[3] And again "Were it worth his while to refer to my political record, he would have found that I was not in favor of secession and was opposed to war; in fact, that I was for the Constitution and the Union established by our forefathers. No one now is more in favor of that Constitution and that Union."[4] When testifying before the Congressional Reconstruction Committee, he was questioned very closely in regard to his attitude toward future possible complications; but his answers, though characteristically reserved, showed nothing but profound loyalty and hope.

That he sympathized with the indignation of his countrymen over the ill-judged and mismanaged methods of so-called reconstruction is probable, though his language is always guarded. As to the great theme of Southern wrath,—the captivity of Davis,—Lee is full of pity for the captive, but does not abuse the captors. And why should he? In the place of Lee and Davis I should have done as they did. But from the Northern point of view they had striven rebelliously to overthrow an established government. They had wasted hundreds of thousands of lives and hundreds of millions of treasure. Any other people in any other age of the world would have hanged both of them without a moment's compunction or delay. It would have been unwise, it would have been impolitic. Who dare say it would have been unhuman? Yet the South complains, because Davis was subjected for a few months to petty annoyance and personal insult.

But whatever his feelings or opinions, Lee absolutely refused to take any part in practical politics. His scrupulous observance of his parole made him unwilling to recognize any continued relation to the Confederacy, as when he declined to share in the remains of the civil service fund from which other officers helped themselves freely.[5] It also made him unwilling to meddle in the political activities going on about him. To be sure, when he was urged by the Reconstruction Committee as to negro suffrage, he spoke out: "My own opinion is that at this time they cannot vote intelligently and that giving them the right of suffrage would open the door to a good deal of demagogism and lead to serious embarrassments in various ways."[6] Are there many people today who think that he was wrong? But in general he was faithful to his established rule: "I must not wander into politics, a subject I carefully avoid."[7] Even a nomination to the highest office in his native state was declined by him, partly on personal grounds: "My feelings induce me to prefer private life, which I think more suitable to my condition and age"; but mainly because he believed such action "would be used by the dominant party to excite hostility towards the State, and to injure the people in the eyes of the country; and I, therefore, cannot consent to become the instrument of bringing distress upon those whose prosperity and happiness are so dear to me."[8]

The desire for retirement and quiet was so strong that Lee avoided, if possible, everything connecting him with the war and all its memories. This does not mean that he had any occasion for regret;

simply that a chapter of terrible agony was closed forever, and he wished his people as well as himself to look forward and not back. Nor does it mean that he forgot his old comrades. On the contrary, he remembered them too well, thinking of them every day and every hour, their unavailing toil, their fruitless sacrifice. "You will meet many of my old soldiers during your trip," he said in 1869, "and I wish you to tell them that I often think of them, try every day to pray for them, and am always gratified to hear of their prosperity."[9]

And they remembered him. Many and many are the stories told of long devotion, of high enthusiasm, of eager desire for a touch, for a glance even, that might be treasured always. The simplest of these stories are the sweetest. When he visited Petersburg in the last years, they thronged round his carriage and tried to take out the horses and so draw him into the city, but he declared if they did so, he should have to get out and help them.[10] Just after the war closed, he received the following letter, which needs no comment: "Dear General: we have been fighting hard for four years, and now the Yankees have got us in Libby Prison. They are treating us awful bad. The boys want you to get us out if you can, but, if you can't, just ride by the Libby, and let us see you and give you a cheer. We will all feel better after it."[11] On one occasion the general was ill and a watchful attendant was taking pains to see that he was in no way disturbed. His room was on the ground floor and the nurse noticed a man step softly to the window and try to open the blinds. "Go away," she said. "That is General Lee's room." The man went, murmuring, "I only wanted to see him."[12]

But though Lee was glad to meet his old soldiers, he was reluctant to talk of the war with them or with any one else. He did, indeed, plan "to write a history of my campaigns, not to vindicate myself and promote my reputation, but to show the world what our poor boys with their small numbers and scant resources had succeeded in accomplishing."[13] But the history was never written, and I do not believe it ever would have been written. As time went on, he would have shrunk from it more and more. For this reason the few comments that he has left us are doubly precious. There is the delightful letter to the Union general, Hunter, who had sought Lee's justification for the line of retreat from Lynchburg: "I am not advised as to the motives which induced you to adopt the line of retreat which you took, and am not, perhaps, competent to judge of the question; but I certainly expected you to retreat by way of the Shenandoah Valley, and was gratified at the time that you preferred the route through the mountains to the Ohio—leaving the Valley open for General Early's advance into Maryland."[14] There are the rare observations on the

Union commanders. As to McClellan: A friend "asked General Lee which in his opinion was the ablest of the Union generals; to which the latter answered, bringing his hand down on the table with emphatic energy, 'McClellan, by all odds.'"[15] As to Grant, the often quoted but probably apocryphal expressions of extravagant eulogy, and the authentic written words showing respect and esteem, "General Grant, who possesses magnanimity as well as ability."[16] There is the characteristic advice to General Early as to the whole subject: "I would recommend, however, that while giving facts necessary for your own vindication, you omit all epithets or remarks calculated to excite bitterness or animosity between different sections of the country."[17]

Anything like interviewing it is needless to say that Lee shunned with disgust and he treated reporters with less civility than he showed to anybody else. "One evening a correspondent of the 'New York Herald' paid him a visit for the purpose of securing an interview. The general was courteous and polite, but very firm. He stood during the interview, and finally dismissed the reporter, saying: 'I shall be glad to see you as a friend, but request that the visit may not be made in your professional capacity.'"[18] Of Swinton he said, "He seemed to be gentlemanly, but I derive no pleasure from my interviews with bookmakers."[19]

And if Lee shunned publicity through the press, he was even more unwilling to be made an object of personal curiosity. On the rare occasions when he was persuaded to appear in public places, he was received with an enthusiasm, a deference, a universal esteem and affection which must have touched him. But his natural modesty and reserve shrank from all such manifestations, whenever possible. He frequently alludes to his feelings on the subject with gentle humor. "They would make too much fuss over the old rebel."[20] "Why should they care to see me? I am only a poor old Confederate."[21] And there is the delicious story of the raffle. "I have had a visit since commencing this letter from Mrs. William Bath, of New Orleans, who showed me a wreath made in part, she says, of my, your [Mrs. Lee's], and Mildred's hair, sent her by you more than two years ago. She says she sent you a similar one at the time, but of this I could tell her nothing, for I remember nothing about it. She says her necessities now compel her to put her wreath up to raffle, and she desired to know whether I had any objection to her scheme, and whether I would head the list. All this, as you may imagine, is extremely agreeable to me, but I had to decline her offer of taking a chance in her raffle."[22]

So, instead of glory and applause and raffles, Lee wanted quiet. He had neighbors, rich and poor, high and humble, who adored him; and their homelike kindness and affection he thoroughly appreciated. His son writes that for days and weeks, after the family was established at Lexington, "supplies came pouring to my mother from the people in the town and country, even from the poor mountaineers, who, anxious to 'do something to help General Lee,' brought in handbags of walnuts, potatoes, and game."[23] He had friends, old and new, who wrote him cordial and admiring letters and drew from him such charming replies as that addressed to the English poet Worsley, and many others. Best of all he had his family circle, the invalid wife to whom he gave constant care and who paid it back in sunshine, the sons and daughters and daughters-in-law, whose serious concerns received his earnest attention and sympathy, and whose lighter doings he followed with the playful jest and kindly merriment under which he took pains to veil the weight that always pressed his heart.

It cannot be said that the many letters preserved from this period often contain frank outpouring, or indicate that Lee gave himself up to any human soul. Yet they are well worth attentive study as showing the constant tenderness of his nature and his watchful devotion to the welfare of those about him. And now and then there is a glimpse of profound emotion, as in the reference to his lost daughter. "I shall go first to Warrenton Springs, North Carolina, to visit the grave of my dear Annie, where I have always promised myself to go, and I think, if I am to accomplish it, I have no time to lose. I wish to witness her quiet sleep, with her dear hands crossed over her breast, as it were in mute prayer, undisturbed by her distance from us, and to feel that her pure spirit is waiting in bliss in the land of the blessed."[24]

Much as Lee liked home and quiet, he was the last man in the world to sit down and fold his hands, to feel that his life's task was done, while his limbs had strength in them. Even as a simple Virginian farmer he would have worked and worked hard. The world had seen too much of his greatness, however, to let him hide it in shadow. During all the years after the war offers kept coming to him, of establishment, of occupation, of possible usefulness and assured emolument. An English nobleman offered him a country-seat in England and an annuity of £3000. Lee answered, "I must abide the fortunes and share the fate of my people."[25] He was urged to emigrate with a Southern colony to Mexico. He answered: "The thought of abandoning the country and all that must be left in it is abhorrent to my feelings, and I prefer to struggle for its restoration and share its fate, rather than give up all as lost."[26]

Many business positions of high trust or dignity were pressed upon him. He uniformly declined them, alleging that his training did not lie in that direction and that his age rendered him incapable of performing such arduous labors. When he was told that no labors were expected of him, that his name was all that would be required, and that a large salary would be paid simply for the use of that, he replied that his name was not for sale.[27]

It was suggested that he should be at the head of a large house in New York to represent Southern commerce, with immense sums of money at his disposal. He said in response: "I am grateful, but I have a self-imposed task which I must accomplish. I have led the young men of the South in battle; I have seen many of them die on the field; I shall devote my remaining energies to training young men to do their duty in life."[28]

For already, within a brief time after the war closed, he had accepted an office which in itself seemed neither very brilliant nor very profitable, at least when compared with the position Lee occupied in the eyes of the whole world. After much hesitation, not as to brilliancy or profit, but as to his own fitness, he had yielded to the request of the trustees of Washington College that he would become their president. "Fully impressed with the responsibilities of the office," he wrote on the 24th of August, 1865, "I have feared that I should be unable to discharge its duties to the satisfaction of the Trustees, or to the benefit of the country. . . . Should you, however, take a different view, and think that my services in the position tendered me by the Board will be advantageous to the college and the country, I will yield to your judgment and accept it."[29]

At that time the college consisted of forty students and four professors.[30] The endowment was unproductive and the salary offered the new president—fifteen hundred dollars—was offered purely on a basis of faith. Lee's great name told at once, and money and students began to appear. But it was by no means his intention to work only with his name. For five years he gave the best of his thought and toil to building up the institution which has most justly coupled him in glory with its great original founder, and all the qualities which had made him famous on the battlefield now displayed themselves with richer and more fruitful effort, in the ways of peace. It may indeed be thought that he did not show quite all the grasping greed of the modern college president when he wrote to a lady who was considering a large legacy, "It is furthest from my wish to divert any donation from the Theological Seminary at Alexandria, for I am well acquainted with the merits of that institution, have a high respect for its professors, and am an earnest advocate of its object. I only give you

Robert E. Lee as college president

the information you desire and wish you to follow your own prefer-
ences in the matter."[31] But perhaps, after all, such methods are not less
effective than some that are more bustling.

And in performing this arduous and useful work for others Lee
doubtless brought happiness to himself also, as is shown by his most
beautiful and striking observation which I have already quoted and
am glad to quote again. "For my own part, I much enjoy the charms
of civil life, and find too late that I have wasted the best part of my
existence."[32] Thus loved, honored, and revered by all, he labored
fruitfully, till the end came, far too soon and doubtless hastened by his
vast cares and vaster sorrows, on the 12th of October, 1870. He was

buried, with simple ceremony, at Lexington, in the chapel which had been erected by his efforts, and which will be an object of pilgrimage to thousands who cherish his memory.

But let us look more closely at what he accomplished in his college presidency for the profoundly interesting light it throws on the various aspects of his character. To begin with, as I have said, he worked. His was no ornamental position. He spent his days regularly in his office and attended personally to his immense correspondence, with so much faithfulness that a newspaper editor, who had occasion to send to a large number of college presidents a circular calling for an answer, relates that General Lee was the only one from whom he received a reply.[33] Nor did he confine himself to the details of the administrative side of his position. He was constant in visiting examinations and recitations, remaining a few moments, asking pertinent and stimulating questions in every sort of subject, then departing with the dignified bow of his grave, old-fashioned courtesy.[34]

And his intellectual interest was much more than a mere routine observation of pedagogical work. As may be seen from his yearly reports to the trustees,[35] he set himself at once to devise large educational plans, which went far beyond the means he had to work with and far beyond the traditions that prevailed about him. Brought up at once in old habits of thought and in modern practical training, he would have saved, if possible, the liberal, classical culture of the past, combined it with the energetic commercial methods of new America.[36] He wanted to develop his scientific courses, his laboratories, begged money for them, sought teachers for them. He designed an elective system which was most broadly in advance of current ideas, yet he saw the necessity of checking such a system by rigid supervision and constraint. In other words, so far as his limited opportunities will allow us to judge, he was a thinker in education as he was a thinker in war.

But these were "worlds not realized," and I find him in his human relations even more worth study. He managed his faculty as he managed his generals, with firmness tempered by an ever-ready sympathy. In their personal welfare he took the kindest and most genuine interest. "My wife reminds me," says Professor Joynes, "that once, when I was detained at home by sickness, General Lee came every day, through a deep Lexington snow, and climbed the high stairs, to inquire about me and to comfort her."[37] At the same time he was minutely exacting himself about matters of duty and wished others to be so. A professor walked into church with his pipestem protruding from his pocket. This caused some comment in the faculty meeting, and the offender took out the pipe and began cutting off the stem. "No, Mr. Harris," said the general, "don't do that; next time leave it at home."[38] The narrow circumstances, not only of the college but of the whole South, seemed, to Lee, at any rate, to demand the closest economy. One day a professor wished to consult a catalogue and was going to tear the wrapper off one that had been prepared for mailing. Lee hastily handed him another already opened. "Take this, if you please."[39] Regularity and punctuality were his cardinal principles and he did not like others to neglect them. A professor who was not always constant at chapel one day spoke of the importance of inducing the students to attend. Lee quietly remarked, "The best way that I know of to induce students to attend is to set them the example by always attending ourselves."[40]

Some of these anecdotes and the many others like them suggest that Lee may have appeared just a little of a martinet, just a little over-particular. I suspect that he did occasionally appear so to some who have forgotten it now, or who do not wish to remember it. Yet the general testimony is that kindness of manner made up for any sharpness of speech; and as we have seen that his greatness in war came from his wide knowledge of all rules and his perfect willingness to fling them aside at the right moment, so we find that in peace he thought nothing of tradition or system when it trammeled the progress of the soul. "Make no needless rules," he told his teachers.[41] Again, "We must never make a rule that we cannot enforce."[42] And when one of them appealed to precedent and urged that "we must not respect persons," Lee replied, "I always respect persons and care little for precedent."[43] Coming from a man whose life was built on law and the reverence for law, I call that magnificent.

On this nice balance of law and liberty his whole discipline of the college was based. It might be supposed that as a military man, brought up in a military school, he would be a firm believer in the military methods of training of which we nowadays hear so much. It is only another instance of his breadth of mind that this was not so. "I have heard him say," writes Professor Joynes, "that military discipline was, unfortunately, necessary in military education, but was, in his opinion, a most unsuitable training for civil life."[44] Without going to any opposite extreme, he believed, as we have seen above, in reducing rules to the minimum, in making rules simple and not vexatious, believed that the highest aim of education is to produce a type of character which shall leave rules unnecessary. "Young gentleman," he said to one newcoming student, "we have no printed rules. We have but one rule here, that every student be a gentleman."[45] And in a general circular issued after some public disturbance he embodied his idea completely. "The Faculty therefore appeal to the honor and self-respect of the students to prevent any similar occurrence, trusting that their sense of what is due to themselves, their parents, and the institution to which they belong, will be more effectual in teaching them what is right and manly than anything they can say."[46]

Such leniency of system sometimes works havoc. Not when it is supported by the personal force which Lee gave it. He used the same methods with his students that he had used with his soldiers. His reprimands were gentle and quiet, but they were effective. They did not sting, but they stirred and touched and inspired. Rough and bitter he could not make them. When some one remonstrated a little on this, he answered: "I cannot help it; if a gentleman can't understand the language of a gentleman, he must remain in ignorance, for a gentleman cannot write in any other way."[47] Nevertheless, it seems that he usually achieved his object. For all his gentleness, the wildest boys were apt to come out of his office in tears. One, who had boasted that this would not happen, underwent the same experience as the rest. "What did he do to you? Did he scold you?" were the eager inquiries. "No; I wish he had. I wish he had whipped me. I could have stood it better. He talked to me about my mother and the sacrifices she is making to send me to college, and before I knew it, I was blubbering like a baby."[48]

As with his officers and soldiers, he had endless ingenious devices of kindly fun for making reproof more tolerable—and more effectual. A student was once called to account for absence. "Mr. M., I am glad to see you better," said the general, smiling. "But, General, I have not been sick." "Then I am glad you have better news from home." "But, General, I have had no bad news." "Ah," said the general, "I took it for granted that nothing less than sickness or distressing news from home could have kept you from your duty."[49] In the same vein Mr. Page has a story of being late for prayers and the general's asking him to "tell Miss – that I say will she please have breakfast a little earlier for you?"[50]

And again, as with the officers and soldiers, back of Lee's discipline there was love. He was not thinking of his own dignity, or even of the reputation of the college. He was thinking first of the boy and of what could be done to save him. And the boy knew it. It is said that often in the faculty meetings, when a case seemed hopeless and expulsion the only remedy, Lee would plead, "Don't you think it would be better to bear with him a little longer? Perhaps we may do him some good."[51]

With scholarship it was as with discipline for conduct. Lee made it a point to know every student, know his character, know his record, know even his marks, when necessary. A boy's name was one day mentioned. "I am sorry to see he has fallen so far behind in his mathematics," the general observed. "You are mistaken, General, he is one of the very best men in my class." "He only got 66 on his last month's report," was the general's answer. Investigation showed that the president was right as to the report, but a mistake had been made in copying 66 for 99.[52]

Reproof, encouragement, exhortation as to study were given in the same vein, with the same tact and ingenious aptness, as for other things. To one parent of a negligent pupil he writes: "I have myself told him as plainly but as kindly as I could that it was necessary for him to change his course, or that he would be obliged to return home. He has promised me that he would henceforth be diligent and attentive, and endeavor to perform his duty. I hope that he may succeed, for I think that he is able to do well if he really makes the effort."[53] Of another similar case he remarked, in his humorous fashion, "He is entirely too careful of the health of his father's son. . . . We do not want our students to injure their health studying, but we want them to come as near to it as it is possible to miss. This young gentleman, you see, is a long way from the danger-line."[54] And again, he offered a like suggestion to the pupil himself: "How is your mother? I am sure you must be devoted to her; you are so careful of the health of her son."[55]

Many of these incidents are doubtless trivial in themselves. They are valuable as showing how entirely Lee was devoted to his work, and that he threw himself into the task of building up a little college with as much zeal as he had given to the creating of a great nation. What counted with all these young men was his personal influence and he knew it. In point of fact, he was creating, or re-creating, a great nation still. His patience, his courage, his attitude towards the past, his attitude towards the future, his perfect forgiveness, his large magnanimity, above all, his hope, were reflected in the eager hearts about him and from them spread wide over the bruised and beaten South, which stood so sorely in need of all these things. I have referred in an earlier chapter to the immense importance of his general influence in bringing about reconciliation and peace. It is almost impossible to overestimate this. We have the high Northern evidence of Grant: "All the people except a few political leaders in the South will accept whatever he does as right and will be guided to a great extent by his example."[56] Perhaps nothing will better illustrate the passionate testimony of Southerners than a simple anecdote. A Confederate

Head from Valentine's recumbent statue of Lee

soldier told General Wise that he had taken the oath of allegiance to the United States. "You have disgraced the family," said Wise. "General Lee told me to do it." "Oh, that alters the case. Whatever General Lee says is all right, I don't care what it is."[57] Does not the knowledge of these things double the pathos of that profoundly pathetic sentence in one of Lee's late letters? "Life is indeed gliding away and I have nothing of good to show for mine that is past. I pray I may be spared to accomplish something for the benefit of mankind and the honor of God."[58] If he had accomplished nothing, what shall be said of some of us?

Yet in spite of all this, it must be admitted that Lee's life will always be regarded as a record of failure. And it is precisely because he failed that I have been interested to make this study of him. Success is the idol of the world and the world's idols have been successful. Washington, Lincoln, Grant, were doubtless very great. But they were successful. Who shall say just how far that element of success enters into their greatness. Here was a man who remains great, although he failed. America in the twentieth century worships success, is too ready to test character by it, to be blind to those faults success hides, to those qualities that can do without it. Here was a man who failed grandly, a man who said that "human virtue should be equal to human calamity," and showed that it could be equal to it, and so, without pretense, without display, without self-consciousness, left an example that future Americans may study with profit as long as there is an America.

A young sophomore was once summoned to the president's office and gently admonished that only patience and industry would prevent the failure that would inevitably come to him through college and through life.

"But, General, you failed," remarked the sophomore, with the inconceivable ineptitude of sophomores.

"I hope that you may be more fortunate than I," was the tranquil answer.[59]

Literature can add nothing to that.

THE END

LEE AND PSYCHOGRAPHY

W hat I have aimed at in this book is the portrayal of a soul. We live in an age of names and a new name has recently been invented—psychography. This means, I suppose, an art which is not psychology, because it deals with individuals, not general principles, and is not biography, because it swings clear of the formal sequence of chronological detail, and uses only those deeds and words and happenings that are spiritually significant.

New names are often attached to old things. This thing is as old as Plutarch, as old as the Bible, as old as the first man who reflected on his fellows and sketched them with one brief word that made others reflect. What a portrait painter was Tacitus, and Clarendon, and Saint-Simon. But the nineteenth century, with its scientific training, brought more method to the work, more patient curiosity, more desire to base its results on deep research, and delicate discrimination. Matthew Arnold's essay on Falkland is an English masterpiece in this kind. Lowell wrote *A Great Public Character*. Mr. Rothschild, in his *Lincoln: Master of Men*, has drawn a full-length with loving care. And there are others too numerous to mention. But the prince of all psychographers is incontestably Sainte-Beuve. He is usually spoken of as a literary critic. In pure literature he has some limitations. As what he himself called "a naturalist of souls"[1] he has never been surpassed, or equaled, or even approached.

The art of painting souls has its difficulties. First, one would wish to be fair-minded, impartial, free from prejudice. This is, I think, impossible, and the impartial historian, or biographer,—that is, he who studies his subject in and for itself, without preconception or prepossession, without an instinctive disposition to misrepresent from one cause or another,—does not exist. There are simply those who think they are impartial and those who know they are not.

To begin with, there is the cruder element of political, or religious, or social partisanship, from which none of us is wholly free. Tacitus can see little good in a Cæsar. Clarendon finds the Devil's finger pushing Cromwell. Saint-Simon hates a parvenu. Mommsen has to justify the imperialism of Prussia in the imperialism of Rome. These are the extremes. Beside them Mr. Rhodes and Gardiner seem fair, dispassionate judges. Are they so? Mr. Rhodes's admirable history is spoken of as perfectly impartial—by Northerners. Southerners usually refer to it as the least partial of Northern histories. Certainly, in spite of all reserves and concessions, Mr. Rhodes throughout takes the Northern view of things—as is natural and right. So Gardiner, for all his fairness, obviously praises the Puritans because they were Puritans, the Cavaliers although they were Cavaliers. Indeed, it is not impossible that the open, avowed, and evident partisanship of Clarendon (discarding, of course, all question as to accuracy of fact) makes safer reading than the disguised, insinuating partisanship of Gardiner.

But these established prepossessions of creed or preference are not the only obstacles to the psychographer's impartiality. He is exposed to another danger which is greater according as his gift of artistic treatment and expression is greater. That is the danger of making his means more than his end, of taking such vigorous and startling measures to attract the attention of his readers and stir their passions that he emphasizes both the good and the evil in his subject far more than nature warrants or justice allows. This is the real weakness of such writers as Macaulay and Froude, far more than their political prejudices, just as, in a different order of literature, it is the weakness of Dickens. Macaulay doubtless loved the Puritans. But he loved a clever rhetorical touch far more than any Puritan. It was well to make his readers delight in the champions of liberty. It was even better to make his readers stare and gasp at the skill with which he painted a champion of liberty or a tool of Satan. Therefore his highlights are very high and his shadows very deep.

"Lord Macaulay had, as we know, his own heightened and telling way of putting things," says Matthew Arnold. Sainte-Beuve also has his tranquil judgment on "the clever and dangerous counsels of M. Macaulay, much in vogue at present. 'The best portraits,' says that great historical painter, 'are those in which there is a slight touch of exaggeration. . . . Something is lost in exactitude, but much is gained in effect. . . . The less important features are neglected, but the great characteristic traits are permanently impressed upon the mind.' It is thus that many great figures are revamped and made over long after they have passed away."[2] I have said that Sainte-Beuve was "a naturalist of souls." Macaulay might well be called "a showman of souls."

In dealing with historical material of all sorts one finds it constantly necessary to be on one's guard against this tendency. Thus, with the innumerable anecdotes bearing on the Civil War, the plain, uncouth narrative of a soldier who has no pretension whatever to literature often gives the impression of being far more reliable than the polished version contributed by a John Esten Cooke or a George Cary Eggleston.

But this is not all. A psychographer may rid himself to a considerable degree of general prejudices. He may by habit and temperament grow to think first, last, and always of his subject, never of his effects (which is the sure cure for rhetoric). And still he may fall into an even more pervasive and treacherous form of misrepresentation: he may be misled by a personal affection for his subject, for his model, for what, in a certain sense, becomes almost his own child. Probably no biographer who is worth much is altogether free from this. It is the obvious cause of the undue partiality which Sainte-Beuve is said to show towards some of his minor figures, such as the Guérins. Gaston Boissier's portrait of Cicero is one of the most lucid, most limpid character studies ever made, absolutely free from any suggestion of rhetorical effect; but on every page you feel the painter's love for his subject, and that the defects which are neither slurred nor palliated are touched in a very different spirit from that in which a lover of Cæsar would have touched them.

In our own war literature Henderson's Jackson is an excellent example of what I mean. There are few saner, more exact, judicial tempers than Henderson's. Not on any account would he deliberately have concealed or misrepresented any flaw or weakness in his hero. Yet, by some subtle, inexplicable alchemy, everything turns to Jackson's credit; and words and acts which might have been used by others only to make him repulsive and ridiculous serve in Henderson to make him heroic and lovable.

Finally, the psychographer has to contend with another humiliating difficulty, the indisposition to change his mind when it is once made up. You labor widely, through thousands of dull pages. Gradually your picture arranges itself in neat order and correct detail. You see your subject as you think it must finally stand. Then comes some little sentence in an out-of-the-way magazine, or some kindly correspondent reveals a flaw you could not have discovered, and large readjustment seems to be indicated. You are ready for it—oh, yes. You accept it, if true—oh, yes. But it is surprising, the amount of ingenuity you expend in convincing yourself that it is not true, that it may be explained, disputed, adapted. When you come to your senses, you laugh at yourself; but you are so ready to do the same thing again!

All these subjective difficulties beset the charming art of the psychographer; but the objective are no less, perhaps greater. Every portrait of a character must be based finally upon that character's own words and actions. As regards actions, it is obvious that we depend entirely upon report, and little study is needed to make it plain that a man's own report is unreliable and that of others much more so. The reliability, indeed, varies. Report at third or tenth hand by incompetent witnesses differs considerably in quality from that transmitted by a trained observer in direct contact. But this latter is difficult to obtain and at the very best must be used with caution. A man's eyes are the servants of his mind and all minds are biased to some degree. Therefore the mass of biographical anecdote and reminiscence has to be sifted and tested by numerous almost instinctive criteria before it can be profitably employed.

When it comes to a man's words, we are on surer ground; that is, to his own written words; for words reported by others belong in a quite different category. If we can consult a manuscript as it was actually penned, we have material which, so far as it goes, is indisputable and invaluable. Unfortunately this is in all cases difficult, in many impossible. For the most part, we are obliged to rely on a printed copy, and printed copies are very far from being verbal facsimiles. Even when we are guaranteed against willful omission or emendation on the part of editors, the danger of error is by no means eliminated. Printers are careless, proof-readers indifferent. No text of historical documents, made before the nineteenth century learned conscientiousness in such matters, is to be used with security, and few since. I do not suppose the most scrupulous historian will ever again consult the original records of the Civil War. Probably the printed copies are to be implicitly relied on. Yet they were made by many people and passed through many hands. Who knows?

Take one very trifling yet significant instance of slight verbal variation. Jones, Fitzhugh Lee, and Captain R.E. Lee all reprint the important letter in which Lee refers to the capture of Mason and Slidell, and they all print differently one little word which might have quite a bearing on Lee's instinctive mental attitude towards his old allegiance. Lee assures Mrs. Lee that the United States will not go to war. "*Her* (R.E.L.) *The* (Jones) *Our* (F. Lee) rulers are not entirely mad." Which did Lee write? None of the three quite commends itself, though Captain Lee's text is probably correct. But the point is that each editor prints his own version with placid indifference and not a hint that there is the slightest doubt about the matter. A trivial thing, you say. So it is. But an inch on a man's character is sometimes prodigious, and it is precisely in the trivial things that the danger lies. Here is another case of the mere variation of a letter. In his eulogy of Lee, B.H. Hill apparently called him "a man without *guile*," and so it stands in some texts; a harmless compliment, surely. But other proof-readers have it "a man without *guilt*," and this calls down upon Hill a page of abuse from Rhett in the *Southern Magazine* for daring to place Lee on a level with Christ.

If we cannot trust a man's own written words, what are we to do about words attributed to him by others? Generally speaking, we can have no confidence in them whatsoever. If you have tried at a half-hour's interval to recall the exact form of some speech that has been made to you, you know the difficulty and how apt you and other auditors are to differ. Yet in these matters of character study the exact form is sometimes all-important. Who can suppose that even trained and conscientious observers like Boswell or the Goncourts really get a stenographical report of the long conversations which they write down so industriously three or four hours after hearing them? And if not they, who? Can any one doubt that these reporters uncon-sciously arrange, adapt, and supply words and phrases which they know to be generally characteristic of the man, but which may never have been uttered in that connection and which the speaker would disown? An admirer declared that the Goncourt conversations "sweated authenticity." But Renan at least energetically disavowed his share in them.

The ancient historians, Livy, Tacitus, even Thucydides, have been abused and ridiculed for inventing the speeches of great historical characters. But I am not at all sure that a thinker and an artist, knowing the man he dealt with, and the occasion, and the substance of the speech, would not produce something more humanly accurate and characteristic than comes from many a stenographic reporter to-day.

Sainte-Beuve has some excellent sentences on this matter of reported speech. "I must, in my turn, point out that from such conversations, reported and repeated at leisure, even when they are reproduced with the utmost sincerity, we can accept only the significant touch and the general drift. As regards the details, inexactitude and guesswork always enter in more or less. And, moreover, memory is a great adapter and arranger (la mémoire aussi est une arrangeuse)."[3]

In estimating the value of words attributed to a historical character, one rule, well known to the critics of classical texts, is often useful; viz., that among several doubtful readings, the least intelligible, the least smoothly conventional, is the most likely to be correct. For example, I feel sure that Lee's eulogy on Stuart, "He never brought me a piece of false information," reads exactly as it was spoken; for no "arranging" memory would have been satisfied with a turn of phrase so baldly inadequate.

Even when there is a reasonable assurance that we have the actual language used, how seldom do we get all the meaning a speaker intended to convey. Words by themselves are so little. The emphasis is so much. The smile or gesture is so much. No reporter succeeds in giving us these; yet how far they go in enhancing or diminishing the bare significance of speech.

Nevertheless, we will assume that we start from an exact knowledge of a man's words and actions. Still, we are only on the threshold, only lifting the latch of the door which leads to the secret of his character. We must get back of word and action to the motive beneath. The deeper one's study, the wider one's experience, the less confidence one has that this can be done. "We may know historical facts to be true, as we know facts in common life to be true. Motives are generally unknown," said Dr. Johnson.[4] Different actions so often spring from the same motive and the same action from different motives. Ambition does the deeds of loving kindness and haughtiness of humility. Greed sometimes squanders and charity pinches itself and those it loves. Again and again a man fails to understand his own motives, even when he tries to disentangle them, errs ludicrously in making an honest attempt to explain them in warm words or in cold print. How, then, can we ever be confident of penetrating the motives of those who lived years ago, with different habits of speech, different habits of thought, viewing them in a mirror so uncertain as we have seen the records of the past to be?

Perhaps I may be permitted another illustration from the subject which has most recently brought all these questions to my mind. General Porter, describing Lee's surrender, says that afterwards, as the general stood on the porch of the McLean house waiting for his horse, he struck his hands together. There can be no question about the fact here. So good an observer as Porter has told us only what actually took place. I have followed Porter further in the assumption that the motive for this gesture was an immense despair. But neither Porter nor I know anything about it, and an uncomfortable suspicion besets me that, after all, Lee may have been only calling for his horse.

But even with a sure knowledge of fact and an unfailing insight into motive, the exact portrayer of character would still have a wide, uncharted course to travel. For he must finally resort to general terms. His subject is honest, generous, frank. Well, an honest man is one who does nothing that is not honest. A generous man does only what is generous. A frank man always speaks the truth. In other words, all traits of character are merely generalizations from habitual action and motive; and on a foundation in itself utterly unstable we must rear an edifice as shifting and fleeting and uncertain as the clouds of heaven. When Macaulay says of Laud, "his understanding was narrow. . . . he was by nature rash, irritable, quick to feel for his own dignity, slow to sympathize with the sufferings of others,"[5] we get a vivid impression which stays with us, but which may have been wholly borne out by the facts, or mainly, or very insufficiently. When Saint-Simon says of La Feuillade, "I don't think there was ever a madder head or a man more radically dishonest to the very marrow of his bones,"[6] we feel that we are beholding a fellow creature damned beyond the limit of human desert. And the weakness of all such soul portrayal is admirably shown in one of Clarendon's most striking specimens of it. "He quickly lost the character of a bold, stout, magnanimous man, which he had been long reputed to be in worse times; and, in his most prosperous season, fell under the reproach of being a man of big looks, and of a mean and abject spirit."[7] We see suggested here how slight is the basis of all our moral generalizations and how uncertain is the interpretation of motives on which even that slight basis rests. "There is," says Sainte-Beuve, "a degree"–and perhaps we may conclude a very limited degree–"of intimacy beyond which it is not given to man to advance in the study of his fellow man! There are secrets which the great Anatomist of heart keeps only for himself."[8] May we not establish one final test of a thorough knowledge of character; that is, the prediction of action under given circumstances? But who of us dares often predict with any certainty the action of others, or even his own?

If, then, the portrayal of character is so difficult–not to say impossible–why persist in it? First, because, largely on account of this very difficulty, it is the most fascinating of human pursuits. The naturalist spends long days or months of patient toil in observing the habits of a bird or an insect. Is not the human soul of more value than many insects? Also, with birds and insects the naturalist rarely attempts to go beyond the species or concern himself with the individual. With humanity the individual is endless in variety, inexhaustible in interest. What a delight, after going through pages that are irrelevant and for one's purpose unprofitable, to find some sentence that, in Sainte-Beuve's phrase, reveals "bare soul"! It is as if one had groped for hours in darkness and then suddenly opened a little window into bright heaven. Such, for example, is the careless touch in Cavour's letters, which sums up a whole glorious career, and stamps the eternal difference between the founders of modern Italy and modern Germany: "Je suis fils de la liberté et c'est à elle que je dois tout ce que je suis."[9] Some writers, as Pepys, are studded thick with these jewels of self-revelation. But perhaps the pleasure of finding them is even greater when they are comparatively rare, as with Lee; and I shall not soon forget my delight in the reported phrase, "It is well that war is so terrible, or else we might grow too fond of it," and the written one, "She is like her papa–always wanting something."

Moreover, the art of character study is recommendable not only for its charm, but for its utility. The knowledge of birds and insects is of merely indirect advantage to us. The knowledge of men and women, obscure, imperfect, incomplete as it necessarily is, profits us from the cradle to the grave. The infant, hardly able to speak, learns whom it can wheedle, and whom not. The child, but little older, knows very well that its parent forgives a fault or grants a privilege more readily after dinner than before. All of us always build and unbuild the character of others, observe, divine, detect, use instinctively every little indication of face, of tone, of gesture. We often blunder, often go far astray. The wisest are those who recognize most clearly their utter lack of exact knowledge and most frequently exclaim,–

> "Oh, that there were an art
> To read the mind's character in the face."

Yet they persist, because they must. And all men and women are, whether they know it or not, if I may say so, mutual psychographers.

For this purpose of mutual self-knowledge some may question whether it is essential or desirable to choose prominent figures rather than the man in the street. They say, it is not the great men, who are remote and above us, who help us to understand ourselves, but those who have lived a little petty life of trifles such as we live.

To begin with, the man in the street is less accessible. He does not leave letters and memoirs. His speech and actions are not jealously observed and faithfully recorded. We may study him for our own profit, daily, as we can. But the permanent portrait painter must look further afield for the material with which to work.

Then, men who have lived large lives and filled great places bring more of their humanity into action. A violin that is played on in only one small portion of one string yields us far less than one that is swept broadly from end to end of its entire compass. A man who for forty years has carried the wide world's burdens on his shoulders may not have finer natural faculties than you or I, but at least he has brought every faculty into use with all the might he has in him.

In other words, the main advantage of studying great men comes not because they are great, but because they are not great. Carlyle wished to exalt a few choice heroes and let the rest of humanity bow down to them. The opposite seems to me the true course, to insist that all men may be heroes if they will. What strikes me most in men who have achieved greatly is not their difference from others but their resemblance to them. They are in all points tempted as we are, laugh as we, weep as we, suffer as we, fail as we, and for the most part are astonished at triumphing as much as we should be. And do not urge that this is the old theory of "no man a hero to his valet," and that in applying it generally I am only displaying a most valet-like spirit. I hope not. For it is not my aim to debase them, but to exalt us. When it is shown that great personages, who left a name behind them, had only qualities like ours, often defects like ours, and that they made their greatness perhaps by a happy balance of qualities or by an extreme development of some particular quality, perhaps even a little by the kindliness of fortune, it seems to me that we should be led to emphasize rather what we may be than what they were not. If Lee had something of my weakness, may I not have better hope of attaining something of Lee's nobleness?

It must be confessed that such a method of studying heroic characters depends for its success largely upon the spirit in which it is carried on. It may easily degenerate into the trivial, the gossiping, or even the scandalous. The distinction between what is humanly significant and mere gossip is not always simple. Even mere gossip may be immensely amusing, but the psychographer is concerned only with that which has a bearing upon character. Thus, if my neighbor's wife falls downstairs and breaks a leg, I may be civilly sympathetic, but I shall feel no scientific interest. But if she runs away with the coachman, the psychological problem attracts my curiosity

181

at once. To take a historical instance. Mrs. Chesnut, in her invaluable *Diary*, tells a long story of a colored waiter who was convulsed by the blank baldness of Joe Johnston. This is entertaining, but it shows me nothing of Johnston's character. On the other hand, she remarks, in one brief sentence, that Johnston spent an afternoon enlarging to her and a friend on Lee's and Jackson's mistakes. Here we have a revelation.

Still, the border line between psychography and gossip is easy to cross, especially when the psychographer is unkindly. Indeed, the art, to have its richest usefulness, should be based upon love. Our observer of birds and insects almost always loves them with a personal tenderness. Much more, I think, will the observer of men gain by loving them. To be sure, there have been great observers who seem to have hated. But the very wisest, richest, deepest—Sophocles, Shakespeare, Cervantes—have always loved; sometimes laughed a little, teased a little, mocked a little, but loved always. Humanity has been to them a strange thing, a pitiable thing, sometimes a deplorable thing; but even in its lowest vice and degradation, as in its height and grandeur, lovable, because they themselves were human.

It is in this point of love that Sainte-Beuve is weakest. He prided himself on understanding everything (le père Beuve avec son touchant désir de tout comprendre) and I think a little on loving nothing. Therefore his very subtlest work is sometimes bitter, and bitterness is no help to psychography or to anything else.

It is an advantage to have a subject like Lee that one cannot help loving. I say, cannot help. The language of some of his adorers tends at first to breed a feeling contrary to love. Persist and make your way through this and you will find a human being as lovable as any that ever lived. At least I have. I have loved him, and I may say that his influence upon my own life, though I came to him late, has been as deep and as inspiring as any I have ever known. If I convey but a little of that influence to others who will feel it as I have, I shall be more than satisfied.

TITLES OF BOOKS MOST FREQUENTLY CITED, SHOWING ABBREVIATIONS USED

Battles and Leaders of the Civil War.	*Battles and Leaders.*
Cooke, John Esten *Life Of General Robert E. Lee.*	Cooke.
Dabney, R.L., *Life And Campaigns Of General T.J. Jackson.*	Dabney.
Davis, Jefferson, *Rise And Fall Of The Confederate Government.*	*Rise and Fall.*
Davis, Varina Howell, *Jefferson Davis.*	Mrs. Davis.
Henderson, G.F.R., *Stonewall Jackson And The American Civil War.*	Henderson.
Jackson, Mary A., *Life And Letters Of General T.J. Jackson.*	Mrs. Jackson.
Jones, J.B., *A Rebel War Clerk's Diary.*	Jones, *Diary.*
Jones, J.W., *Life And Letters Of General Robert E. Lee.*	Jones, *Life.*
Jones, J.W., *Personal Reminiscences, Anecdotes, And Letters Of General Robert E. Lee.*	Jones, *Rem.*
Lee, Fitzhugh, *General Lee.*	F. Lee.
Lee, R.E., *Recollections And Letters Of General Robert E. Lee.*	R.E.L.
Long, A.L., *Memoirs Of Robert E. Lee.*	Long.
Mason, E.V., *Popular Life Of General Robert E. Lee.*	Mason.
McCabe, J.D., *Life And Campaigns Of General Robert E. Lee.*	McCabe.
Military Historical Society Of Massachusetts, *Publications.*	*M.H.S. of M.*

Official Records Of The Union And Confederate Armies (Quoted By Serial Nos. Throughout). — O.R.

Pollard, E.A., *Life Of Jefferson Davis.* — Pollard,*Davis.*

Pollard, E.A., *The Lost Cause.* — Pollard, *L.C.*

Rhodes, J.F., *A History Of The United States, From The Compromise Of 1850.* — Rhodes, *U.S.*

Southern Historical Society Papers. — S.H.S.P.

White, H.A., *Robert E. Lee And The Southern Confederacy.* — White.

Wood, W.B., and Edmunds, J.E., *History Of The Civil War In The United States.* — Wood and Edmunds.

NOTES

CHAPTER I

1. For an exhaustive discussion of the Lee genealogy, see *Lee of Virginia*, by Edmund Lee. (Philadelphia, 1895.)

2. *S.H.S.P.*, vol. IX, p. 198.

3. F. Lee, p. 2. In his memoir of his father, however, the general goes quite extensively into the English affiliations.

4. Jones, *Life*, p. 33.

5. To Mrs. Lee, in F. Lee, p. 22.

6. *Works* (ed. Ford), vol. X, p. 222.

7. Jones, *Life*, p. 154.

8. Long, p. 23.

9. Charles Lee, quoted in Lee's memoir of his father, p. 29.

10. Long, p. 19.

11. Jones, *Rem.*, p. 118.

12. G. M. Sorrel, *Recollections of a Confederate Staff Officer*, p. 74.

13. *Manassas to Appomattox*, p. 287.

14. Mason, p. 24.

15. To Cabell, November, 1820, *Works* (ed. Ford), vol. X, p. 165.

16. Writer in *Putnam's Monthly*, quoted in Olmsted, *Journey to the Seaboard Slave States*, p. 245.

17. *Ibid.*

18. Jones, *Life*, p. 24.

19. Jones, *Life*, p. 27.

20. John Quincy Adams, *Diary*, vol. VII, p. 209.

21. Thomas Nelson Page, *The Old South*, p. 184.

22. *Journey to the Seaboard Slave States*, p. 247.

23. Long, p. 33.

24. Jones, *Rem.*, p. 291.

25. Jones, *Rem.*, p. 290.

26. Testimony at Pillow Inquiry, Senate Doc., 30th Congress, First Session, vol. VIII, p. 73.

27. Report in Senate Doc. as above, vol. I, p. 332.

28. Report in Senate Doc. as above, vol. I, p. 306.

29. Report in Senate Doc. as above, vol. I, p. 315.

30. Long, p. 61.

31. *Ibid.*

32. Colonel Preston, direct from Scott, in "Lee Memorial Address," printed in Mason, p. 382. I find in F. Grasset's *La Guerre de la 'Sécession*, vol. II, p. 59, a saying attributed to Scott, which I have not been able to trace to an American source, but which, if not a prophecy manufactured after the event, has a good deal of interest: "*Défiez-vous de Lee quand il avance et de Johnston lorsqu'il recule, car le diable lui-même se ferait battre, s'il les attaquait dans ces conditions.*"

33. Senate Doc. as above, vol. I, p. 337.

34. Senate Doc. as above, vol. I, p. 344.

35. Senate Doc. as above, vol. I, p. 404.

36. Jones, *Life*, p. 32.

37. Jones, *Life*, p. 54.

38. Jones, *Life*, p. 54.

39. Jones, *Life*, p. 56.

40. Jones, *Life*, p. 57.

41. Mrs. Davis, vol. I, p. 413.

42. White, p. 47.

43. White, p. 48.

44. C.C. Chesney, *A Military View of the Recent Campaigns in Virginia and Maryland*, p. 50.

45. R.E.L., p. 13.

46. Jones, *Life*, p. 84.

47. Jones, *Life*, p. 92.

48. Jones, *Life*, p. 113.

49. Mason, p. 58.

50. Jones, *Life*, p. 116.

51. Jones, *Life*, p. 105.

52. Reports of Committees, 36th Congress, First Session, no. 278, p. 42.

53. R.E.L., p. 19.

54. Ed. Keyes, *Fifty Years' Observation of Men and Events*, p. 204.

55. Colonel Venable, in *Battles and Leaders*, vol. IV, p. 242.

56. White, p. 31.

57. White, p. 32.

58. Mason, p. 381.

59. Jones, *Life*, p. 71.

60. J.S. Wise, *The End of an Era*, p. 342.

61. Jones, *Life*, p. 135.

CHAPTER II

1. J.K. Hosmer, *The Appeal to Arms*, p. 29.

2. Long, p. 27.

3. Long, p. 29.

4. *U.S.*, vol. III, p. 413.

5. Jones, *Life*, p. 437.

6. Mrs. Pickett, in *Lippincott's Magazine*, vol. 79, p. 52.

7. Jones, *Life*, p. 118.

8. F. Lee, p. 84.

9. To Reverdy Johnson, F. Lee, p. 85.

10. *Ibid.*

11. Long, p. 92.

12. Long, p. 94.

13. E. Townsend, *Anecdotes of the Civil War*, p. 29.

14. F. Lee, p. 94.

15. Jones, *Life*, p. 162.

16. Senator Culberson calls my attention to another error in Townsend's narrative. He says Lee was "on leave" at Arlington. Investigation of the War Office records does not bear out this statement, but shows rather that he was awaiting orders.

17. F. Lee, p.88.

18. Grandson of Rawle to Deering, in J.R. Deering, *Lee and his Cause*, p. 37.

19. See General J.W. Latta's pamphlet, *Was Secession taught at West Point?* Also the *Century Magazine* for August, 1909.

20. William Rawle, *A View of the Constitution of the United States of America*, 1825, p. 289.

21. *Works*, Sparks, vol. IX, p. 119.

22. Jones, *Life*, p. 121.

23. *Reports of House Committees*, 38th Congress, vol. II. pt. II. p. 136.

24. Jones, *Life*, p. 130.

25. Jones, *Life*, p. 125.

26. Longstreet, *From Manassas to Appomattox*, p. 29.

27. Page 18.

28. *Outlook*, vol. 74, p. 888.

29. Letter in Jones, *Rem.*, p. 218.

30. *O.R.*, vol. 96, p. 1230.

31. John B. Gordon, *Reminiscences of the Civil War*, p. 434.

32. See Rhodes, *U.S.*, vol. V, p. 71.

33. To Gilman, December, 1860, in Rhodes, *U.S.*, vol. III, p. 161.

34. R.E.L., p. 168.

35. R.E.L., p. 306.

36. *O.R.*, vol. 129, p. 1012.

37. Jones, *Life*, p. 83.

38. *New York Herald* reporter, quoted in Avary, *Dixie After the War*, p. 71.

39. *Mixed Essays* (New York, 1883), "Falkland," p. 170.

40. Burke's *Works* (Bohn ed.), vol. I, p. 467.

41. Jones, *Life*, p. 132.

42. *O.R.*, vol. 6, p. 43.

43. *O.R.*, vol. 31, p. 1086.

44. Long, p. 485.

45. *O.R.*, vol. 5, p. 192.

46. *O.R.*, vol. 5, p. 785.

47. *O.R.*, vol. 31, p. 556.

48. Jones, *Life*, p. 376.

49. R.E.L., p. 225.

50. Quoted verbally in *S.H.S.P.*, vol. XI, p. 360.

51. Jones, *Life*, p. 436.

52. Quoted in *S.H.S.P.*, vol. XI, p. 360.

53. Jones, *Life*, p. 140.

CHAPTER III

1. J.J. Craven, *The Prison Life of Jefferson Davis*, p. 283.

2. *Davis Memorial Volume*, p. 387.

3. Mrs. Davis, vol. I, p. 580.

4. *S.H.S.P.*, vol. XXIV, p. 372.

5. Mrs. Davis, in P. Butler's *Judah P. Benjamin*, p. 332.

6. Mrs. Davis, vol. I, p. 356.

7. Mrs. Davis, vol. II, p. 163.

8. Mrs. Davis, vol. II, p. 163.

9. Pollard, *Davis*, p. 126; also Mrs. J. Chesnut, *A Diary from Dixie*, p. 318.

10. Pollard, *Davis*, p. 222.

11. Mrs. Davis, vol. II, p. 155.

12. Mrs. Davis, vol. I, p. 178.

13. Mrs. Davis, vol. I, p. 78.

14. Quoted in Rhodes, *U.S.*, vol. III, p. 459.
15. Jones, *Diary*, vol. II. p. 205.
16. *Davis Memorial Volume*, p. 41.
17. Pollard, *Davis*, p. 231.
18. *O.R.*, vol. 40, p. 726.
19. *O.R.*, vol. 28, p. 600.
20. *O.R.*, vol. 31, p. 1029.
21. *Ibid.*
22. *O.R.*, vol. 40, p. 810.
23. *Story of the Civil War*, vol. I, p. 131.
24. *Battles and Leaders*, vol. III, p. 711.
25. *O.R.*, vol. 26, p. 1083.
26. Mrs. Davis, vol. II, p. 393.
27. Cecil Battine, *The Crisis of the Confederacy*, p. 110.
28. Henderson, vol. II, p. 601.
29. *O.R.*, vol. 108, p. 752.
30. *O.R.*, vol. 108, p. 741.
31. Meigs, in Long, p. 44.
32. *Rise and Fall*, vol. II. p. 133.
33. *O.R.*, vol. 14, p. 635.
34. *O.R.*, vol. 28, p. 619.
35. John J. Craven, *The Prison Life of Jefferson Davis*, p. 106.
36. *O.R.*, vol. 28, p. 600.
37. *O.R.*, vol. 45, p. 881.
38. Long, p. 587.
39. *O.R.*, vol. 28, p. 644.
40. *O.R.*, vol. 129, p. 247.
41. *O.R.*, vol. 96, p. 1256.
42. *O.R.*, vol. 89, p. 1213.
43. *Ibid.*
44. Jones, *Life*, p. 152.
45. John J. Craven, *The Prison Life of Jefferson Davis*, p. 322.
46. *Rise and Fall*, vol. II, p. 152.
47. *Diary*, vol. I, p. 121.
48. Mrs. Davis, vol. II, p. 320.
49. *O.R.*, vol. 28, p. 634.
50. Quoted in R.E.L., p. 53.
51. Jones, *Rem.*, p. 340.
52. R.E.L., p. 220
53. R.E.L., p. 268.
54. Long, p. 266.
55. J.B. Gordon, *Reminiscences of the Civil War*, p. 393.

56. *Examiner*, August 5, 1863.

57. Quoted in Mrs. Chesnut, *A Diary from Dixie*, p. 162.

58. *Diary*, p. 151.

59. *O.R.*, vol. 110, p. 808.

60. Quoted in Pollard, *Davis*, p. 446.

61. *Diary*, January 1, 1865.

62. A.B. Hart, *Essays on American Government*, p. 283.

63. *A Diary from Dixie*, p. 108.

64. *Diary*, vol. I, p. 189.

65. *Diary*, January 1, 1865.

66. *A Diary from Dixie*, p. 108.

67. Cf. *Southern Review*, July, 1867.

68. *New York Tribune*, April 14, 1860, in Rhodes, *U. S.*

69. Mrs. Davis, vol. I, p. 191.

70. *Davis Memorial Volume*, p. 205.

71. Mrs. Davis, vol. II. p. 163.

72. Mrs. Davis, vol. II. p. 923.

73. Pollard, *Davis*, p. 437.

74. *O.R.*, vol. 96, p. 1199.

75. R.E.L, p 287.

76. Davis, in *S.H.S.P.*, vol. 17, p. 372.

CHAPTER IV

1. Jones, *Life*, p. 135. Differently worded in R.E.L., p. 28.

2. Quoted in Jones, *Life*, p. 136.

3. C.C. Greville, *Journals of the Reign of Queen Victoria* (Am. ed.), vol. I, p. 509.

4. Saunders, in R.E.L., p. 231.

5. F. Lee, p. 408.

6. Reports of Committees, 39th Congress, vol. II, pt. II, p. 129.

7. See *O.R.*, vol. 120, pp. 1010, 1018.

8. *O.R.*, vol. 13, p. 936.

9. *O.R.*, vol. 14, p. 636.

10. Jones, *Life*, p. 292.

11. *O.R.*, vol. 60, p. 1279.

12. Jones, *Life*, p. 226.

13. Jones, *Life*, p. 331.

14. *O.R.*, vol. 40, p. 687.

15. *O.R.*, vol. 96 p. 1143.

16. G.C. Eggleston, *A Rebel's Recollections*, p. 214.

17. Jones, *Diary*, vol. I, p. 135.

18. *O.R.*, cited in J.C. Schwab, *The Confederate States of America*, p. 262.

19. *O.R.*, in Schwab, p. 92.

20. *O.R.*, vol. 129, p. 257.

21. Pollard.

22. Quoted by General Mosby, in *S.H.S.P.*, vol. XXVII, p. 317.

23. Jones, *Life*, p. 279.

24. *Correspondence de Napoléon*, vol. XVI, p. 560.

25. Jones, *Life*, p. 227.

26. *O.R.*, vol. 129, p. 1012.

27. In *Richmond Examiner*, February 16, 1865.

28. *Ibid.*

29. *Richmond Examiner,* January 5, 1865.

30. Pollard, *L.C.*, p. 655.

31. January 1, 1865.

32. Sherman, *Memoirs*, vol. II, p. 224.

33. April 21, 1887.

34. See page 24+.

35. Pollard, *L.C.*, p. 655.

36. Pollard, *L.C.*, p. 429.

37. *Ibid.*

38. Quoted in Jones, *Rem.*, p. 341.

39. *O.R.*, vol. 19, p. 523.

40. Volume XI, p. 523.

41. *Galaxy*, vol. XII, p. 628.

42. Jones, *Life*, p. 84.

43. Cited in Cooke, p. 476.

44. J. Scheibert, *Der Bürgerkrieg in den nordamerikanischen Staaten*, p. 39.

45. *O.R.*, vol. 108, p. 738.

46. Long, p. 454.

47. Towards the end of the war disaffected persons in the South began to see the prospect more clearly. The *Augusta Chronicle* for March 3, 1864 copies from the *Richmond Whig* the following statement of principles of the peace party in Georgia: "It is contended that two rival Confederacies, each with a standing army, cannot exist side by side on this continent; that constant wars will occur and one eventually absorb the other. It is contended that a sectionally consolidated South will necessitate a similarly consolidated North, and that the two armed powers, acting and reacting upon each other, will produce endless strife and bloodshed."

48. Pollard, *Davis*, p. 426.

49. Jones, *Life*, p. 121.

50. *Ibid.*

51. *O.R.*, vol. 6, p. 350.

52. Bishop Wilmer, in *Memorial Address*, printed in Jones, *Life*, p. 438.

53. *O.R.*, vol. 45, p. 880.

54. Jones, *Life*, p. 249.

55. *O.R.*, vol. 99, p. 1270.

56. *A Diary from Dixie*, p. 373.

57. R.E.L., p. 65.

58. Collyar, in *The Confederate Veteran*, vol. I, p. 324.

59. *S.H.S.P.*, vol. IV, p. 309.

60. *New York Herald* reporter in M.L. Avary, *Dixie after the War*, p. 71.

61. Quoted by Mrs. Roger A. Pryor, *Reminiscences of War and Peace*, p. 358.

62. C.F. Adams, *The Confederacy and the Transvaal.*

63. J.S. Wise, *The End of an Era*, p. 344.

64. Jones, *Life*, p. 372.

65. R.E.L., p. 163.

66. R.E.L., p. 410.

67. Jones, *Life*, p. 387.

68. E.L. Childe, *Life and Campaigns of General Lee* (trans. from French), p. 331.

CHAPTER V

1. General Palfrey, in *M.H.S. of M.*, vol. I, p. 220.

2. *O.R.*, vol. 17, p. 919

3. To Northrop, *O.R.*, vol. 60, p. 1065.

4. Marshall, in R.E.L., p. 119.

5. Quoted in F. Lee, p. 364.

6. *O.R.*, vol. 48, p. 408.

7. *O.R.*, vol. 28, p. 722.

8. Mangold, in *S.H.S.P.*, vol. II, p. 65.

9. *S.H.S.P.*, vol. XVII, p. 37.

10. *O.R.*, vol. 108, p. 994.

11. Before Committee on the Conduct of the War, quoted in Jones, *Rem.*, p. 28.

12. Long, p. 166 (from diary).

13. Scheibert, *Der Bürgerkrieg in den nordamerikanischen Staaten*, p. 42.

14. *O.R.,* vol. 2, p. 828.
15. Diary of Cobb, in *S.H.S.P.,* vol. XXVIII, p. 295.
16. *O.R.,* vol. 29, p. 722.
17. As to brutality, Lee is reported to have said to a soldier who was abusing some captured negroes: "If I ever hear of your mistreating a prisoner again, be he as black as Erebus, I will hang you to the nearest tree." Judge D.G. Tyler, *Lee Birthday Address,* 1911, p. 6. But the naked energy of this phraseology does not sound like Lee.
18. *O.R.,* vol. 49, p. 807.
19. *O.R.,*vol. 40, p. 844.
20. *O.R.,* vol. 10, p. 303.
21. G.M. Sorrel, *Recollections of a Confederate Staff Officer,* p. 279.
22. *O.R.,* vol. 89, p. 1268.
23. *O.R.,* vol. 96, p. 1276.
24. *Battles and Leaders,* vol. II, p. 666.
25. *O.R.,* vol. 40, p. 792.
26. *S.H.S.P.,* vol. II, p. 65.
27. McCabe, p. 602.
28. D.H. Maury,*Recollections of a Virginian in the Mexican, Indian, and Civil Wars,* p. 238.
29. In *Harper's Magazine,* February, 1911.
30. Jones, *Life,* p. 455.
31. *S.H.S.P.,* vol. XXIII, p. 208.
32. G.C. Eggleston, *A Rebel's Recollections,* p. 52.
33. *O.R.,* vol. 40, p. 820.
34. R. Stiles, *Four Years under Marse Robert,* p. 20.
35. Long, p. 102.
36. *O.R.,* vol. 108, p. 994.
37. *Ibid.*
38. Jones, *Rem.,* p. 185.
39. *O.R.,* vol. 2, p. 837.
40. R. Stiles, *Four Years under Marse Robert,* p. 264.
41. *O.R.,* vol. 5, p. 868.
42. G.M. Sorrel, *Recollections of a Confederate Staff Officer,* p. 88.
43. Jones, *Life,* p. 267.
44. Long, p. 229.
45. Long, p. 278.
46. Long, p. 301.
47. *O.R.,* vol. 108, p. 994.
48. Henderson, vol. I, p. 537.
49. *Battles and Leaders,* vol. IV, p. 240.
50. *Ibid.*

51. September 16.

52. Mrs. Pickett, in *Lippincott's Mazagine*, vol. LXXIX, p. 55.

53. Jones, *Rem.*, p. 162.

54. *Ibid.*

55. G.M. Sorrel. *Recollections of a Confederate Staff Officer*, p. 182.

56. Cooke, p. 368.

57. Jones, *Rem.*, p. 232.

58. McCormick, in the *Outlook*, vol. LVI, p. 684.

59. Jones, *Rem.*, p. 237.

60. *O.R.*, vol. 108, p. 994

61. Long, p. 227.

62. W. H. Taylor, *Four Years with General Lee*, p. 141.

63. *Ibid.*

64. *Confederate Veteran*, vol. VI, p. 12.

65. A.L. Fremantle, *Three Months in the Southern States*, p. 276.

66. Quoted in G.M. Sorrel, *Recollections of a Confederate Staff Officer*, p. 307.

67. E.P. Alexander, *Military Memoirs of a Confederate*, p. 154.

68. *O.R.*, vol. 6, p. 366.

69. *O.R.*, vol. 26, p. 847.

70. *O.R.*, vol. 69, p. 896.

71. Long, p. 626.

72. G.C. Eggleston, *A Rebel's Recollections*, p. 145. Mr. Allen C. Redwood writes me of similar impressions: "I cannot recollect ever having heard the men cheer General Lee. They would stand quietly and as he passed by their lines take off their hats. and stand looking at him with the greatest veneration."

73. *Examiner*, August 19, 1864.

74. Charles Marshall, quoted in R.E.L., p. 138.

75. E.P. Alexander, *Military Memoirs of a Confederate*, p. 504.

76. Napier, *A History of the Peninsula War*, vol. V, p. 250.

77. Jones, *Rem.*, p. 161.

78. *O.R.*, vol. 28, p. 597.

79. To Hood, in Jones, *Life*, p. 247.

80. Jones, *Rem.*, p. 400.

CHAPTER VI

1. Quoted in Cooke, p. 353.

2. Henderson, vol. II, p. 88.

3. Dabney, vol. I, p. 62.

4. Mrs. Jackson, p. 47.

5. Mrs. Jackson, p. 70.

6. Mrs. Jackson, p. 57.

7. E.P. Allan, *Life and Letters of M.J. Preston*, p. 83.

8. Dabney, vol. II, p. 521.

9. Dabney, vol. II, p. 522.

10. Mrs. Jackson, p. 43.

11. Cooke, p. 248.

12. Cooke, p. 355.

13. Mrs. Jackson, p. 54.

14. F. Lee, p. 142.

15. Henderson, vol. I, p. 46.

16. E.P. Allan, *Life and Letters of M.J. Preston*, p. 80.

17. Cooke, p. 275.

18. Mrs. Jackson, p. 68.

19. Mrs. Jackson, p. 63.

20. Mrs. Jackson, p. 75.

21. Mrs. Jackson, p. 69.

22. Mrs. Jackson, p. 249.

23. *O.R.*, vol. 2, 825.

24. Mrs. Jackson, p. 237.

25. Dabney, vol. II, p. 346.

26. Mrs. Jackson, p. 310.

27. McGuire, in Henderson, vol. II, p. 401.

28. Dabney, vol. II, p. 130.

29. Henderson, vol. II, p. 589.

30. To Mrs. Jackson, in Dabney, vol. I, p. 213.

31. Jones, *Life*, p. 71.

32. McGuire, in Mrs. Jackson, p. 452.

33. Jones, *Life*, p. 240.

34. Dabney, vol. II, p. 637.

35. Dabney, vol. I, p. 335.

36. Mrs. Jackson, p. 313.

37. Dabney, in Henderson, vol. II, p. 95.

38. Cooke, p. 212.

39. Jackson's constant devotion to the study of everything connected with Napoleon gives a certain plausibility to Grasset's assertion (*Guerre de la Sécession*, vol. II, p. 95) that this saying was taken from one of *Kléber's* in regard to the great emperor.

40. R.E.L., p. 94.

41. Mrs. Jackson, p. 394.

42. Lee to Davis, *O.R.*, vol. 27, p. 643.

43. G.C. Eggleston, *A Rebel's Recollections*, p. 153.

44. *O.R.*, vol. 17, p. 910.

45. Jones, *Life*, p. 237.

46. Lawley, in Henderson, vol. II, p. 58.

47. R.E.L., p. 94.

48. Dabney, vol. II, p. 507.

49. Cooke, p. 440.

50. *O.R.*, vol. 18, p. 926.

51. *O.R.*, vol. 18, p. 878.

52. *O.R.*, vol. 18, p. 919.

53. Henderson, vol. II, p. 142.

54. *O.R.*, vol. 31, p. 1044.

55. *O.R.*, vol. 2, p. 814.

56. D.H. Hill, in *Battles and Leaders*, vol. II, p. 390.

57. *Ibid.*

58. *O.R.*, vol. 40, p. 647.

59. Mrs. Jackson, p. 234.

60. Henderson, vol. I, p. 197.

61. Quoted in Mrs. Jackson, p. 204.

62. Cooke, p. 459.

63. McGuire, in Henderson, vol. II, p. 71.

64. F. Lee, p. 142.

65. Dabney, letter in Henderson, vol. II, p. 88.

66. Cooke, p. 205 (not verbal).

67. Henderson, vol. II, p. 453.

68. Cooke, p. 387.

69. E.P. Alexander, *Memoirs of a Confederate*, p. 181.

70. *O.R.*, vol. 28, p. 733.

71. D.H. Maury, *Recollections of a Virginian*, p. 72.

72. *Ante*, p. 140.

73. *O.R.*, vol. 31, p. 1033.

74. Jones, *Life*, p. 232.

75. H. von Borcke, *Memoirs of the Confederate War for Independence*, vol. II, p. 260.

76. Henderson, vol. II, p. 573.

77. Henderson, vol. II, p. 582.

78. Jones, *Life*, p. 236.

79. Mrs. Jackson, p. 71.

CHAPTER VII

1. Jones, *Life*, p. 242.
2. J. Scheibert, *Der Bürgerkrieg in den nordamerikanischen Staaten*, p. 39.
3. R.E.L., p. 386.
4. Long, p. 240.
5. Wood and Edmunds, p. 137.
6. In *Battles and Leaders*, vol. II. p. 366.
7. Jones, *Life*, p. 53.
8. R.E.L., p. 89.
9. Jones, *Life*, p. 53.
10. Jones, *Life*, p. 208.
11. Scheibert, *Der Bürgerkrieg in den nordamerikanischen Staaten*, p. 39.
12. *S.H.S.P.*, vol. XVII, p. 242.
13. H. von Borcke, *Memoirs of the Confederate War for Independence*, vol. II, p. 197.
14. Jones, *Rem.*, p. 164.
15. J.B. Gordon, *Reminiscences of the Civil War*, p. 430.
16. Gracie's son, in *Confederate Veteran*, vol. V, p. 432.
17. Jones, *Rem.*, p. 182.
18. J. B. Gordon, *Reminiscences of the Civil War*, p. 278, and many other authorities.
19. J. Longstreet, *From Manassas to Appomattox*, p. 384.
20. *S.H.S.P.*, vol. V, p. 92.
21. In Longstreet, *From Manassas to Appomattox*, p. 357.
22. *Harper's*, February, 1911.
23. See *M.H.S. of M.*, vol. VI, p. 471.
24. Henderson, vol. II. p. 323.
25. A.L. Fremantle, *Three Months in the Southern States*, p. 254.
26. E.P. Alexander, *Memoirs of a Confederate*, p. 356.
27. Fremantle, *Three Months in the Southern States*, p. 268.
28. *Ibid.*
29. *Ibid.*
30. In *Galaxy*, vol. XI, p. 509.
31. J.B. Gordon, *Reminiscences of the Civil War*, p. 279.
32. *S.H.S.P.*, vol. XXXII, p. 201.
33. *S.H.S.P.*, vol. VIII, p. 565,
34. Thomas Nelson Page, *Robert E. Lee the Southerner*, p. 206.
35. *Memorial Address*, in Mason, p. 361.
36. G. C. Eggleston, *A Rebel's Recollections*, p. 147.

37. Jones, *Life*, p. 380.

38. Colonel Venable, *Memorial Address*, in Jones, *Life*, p. 369.

39. *Ibid.*

40. General Horace Porter, in *Battles and Leaders*, vol. IV, p. 743.

CHAPTER VIII

1. *Letters* (1894 edition), vol. II, p. 200.

2. J.C. Ropes, *The Story of the Civil War*, vol. II. p. 158.

3. Jones, *Rem.*, p. 258.

4. Quoted in Jones, *Rem.*, p. 223.

5. Quoted in Jones, *Rem.*, p. 50.

6. *Life*, p. 381.

7. E.A. Pollard, *A Southern History of the War*, vol. I, p. 168.

8. E.A. Pollard, *A Southern History of the War*, vol. I, p. 354.

9. H.D. Longstreet, *Lee and Longstreet at High Tide*, p. 83.

10. *Battles and Leaders*, vol. III, p. 350.

11. *S.H.S.P.*, vol. V, p. 61.

12. *S.H.S.P.*, vol. V, p. 72.

13. *Battles and Leaders*, vol. III, p. 349.

14. Jones, *Rem.*, p. 266.

15. Adam Badeau, *Military History of U.S. Grant*, vol. II, p. 524.

16. Badeau, vol. II. p. 166.

17. Badeau, vol. II. p. 220.

18. Badeau, vol. II, p. 227.

19. Badeau, vol. II, p. 132.

20. Colonel T. Lyman, in *M.H.S. of M.*, vol. III, p. 171.

21. J.R. Young, *Around the World with General Grant*, vol. II, p. 459.

22. J.G. Wilson, *General Grant*, p. 367.

23. Criticism, taking, in a more or less modified form, the view of
Badeau and Grant, is, of course, still often met with. Colonel T.L.
Livermore's clear and forcible discussions in the volumes of the
Military Historical Society of Massachusetts are perhaps the best
examples of it. Colonel Livermore, in summing up the Appomattox
Campaign, says: "No fault appears in Grant's generalship. To Lee's
failure to make timely retreat from Petersburg and Richmond, and
perhaps his delay in ordering supplies to Amelia Court House, must
be attributed his failure to reach the Roanoke." (Vol. VI, p. 501.) It
may be worthwhile to refer here to the very remarkable anecdote told
by the Reverend Dr. McKim (*A Soldier's Recollections*, p. 258) of
Grant's having discovered in a waste-basket a sketch of Lee's plan of

retreat from Petersburg. The story seems well authenticated, but is rather difficult to accept.

24. *O.R.*, vol. 60, p. 1185.
25. R.E.L., p. 416.
26. Jones, *Life*, p. 152.
27. Quoted in Sainte-Beuve, *Nouveaux Lundis*, vol. XIII, p. 96.
28. A. Doubleday, *Chancellorsville and Gettysburg*, p. 158.
29. Page 112.
30. J.C. Ropes, *The Army under Pope*, p. 111.
31. J.C. Ropes, *The Story of the Civil War*, vol. II p. 468.
32. Colonel W.R. Livermore, *Gettysburg,*Mass. Hist. Soc. Proceedings, 1910, p. 232.
33. J.C. Ropes, *The Story of the Civil War*, vol. II, p. 352.
34. *Battles and Leaders*, vol. III, p. 293.
35. J.C. Ropes, *The Story of the Civil War*, vol. II. p. 454.
36. T.A. Dodge, *A Bird's-Eye View of Our Civil War*, p. 218.
37. *Battles and Leaders*, vol. IV, p. 162.
38. W. R. Livermore, *Lee's Conduct of the Wilderness Campaign*, Am. Hist. Assoc. Papers, 1910, p. 236.
39. *Wilderness Campaign*, p. 233.
40. *Wilderness Campaign*, p. 243.
41. R.M. Bache, *Life of Meade*, p. 549.
42. Mass. Hist. Soc. Proceed., 1910, p. 230.
43. J.C. Ropes, *The Army Under Pope*, p. 35.
44. T. Roosevelt, *Gouverneur Morris*, p. 52.
45. T. Roosevelt, *Thomas H. Benton*, p. 38.
46. Field Marshal Viscount Wolseley, *Story of a Soldier's Life*, vol. I, p. 135.
47. Cecil Battine, *The Crisis of the Confederacy*, p. 19.
48. Battine, p. 322.
49. Battine, p. 207.
50. Wood and Edmunds, p. 242.
51. G.F.R. Henderson, *The Science of War*, p. 305.
52. Henderson, *Science of War*, p. 330.
53. Henderson, *Jackson*, vol. II, p. 231.
54. *The Wilderness Campaign*, p. 124.
55. Cecil Battine, *The Crisis of the Confederacy*, p. 380.
56. G.F.R. Henderson, *The Science of War*, p. 314.
57. Cecil Battine, *The Crisis of the Confederacy*, p. 114.
58. American Historical Association, *Annual Report*, 1910, p. 246.
59. H.E. Shepherd, *Life of R.E. Lee*, p. 117.
60. E.P. Alexander, *Military Memoirs of a Confederate*, p. 110.

61. *O.R.*, vol. 14, p. 590.
62. *O.R.*, vol. 45, p. 868.
63. W. Allan, *The Army of Northern Virginia in 1862*, p. 200.
64. *Correspondance de Napoléon*, vol. XVIII, p. 218.
65. G.F.R. Henderson, *The Science of War*, p. 4. It is interesting to compare with this remark of Henderson, Scheibert's assertion that Lee in some points anticipated the later tactics of the Prussian army.
66. F. Lee, quoted by Colonel W.R. Livermore, *Wilderness Campaign*, p. 239.
67. Sir E. B. Hamley, *The Operations of War*, p. 95.
68. Field Marshal Viscount Wolseley, *The Decline and Fall of Napoleon*, p. 30.
69. General W.F. Smith in *M.H.S. of M.*, vol. III, p. 115.
70. Vol. I, p. 294.
71. *Rise of Wellington*, p. 186.

CHAPTER IX

1. *Southern Magazine*, vol. XV, p. 604.
2. Quoted in *Nation*, vol. XLIV, p. 322.
3. *Personal Memoirs*, vol. II, p. 184.
4. *A Diary from Dixie*, p. 94.
5. Long, p. 433.
6. *Ibid.*
7. Mrs. Davis, vol. II, p. 207.
8. Cooke, p. 206.
9. G.M. Sorrel, *Recollections of a Confederate Staff Officer*, p. 74.
10. Jones, *Life*, p. 296.
11. *Charleston Courier*, March 10, 1864.
12. Mrs. Guild, in *Confederate Veteran*, vol. VI, p. 12.
13. W.P. Johnston, in R.E.L., p. 315.
14. Long, p. 37.
15. Jones, *Life*, p. 205.
16. R.E.L., p. 201.
17. R.E.L., p. 395.
18. *A Diary from Dixie*, p. 94.
19. R.E.L., p. 380.
20. Collyar, in *Confederate Veteran*, vol. I, p. 265.
21. Long, p. 35.
22. W.P. Johnston, in R.E.L., p. 315.
23. Daves, in *S.H.S.P.*, vol. XXVI, p. 119. I have already quoted in different connections remarks similar to this. The authenticity of

some of them has been doubted and perhaps with reason. But there are so many instances that Lee's rather peculiar habit of addressing himself to minor subordinates cannot be questioned. Judge Garnett (*S.H.S.P.*, vol. XXVIII, p. 110) suggests an interesting explanation. "And here for the first time I experienced what I afterwards learned was almost a habit with General Lee–to think aloud. He murmured to himself as if addressing me; 'Well, Captain, what shall we do?' To which inquiry I am pleased to say I had sense enough to make no reply, and, indeed, to appear as if I had not heard it." Again Judge Garnett says that when a message was brought to the general during the Wilderness fighting and another at Five Forks, "I heard his deep bass voice ask, 'Well, Captain, what shall we do?'" Absence of mind may easily have played a part here; but I think it quite consonant with all we know of Lee that he should ask a subordinate's opinion and should even take a genuine interest in it.

24. Hunt, in Long, p. 70.
25. *Battles and Leaders*, vol. I, p. 226.
26. *Battles and Leaders*, vol. I, p. 259.
27. Eveleth, in Long, p. 35.
28. In Jones, *Life*, p. 36.
29. Mason, p. 24.
30. Wise, quoted in *Battles and Leaders*, vol. II. p. 276.
31. Jones, *Life*, p. 287.
32. Jones. *Life*, p. 102.
33. Jones, *Rem.*, p. 213.
34. Mason, p. 22.
35. Mason, p. 23.
36. *Ibid.*
37. F. Lee, p. 66.
38. Jones, *Life*, p. 42.
39. R.E.L., p. 9.
40. Jones, *Life*, p. 448.
41. Jones, *Life*, p. 94.
42. Jones, *Life*, p. 34.
43. Jones, *Life*, p. 154.
44. R.E.L., p. 15.
45. Jones, *Life*, p. 286.
46. Jones, *Life*, p. 91.
47. Jones, *Life*, p. 90.
48. R.E.L., p. 342.
49. R.E.L., p. 324.
50. Jones, *Life*, p. 99.

51. Jones, *Life*, p. 300.
52. R.E.L, p. 303.
53. R.E.L, p. 140.
54. R.E.L., p. 343.
55. R.E.L., p. 374.
56. R.E.L., p. 9.
57. R.E.L., p. 405.
58. R.E.L., p. 11.
59. Jones, *Life*, p. 122.
60. R.E.L., p. 325.
61. Jones, *Life*, p. 35.
62. Jones, *Life*, p. 84.
63. It seems to me that I catch a wistful sense of the element of character I am trying to suggest, without emphasizing it too much, in these words from an unpublished letter of Mrs. Lee: "I hope the Gen'l will be able to take a little rest. I think he rather prefers lonely rides among the mountains on his favourite grey."
64. R.E.L., p. 88.
65. R.E.L., p. 325.
66. R.E.L., p. 266.
67. R.E.L., p. 6.
68. Collyar, in *Confederate Veteran*, vol. I, p. 265.
69. R.E.L., p. 193.
70. R.E.L., p. 324.
71. Jones, *Life*, p. 110.

CHAPTER X

1. Jones, *Rem.*, p. 214.
2. Jones, *Life*, p. 117.
3. H. Lee, *Memoirs of the War in the Southern Department of the United States*, new edition with a biography of the author by Robert E. Lee, p. 50.
4. *O.R.*, vol.60, p. 117.
5. Professor Joynes, in *S.H.S.P.*, vol. XXVIII, p. 246.
6. Judge D. Gardner Tyler, in *Address* at William and Mary College, p. 10.
7. R.E.L., p. 248.
8. Jones, *Life*, p. 35.
9. R. E. L., p. 39.
10. *Battles and Leaders*, vol. IV, p. 240.
11. *Ibid.*

12. W.H. Taylor, *Four Years with General Lee*, p. 16.
13. McCormick, in *Outlook*, vol. LVI, p. 586.
14. Jones, *Life*, p. 156.
15. Collyar, in *Confederate Veteran*, vol. I, p. 265.
16. W.H. Taylor, *Four Years with General Lee*, p. 76.
17. R.E.L., p. 263.
18. R.E.L., p. 317.
19. *Ibid.*
20. Old Teacher, in Long, p. 28.
21. R.E.L., p. 289.
22. *O. R.*, vol. 117, p. 843.
23. Jones, *Life*, p. 307.
24. D. Maury, *Recollections of a Virginian*, p. 239.
25. Adam Badeau, *Military History of U.S. Grant*, vol. III, p. 615.
26. *History of the United States* (ed. 1876), vol. V, p. 389.
27. Jones, *Rem.*, p. 239.
28. Jones, *Rem.*, p. 288.
29. *Essays on Great Writers*, p. 343.
30. Jones, *Life*, p. 444.
31. Professor Humphreys, in E.S. Joynes, *Lee the College President*, p. 23.
32. Jones, *Life*, p. 57.
33. Jones, *Life*, p. 81.
34. Jones, *Rem.*, p. 168.
35. *S.H.S.P.*, vol. XXV, p. 179.
36. *O.R.*, vol. 108, p. 1076.
37. R.E.L., p. 37.
38. Jones, *Life*, p. 150.
39. Jones, *Life*, p. 423.
40. J.W. Jones, *Christ in the Camp*, p. 79.
41. In Long, p. 67.
42. R.E.L., p. 317.
43. Pendleton, in *Southern Magazine*, vol. XV, p. 605.
44. J.W. Jones, *Christ in the Camp*, p. 59.
45. *Christ in the Camp*, p. 60.
46. *Christ in the Camp*, p. 79.
47. B.H. Hill, in Jones, *Rem.*, p. 283.
48. Jones, *Life*, p. 144.
49. Jones, *Christ in the Camp*, p. 50.
50. Jones, *Life*, p. 468.
51. *Ibid.*
52. Jones, *Rem.*, p. 196.

53. *Ibid.*

54. *Ibid.*

55. J. W. Jones, *Christ in the Camp*, p. 66.

56. Jones, *Rem.*, p. 323.

57. *O.R.*, vol. 60, p. 1150.

58. Jones, *Christ in the Camp*, p. 79.

59. Among the innumerable Lincoln anecdotes is this one told by General James F. Rusling, in his *Men and Things I saw in the Civil War Days* (p. 15). Lincoln said to him: "The fact is, in the very pinch of the campaign there, I went into my room one day and got down on my knees, and prayed Almighty God for victory at Gettysburg. I told Him that this was His country, and the war was His war, but that we really couldn't stand another Fredericksburg or Chancellorsville. And then and there I made a solemn vow with my Maker that if He would stand by you boys at Gettysburg, I would stand by Him."

60. R.E.L., p. 45.

61. R.E.L., p. 108.

62. J.W. Jones, *Christ in the Camp*, p. 60.

63. Jones, *Christ in the Camp*, p. 52.

CHAPTER XI

1. R.E.L., p. 170.

2. Collyar, in *Confederate Veteran*, vol. I, p. 263.

3. Jones, *Rem.*, p. 205.

4. Jones, *Rem.*, p. 273.

5. Captain Ranson, in *Harper's Magazine*, February, 1911.

6. Quoted in Cooke, p. 476.

7. Jones, *Rem.*, p. 274.

8. Jones, *Life*, p. 396.

9. Jones, *Rem.*, p. 323.

10. R.E.L., p. 289.

11. Jones, *Rem.*, p. 321.

12. R.E.L., p. 276.

13. John W. Daniel, in *S.H.S.P.*, vol. XI, p. 363.

14. Jones, *Life*, p. 454.

15. Long, p. 233. Professor White (quoted in *Bright Skies and Dark Shadows*, by H.M. Field, p. 304) questions an anecdote similar to this, on account of the emphatic gesture, so unlike Lee. Professor White may be correct, but the independent report of two observers seems to deserve some credit.

16. R.E.L., p. 334.

17. Jones, *Rem.*, p. 221.
18. R.E.L., p. 351.
19. R.E.L., p. 261.
20. R.E.L., p. 348.
21. R.E.L., p. 389.
22. R.E.L., p. 367.
23. R.E.L., p. 204.
24. R.E.L., p. 386.
25. Jones, *Life*, p. 445.
26. Jones, *Life*, p. 389.
27. Jones, *Life*, p. 445.
28. R.E.L., p. 375.
29. Jones, *Life*, p. 409.
30. Jones, *Life*, p. 406.
31. R.E.L., p. 335.
32. To Ewell, in Jones, *Life*, p. 430.
33. Jones, *Life*, p. 422.
34. Professor E.S. Joynes, *Lee the College President*, p. 25.
35. Kindly communicated to me by Mr. J.L. Campbell, Secretary of Washington and Lee University.
36. Professor Joynes, pp. 27, 28.
37. Page 19.
38. R.E.L., p. 316.
39. *Ibid.*
40. Jones, *Life*, p. 412.
41. Professor Joynes, p. 33.
42. *Ibid.*
43. *Ibid.*
44. Professor Joynes, p. 23.
45. Collyar, in *Confederate Veteran*, vol. I, p. 265.
46. Jones, *Life*, p. 422.
47. Jones, *Rem.*, p. 286.
48. Jones, *Life*, p. 411.
49. Professor Joynes, *Lee the College President*, p. 35.
50. Thomas Nelson Page, *Robert E. Lee, the Southerner*, p. 276.
51. R.E.L., p. 331.
52. Jones, *Life*, p. 412.
53. R.E.L., p. 296.
54. Jones, *Life*, p. 411.
55. Professor Joynes, p. 35.
56. *O.R.*, vol. 121, p. 536.
57. M.L. Avary, *Dixie After the War*, p. 71.

58. R.E.L., p. 189.

59. Thomas Nelson Page, *Robert E. Lee, the Southerner*, p. 271.

APPENDIX

1. *Portraits Littéraires*, vol. III, p. 546.

2. Sainte-Beuve gives no authority for this quotation from Macaulay and I have not been able to trace it exactly. Mr. Norris E. Pierson and other correspondents have pointed out to me passages somewhat similar in the essay on "History." "Those are the best pictures and the best histories which exhibit such parts of the truth as most nearly produce the effect of the whole" (paragraph 16); and again, "Some events must be represented on a large scale, others diminished; the great majority will be lost in the dimness of the horizon; and a general idea of the joint effect will be given by a few slight touches" (paragraph 17). But Sainte-Beuve appears to be quoting literally, and if he is paraphrasing these passages in form, he really betrays them in sense. See Sainte-Beuve, *Premier Lundis*, vol. III, p. 163.

3. *Nouveaux Lundis*, vol. XIII, p. 78.

4. Boswell, vol. I, p. 449 (American ed. 1807).

5. *History of England* (Harper's ed., 1853), vol. I, p. 67.

6. *Mémoires* (éd. Hachette, 1884), vol. III, p. 326.

7. *The History of the Rebellion* (American ed., 1827), vol. I, p. 114.

8. *Causeries du Lundi*, vol. IX, p. 229.

9. Volume IV, p. 25.

INDEX

Adams, C. F., 68; on Lee's decision to leave the Union, 32.

Alexander, General E.P, on Lee's surrender, 83; concrete instance of Lee's personal influence given by, 84; his description of Lee at Gettysburg, 104; on Lee after Chancellorsville, 108; his estimate of Lee's generalship, 115; his account of General Ives's estimate of Lee before the war, 124.

Allan, William, his estimate of Lee's generalship, 115.

Anderson, Charles, on Lee's manner in society, 129.

Anderson, General R.H., on Lee at Gettysburg, 107.

Antietam, Lee at, 104, 106; Lee on the Potomac after the battle of, 107, 108.

Army, Lee's, devoted to its commander, 71; treated as a human body, for, 72; discipline in, 72-76; the question of promotion in, 76-78.

Arnold, Matthew, quoted, 29, 35; his essay on Falkland, a model of psychography, 173; on Macaulay, 174.

Ashby, General Turner, 97.

Bache, R.M., his *Life of Meade* quoted in commendation of Lee, 120-121.

Badeau, General Adam, 148; his estimate of Lee's generalship, 117; his charge of duplicity against Lee, 149.

Bancroft, George, on Washington's power of secrecy, 148.

Battine, Captain Cecil, on the relation of Lee and Davis, 43; criticises Lee, 121-122; on the Wilderness campaign, 122; his estimate of Lee's character, 123.

Battle, the commander's place in, 103; Lee's conception of his duty and his place in, 103-104; Lee's courage and coolness in, 105-108. *See* Antietam, Gettysburg, etc.

Beauregard, General P.G.T., indorsement by Davis on letter of, 42; letter of Lee to, quoted, 133.

Benjamin, Secretary, clash between Jackson and, 95.

Berkeley, Sir William, governor of Virginia, undemocratic views of, 15.

Blair, Francis P., offers Lee the command of the United States Army, 27.

Bledsoe, Dr. A.T., letter of Lee to, 99-100.

Boissier, Gaston, his portrait of Cicero, 175.

Bragg, General Braxton, 49-50, 57.

Breckinridge, General John C., on Jefferson Davis, 40.

Brown, John, Lee's connection with the affair of, 22-23, 26.

Buena Vista, Lee at, 18.

Bull Run, 98, 119, 122, 133.

Burke, Edmund, quoted, 35.

Cæsar, Julius, 23, 175.

Campbell, J.L., Secretary of Washington and Lee University, 205.

Cavour, Count Camillo di, 180.

Chancellorsville, 46, 108; the responsibility for, as between Lee and Jackson, 98-100; Lee at, 105, 107, 108.

Charleston Harbor, 36.

Chesney, Colonel C. C., his testimony to Lee's efficiency as superintendent of the West Point Academy, 21.

Chesnut, Mrs. J., quoted, 49, 50, 67, 130, 132, 133, 140; on Lee's manner, 129; cited, 182.

Chesterfield, Lord, his theory that attention is the most exquisite element of courtesy, 81.

Clarendon, Earl of, 173, 174, 179.

Collyar, J.B., on Lee's manner, 132; on Lee's horse, Traveler, 142; on Lee's sadness after the war, 159.

Confederate Congress, criticised by Lee, 59; votes to allow slaves to serve as soldiers, 59-60.

Confederate Government, Lee's attitude of non-interference with, 55, 61-69; its possible future, had it been victorious, 191.

Cooke, John Esten, 175; on Lee's memory, 81; on Jackson's love of action, 89.

Craven, John J., 40, 46.

Culberson, Senator, 187.

Custis, Miss, marries Lee, 16. *See* Lee, Mrs. Robert E.

Dabney, R.L., on Jackson, 88, 95.

Davis, Jefferson, and Lee, the most prominent figures of the Confederacy, 39; material for the study of his character, 39; his *The Rise and Fall of the Confederate Government* unsatisfactory, 39; his oratory, 39-40; his character, 40-41; his relations to the officers of the Confederate Army, 41-43; his self-confidence, 41, 43; his confidence and affection retained by Lee, 42, 47-48; Lee's solicitude for, and deference to, 42-45, 47; conflicts of opinion between Lee and, 45-47; snubs Lee, 47; esteemed and admired by Lee, 48, 49; change of feeling toward, as the war progressed, 49, 50; over-parted in his rôle, 50-51; his cabinet, 51-52; appoints Lee commander-in-chief of Confederate armies, 52; remained in harmony with Lee to the end, 52-53; quoted

Read More About the
War Between the States

American Jewry and the Civil War — Bertram W. Korn — 0-89176-087-3
— R. Beemis Publishing   12.95
> Before the fall of Fort Sumter, Jews had no common position on the subject of slavery. But when the War came, the Rabbis of the North offered prayers for the preservation of the Union, and the Southern Rabbis for the Confederacy; and at least one Rabbi offered prayers for both sides. This book is a biography of the Jewish community in the North, South, and West, and its struggle for equality and dignity in this time of conflict. 6x9, paper, 330 pages.

Annals of the Army of Tennessee and Early Western History — 1-55793-034-1
— Guild Bindery Press   33.00
> April through December 1878, a summary of battles from Sherman's memoirs, diaries, letters, and reports of officers, Tennessee Historical Society papers, and a chronological summary of engagements and battles in the western armies of the Confederacy. 6 x 9, 532 pages, hardback.

The Artillery of Nathan Bedford Forrest's Cavalry — J. W. Morton — 1-55793-019-8
— Guild Bindery Press   31.50 (hardback) —R. Beemis Publishing   12.95 (trade paper)
> A detailed and absorbing account of the role played by Forrest's artillery in the Civil War and the daring way in which General Forrest utilized his artillery for many victories. The author was one of Forrest's officers in the war. 6 x 9, 374 pages, hardback with dust jacket, illustrations.

Autobiography of Arab — E. Prioleau Henderson — 1-55793-033-3
— Guild Bindery Press   30.00
> A reprint of a unique story about Arab, a cavalry horse of the Civil War. A rare title in that the horse wrote the book! Henderson, Arab's master for many years, slips easily from horse to human voice in recounting of their phenomenal experiences together. 6 x 9, 170 pages, hardback.

Butler and His Cavalry in the War of Secession 1861-1865–U.R. Brooks–1-55793-028-7
— Guild Bindery Press   30.00
> A recounting of skirmishes and battles, tales of courage, bravado, unforgettable deeds, and sorrow for lost comrades. First-hand observations and stories of soldiers by soldiers. 6 x 9, 591 pages, hardback, illustrated.

Captain Alexander Hamilton Boykin — Richard Manning Boykin — 1-55793-032-5
— Guild Bindery Press   18.00
> A sketch of Boykin, 1815-1866, written by his grandson, to memorialize his record of service as a well-to-do planter, influential citizen, wise legislator, and brave, patriotic soldier. Authentic data and illustrations. 6x9, 264 pages, hardback.

Dark Days of the Rebellion — Benjamin F. Booth & Steve Meyer — 0-9630284-5-6
— Meyer Publishing   24.95
> Benjamin F. Booth wrote notes on scraps of paper while he was a prisoner of war in the Confederate prison at Salisbury, N.C. Revealed are the agonies inflicted on Americans by Americans. 6 x 9, 266 pages, hardback, illustrations.

The Defense of Charleston Harbor–John Johnson–1-55793-048-1–Guild Bindery Press   30.00
> The military operations by land and water around Charleston, S.C. during the Civil War led a foremost military authority to claim, "... that the defense of Fort Sumter and that of Wagner are feats of war unsurpassed in ancient or modern times." Written by engineer-in-charge from private notes, sketches, and diaries, and journals. Complete with charts, illustration, and maps. 6 x 9, 478 pages.

Alexander Books™ •65 Macedonia Road • Alexander, NC, 28701
Orders: 800-472-0438 • Fax: 828 255-8719 • Visa and MasterCard accepted.
Shipping and handling: $3 for the first book, $1 for each additional book.

Edisto Rifles — William Valmore Izlar —1-55793-031-7 — Guild Bindery Press   25.00

Organized in 1851, the Rifles represented some of the best blood of the Orangeburg District and South Carolina. First seen as a social effort, the activities of the Rifles gave way to the realities of a bitter war. They served in the regiment defending Charleston Harbor, the fields of Virginia, and the muddy trenches of Petersburg. Returned in 1865 to build the foundation of what is the Orangeburg County of today. 6 x 9, 168 pages, hardback, illustrations.

Four Years Under Marse Robert — Robert Stiles — 0-89176-046-6
— R. Beemis Publishing   12.95

This book is a moving firsthand account of four years in the Confederate Army, and a glowing and vivid tribute to Robert E. Lee, the man and the general. Robert Stiles serves as a Major of the Army of Northern Virginia, under the direct command of Lee, from First Manassas to Appomattox. 6x9, paper, 378 pages.

General Lee and Santa Claus — Mrs. Louise Clack — 1-55793-106-2
— Guild Bindery Press   9.95

Fantastic collectible! Facsimile of an 1867 children's book. Robert E. Lee's transformation from Rebel general to American icon took place in the public consciousness due in large part to artifacts such as this book. A bestseller! 40 pages, 6x8, illustrated.

General Lee and Santa Claus, an Adaptation — Randall Bedwell — 1-889709-01-8
— Spiridon Press   9.95

When two of the most renowned and esteemed characters in history—General Robert E. Lee and Santa Claus— join together to fulfill three little girls' request, the result is a holiday classic. 5.5x7, 40 pages, trade paper, illustrated.

I Rode With Stonewall — Henry Kyd Douglas — 0-089176-040-7
— Mockingbird Books   5.95

The war experiences of Henry Kyd Douglas, the youngest member of Jackson's staff from the John Brown Raid to the hanging of Mrs. Surratt. His position on Jackson's staff gave him an opportunity to observe the high command; his ready good nature and charm of manner made it easy for him to meet civilians. 4.25x7, paper, 384 pages.

May I Quote You, General Forrest? — Randall Bedwell — 1-888952-35-0
— Cumberland House   7.95

Captures the spirit and brilliance of this Confederate maverick in illuminating quotations from Forrest and his contemporaries on both sides of the battle lines. Beloved by his men and renowned for his many victories, Nathan Bedford Forrest's reputation as a cunning tactician and commander has only increased over time. 5.5 x 7, 96 pages, illustrated.

May I Quote You, General Lee? — Randall Bedwell — 1-888952-34-2 — Cumberland House   7.95

The Southern generals of the Civil War spoke of honor, duty, and the courage to fight for one's beliefs. While their cause was trampled on the battle fields of Dixie, their names live on in glory. Robert E. Lee, the preeminent Southern general was a "wholly human gentleman." This book reveals the spirit of Lee and those who followed him to greatness. 5.5 x 7, 96 pages, illustrated.

May I Quote You, General Longstreet? — Randall Bedwell — 1-888952-37-7
— Cumberland House   7.95

Tells the story of this tarnished warrior through his own words and the words of those who fought beside him. The praise of superiors and subordinates depicts a man of honor and resolve, qualities that inspired confidence and trust. Ironically, it was during peacetime that Longstreet was forced to defend his name. Yet he fervently believed in the end he would be victorious in this, his final battle. 5.5 x 7, 96 pages, illustrated.

May I Quote You, Stonewall Jackson? — Randall Bedwell — 1-888952-36-9
— Cumberland House   7.95

Vividly portrays a hero of the South through his own words and words of those who knew him. Jackson's remarks about the war and its soldiers paint a lucid portrait of the era and one of its most celebrated leaders. 5.5 x 7, 96 pages, illustrated.

Price and availability is subject to change without notice.

Alexander Books™ •65 Macedonia Road • Alexander, NC, 28701
Orders: 800-472-0438 • Fax: 828 255-8719 • Visa and MasterCard accepted.
Shipping and handling: $3 for the first book, $1 for each additional book.

Memoirs of the War of Secession — Johnson Hagood — 1-55793-027-9
— Guild Bindery Press   30.00

Johnson Hagood felt strongly that the service and courage of the Confederate Soldier should be recorded. This book gives thrilling incidents of the skill of the gallant General and of the valor of the brave men who dared to follow where he dared to lead. General Hagood was one of South Carolina's most distinguished sons, a planter, comptroller, banker, and governor. 6 x 9, 480 pages, hardback, illustrated.

Mosby's War Reminiscences — John S. Mosby — 1-887269-09-6
— John Culler and Sons   12.95

The story of the south's greatest partisan leader and raider, John S. Mosby. Acknowledged as one of the geniuses of the Civil War, Mosby operated behind Union lines destroying supplies, taking prisoners, reeking havoc on the Federal Army of the Potomac. Despite having no military training, Private Mosby instinctively developed hit and run tactics that kept thousands of Federal soldiers away from the front. 5 x 8, 264 pages, trade paper.

Old Enough to Die — Ridley Wills II — 1-881576-81-7 — Hillsboro Press   23.95

Old Enough to Die is a fascinating story about a southern family, their lives, their devotion to the South, and their conviction that what they were doing was right. It's the story of the Bostick family—four brothers, their sisters and mother, plus several in-laws and first cousins—primarily thorugh their letters, with background on what was happening to the family in the larger world of American history. 6x9, illustrations, hardback, 180 pages.

Prince of Edisto —James K. Swisher — 1-883522-10-2 — Rockbridge   25.00

Micah Jenkins, son of a wealthy cotton grower on Edisto Island, SC left his work in education to help organize the 5th South Carolina Infantry and was appointed its colonel in June, 1861. Jenkins was one of the truly outstanding regimental, brigade, and divisional leaders in the Southern army and died on the field of battle. 6 x 9, 188 pages, hardback with dust jacket, illustrated.

Rebel Rose— Ishbel Ross — 0-89176-026-1 — Mockingbird Books   4.95

Rose O'Neal Greenhow was adept at political intrigue and often involved in scandal. During her long Washington career she knew nine Presidents and was the intimate friend and advisor of one—James Buchanan. But it was the great South Carolina statesman John C. Calhoun who shaped her political philosophy and influenced her to work heart and soul for the Confederacy. 4.25x7, paper, 244 pages.

Saddle Soldiers — Lloyd Halliburton — 0-87844-115-8 — Sandlapper   22.00

The story of the 4th South Carolina Cavalry from General William Stokes' personal correspondence and memorabilia. Since little exists in National Archives, this book fills a gap in the preservation of the experiences of a brave commander who provided model conduct and leadership. 6 x 9, 266 pages, hardback with dust jacket, illustrated.

Sketch of Cobb Legion Cavalry — Wiley C. Howard — Booklet   9.00

A reprint of a booklet about a regiment first known as Cobb's Legion raised by Colonel, afterwards, Brigadier-General Thomas Roots Reed Cobb, of Athens, Georgia. A sketch of some of the regiment's encounters during the Civil War. 5.5 x 8.5, 20 pages, paper.

A Southern Woman's Story — Phoebe Yates Pember — 0-89176-024-5
— Mockingbird Books   3.95

From 1862 to 1865 Phoebe Pember served as matron of a division of Chimborazo Hospital in besieged Richmond. This hospital was the largest ever built in the Western Hemisphere. Phoebe's account of her experiences there is filled with scandals, gossip, greed, selfishness as well as courage and the needless suffering of the wounded soldiers in that dark age of medicine. 4.25x7, paper, 152 pages.

Stories of the Confederacy — U.R. Brooks — 1-55793-029-5 — Fox   30.00

Sketches of Hampton's Cavalry, Hart's Battery, Story of Brook's Battalion, a brief history of the Third South Carolina Cavalry, Bachman's Battery, and a brief look at the German Fusilliers, in addition to the homefront. 6 x 9, 410 pages, hardback with dust jacket.

Order on the Worldwide Web using SECURE credit card transactions: http://www.abooks.com.

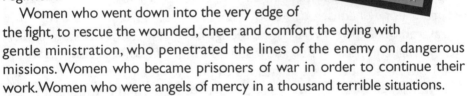